PADDINGTON
STORIES

PADDINGTON STORIES

by
Andrew Starr
and
Janet Morice

Publisher
Andrew Starr and Associates
11 Prospect Street, Paddington NSW, 2021, Australia

andrewstarrheritage@bigpond.com

First Published 2000

ISBN 0-646-40403-2

Typeset and printed by Southwood Press Pty Limited, Marrickville, NSW

Cover Design by the Bloke up the Road.

Cover Photograph Tamsin O'Neill, Elsternwick, Victoria.

Restoration of photographs from private collections by Platinum Imaging, 54 Oxford Street Paddington, NSW

National Library of Australia Cataloguing-in-Publication Data

Starr, Andrew Peter, 1963–
Paddington Stories

Bibliography
ISBN 0-646-40403-2

1. Cities and towns — New South Wales — Sydney — Growth.
2. Paddington (N.S.W.) — History. 3. Paddington (N.S.W.) — Social conditions.
I. Morice, Janet, 1940–. II. O'Neill, Tamsin, 1964–. III. Title.

994.41

Table of Contents

for Max Kelly
1935–1996

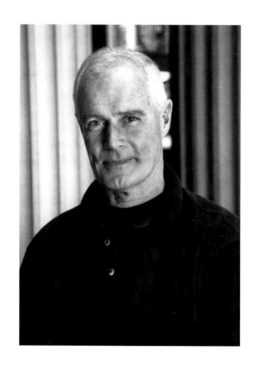

Prologue

Our neighbour, John Blacker says that when he was a child, he could hear the roar of lions at the Taronga Park Zoo across the harbour.

We believe him.

On many nights, Paddington is still so quiet you can hear the fog horns of ships on the harbour and the trains as they pass Rushcutters Bay. Bats rustle Moreton Bay Figs, as they rummage for food by the flood-lit Barracks' wall. Sometimes we can imagine the sound of clapsticks and a low chanting of the ghosts of the Cadigal tribe, Coalbee's songs.

On other nights, the streets are full of madness. Sirens scream towards a boy shot outside a night club. Drunken backpackers serenade the neighbourhood, an old Paddington tradition continued. The Redcoats from Devon, during their occupation of the Barracks in the 1840's, sang their own tunes on forays between bars and brothels. The Salvation Army Band, in the 1930's, marched the victims of the 'six o'clock swill' to their Temple in Glenmore Road.

'The Age of Aquarius' blared out of the hi-fi in the orange, shag-pile carpeted Seventies. Twenty years earlier, the O'Reilly sisters sang, 'Goodnight Sweetheart', as they danced along the pavement at midnight. On the morning after the Sleaze Ball, in the nineties, neighbours stagger home, ears ringing, as Joyce, Bonnie and Mac in Sunday best, head off to Mass.

Paddington smells. On spring nights the jasmine is strongest — great waves of it in September. Frangipani is sweeter. Young girls, and boys too, wear a waxen flower behind their ear. There are smells of chops, sausages, saté, butter chicken and spaghetti marinara. The service lanes hold memories of a Paddington 'on the nose' when the residents relied on the night cart.

The doorways are open — the light, golden, in hallways and windows.

Paddington is colourful. The red and white of 30,000 Sydney Swans' supporters as they make their way to the Sydney Cricket Ground, the lavender blue of the jacarandas in November. The honey colour of sandstone. The drab colours of the terraces in the 1940's have been replaced by a wider palate, but the bright orange clothes of the Rajneesh have vanished. In their place are grey flannel suits, and on weekends, checked baggy shorts and brown boatshoes beside skin tight skirts and navel rings.

The older residents mourn the loss of the ham and beef shops, the butchers, and variety stores. In their place are boutiques, galleries and espresso bars.

Paddington can be a bit rough round the edges. It has been home for rogues and rascals, wharfies and bankclerks, bohemians and businessmen. This book tells their stories.

Andrew Starr and Janet Morice

Authors' Note

Max Kelly gave us our inspiration for this book. He discussed his plans with us, for a companion book to Paddock Full of Houses, which described the economic history of Paddington to the 1890's. The new one would have discussed economic changes in the twentieth century, and he asked us to collect some oral histories for him, because he was concerned that without them, part of the history of the suburb would be lost. Max died in 1996. It was not until late 1997 that we decided to begin the Paddington Project.

Neither of us are economists so we were faced with a number of questions. What was to be the scope of the book? What were we interested in writing about? The project, at first, was to be an architectural and social history of the suburb. We intended to trace the effect that the lives of the residents had on the suburb's architecture. Work was to be divided between us, one working on the architectural history of the suburb, the other on its social history. We wanted to tell the whole story, from the landing of the First Fleet to the present. We wanted to discuss how this suburb reflected changes that were happening in other parts of inner urban Australia, even the world! Elements remain of those ideas, but in fact the book developed in another direction.

Why? It happened through the people we met as we collected the oral histories. We were privileged to hear their stories. It was an intimate experience. We have shared so much. They have become our friends. The book is about real lives, told by the people who have lived in Paddington for eighty years, or eight. It is a social history.

We respect these memories, so pseudonyms have been used in most cases. The thoughts, ideas, and opinions are important, not that we know which of our neighbours spoke them. They are diverse — as in life, and no reader will agree with everything they have to say.

This history is a one of ongoing class conflict, interaction and resolution. We have endeavoured to describe the swings in the status of the suburb, and changes in lifestyle of its population, through the voices of those who live here. 104 oral histories were collected from a wide range of residents and ex-residents over three years, 1997–2000. Some of these people have been important in local politics, others have lived here quietly for more than eighty years. Many of the views of our interviewees are contradicted by others. We hope that these contradictions help to illuminate the messy, wonderful, history of the suburb.

Andrew Starr and Janet Morice

Chapter One
The Wilderness to the East

Paddington is situated on Cadigal tribal land,[1] which extends from Cockle Bay to South Head, but it was not named until sixty years after the settlement of Sydney in 1788. Nor was it formally demarcated until 1861, when the Municipality of Paddington was created. Until that time, the area to the east of the settlement to a distance of two or three miles was known by a variety of names — Woolloomooloo, Woolloomooloo Hill, West's Bush, Darlinghurst, Underwood's Paddocks, Frog Hollow, Rushcutting Bay, and Sydney Common. In 1839, there was another — Paddington Hill. James Underwood had sold part of his property for housing blocks, and called it the Paddington Estate. However the eastern boundary of what was to become Paddington, never extended further than the edge of Captain Piper's estate, the Point Piper Road. [now Jersey Road.]

Paddington is dominated by a high sandstone ridge. In the eighteenth century several valleys, eroded by streams, led to a marshy rush-filled cove, a mile or so to the east of the main settlement. The cove was shallow and unsuitable for ships, and as the hills were steep and rocky, the area was ignored by the newcomers, except for collecting rushes for thatch.

Aboriginal tribes lived around the harbour's edge. In July 1788, John Hunter, Captain of the 'Sirius', counted 67 canoes and more than 150 people around the shores of Port Jackson, 'which is by no means a just account of the numbers who at that time lived in and about the harbour.'[2] Watkin Tench, a young officer of the 'Sirius', described the aboriginal families as they fished and cooked in flimsy bark canoes. 'The child is placed on its mother's shoulders, entwining its little legs around her neck and closely grasping her hair with its hands. The mother tends the child, keeps up her fire, which is laid on a small patch of earth, paddles the boat and broils the fish … Her husband, silent and watchful, fishes with a spear by the shore'.[3]

The relations between observer and observed were not always peaceful. Two rushcutters were killed in May 1788, and local myth places the two murders at Rushcutting Bay. [now Rushcutters Bay] 'Captain Campbell of the Marines, who had been up the harbour to procure some rushes for thatch, brought to the hospital the bodies of William Okey and Samuel Davis, two rushcutters, whom he had found murdered by the natives in a shocking manner.'[4] However, both Tench's, and Surgeon White's journals, refer to the event taking place 'up' the harbour, and Tench recorded that when Phillip set out to find the people responsible, he left from the 'head of the harbour.'[5] So the murders were more likely to have taken place on the western rather than the eastern side of the settlement.

A year later, when Captain Hunter returned from the Cape of Good Hope, he was 'much surprised at not having seen a single native on the shore or a canoe as we came up in the ship.'[6] Smallpox had catastrophically reduced the local aboriginal population by more than half in two years, and caused drastic social disruption. The death rate around Sydney was so great, that traditional burial customs were discontinued. In an effort to investigate and check the growth and consequences of the disease, four of the Cadigal were captured and treated by Surgeon White. An old man and a younger one died, but a boy of eight, Nanbaree, and a girl of perhaps thirteen, Abaroo, recovered, and continued to live in the settlement.

In 1789, Governor Phillip was eager for more contact with the aboriginal groups. The Europeans wanted to learn the language, understand more about their culture, and gain information about the country surrounding the settlement. So Phillip sent Lieutenant Bradley and a party of men down the harbour to capture aborigines. Two men were taken, Coalby and Banelon. Lieutenant Bradley wrote, 'The noise of the men, the crying and screaming of the women and children, together with the situation of the two miserable wretches in our possession, was really a most distressing scene. It was by far the most unpleasant service I was ever ordered to execute.'[7]

Coalby, one of the men taken back to Sydney Cove, was 'a chief or distinguished person among those of the tribe of Cadigal.'[8] 'He was perhaps thirty, of a less sullen appearance than his comrade, considerably shorter, and not so robustly framed, though better fitted for purposes of activity. They had both evidently had the smallpox; indeed Coalby's face was thickly imprinted with the marks of it.'[9]

Both escaped. Over the next few months they were seen by various groups, but said they would return to the settlement only if Governor Phillip himself invited them. This meeting finally occurred on September 7 1790, on the north shore. They were given jackets and invited to Government House.

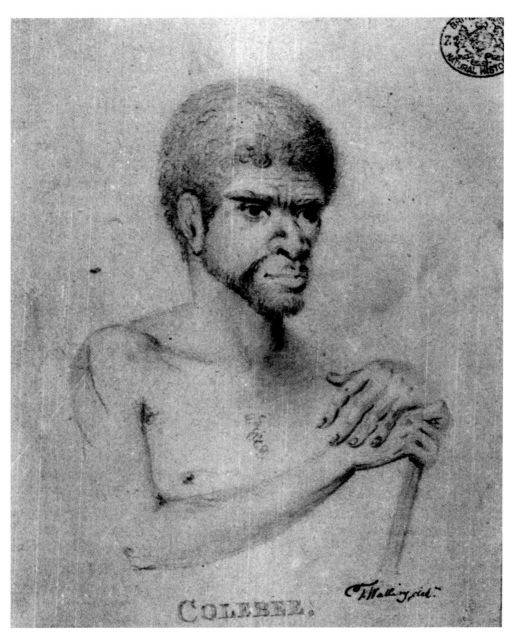

COLEBEE.

Thomas Watling, The Natural History Museum, London

Unfortunately, as the Governor was leaving, he was speared by an aborigine he had not met before, and took six months to fully recover.

The two men did visit the settlement in the following months, often staying the night. 'Banelon and Coalby, with their wives, dined at the Governor's... and came in as usual to have a glass of wine or a dish of coffee after which they left to go and sleep at Banelon's hut on the point.'[10]

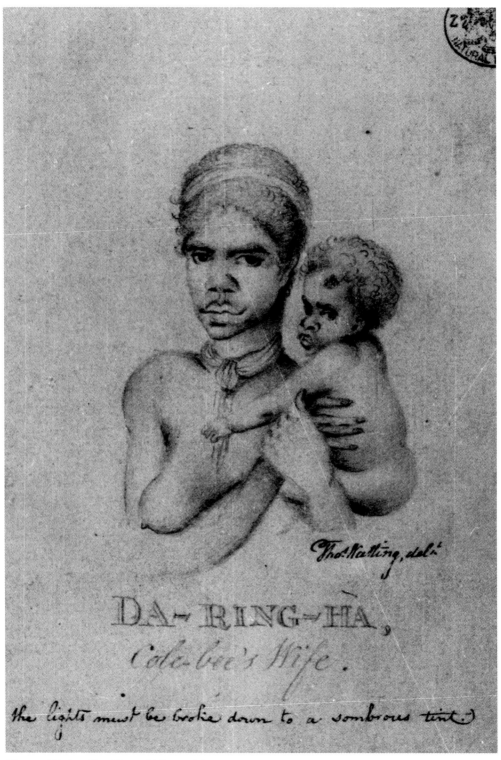

DA~RING~HA,

Cole-bee's Wife.

the lights must be broke down to a sombrous tint.)

Thomas Watling, The Natural History Museum, London

They, in turn, invited the Governor and his company to visit them. Captain Hunter, who was educated in the classics and music, wrote of a special entertainment when some of the officers were invited by Coalby and Banelon to watch a ceremony on the eastern side of Sydney Cove. 'Their dance was truly wild and savage, yet in many parts, there appeared order and regularity…They exhibited with the utmost skill and agility, all the various motions which with them, seemed to constitute the principal beauties of dancing. One of the most striking was that of placing their feet very wide apart, and by an extraordinary exertion of muscles of the thighs and legs, moving the legs in a trembling and very surprising manner, such as none of us could imitate, which seemed to show that it required much practice to arrive at any degree of perfection in this singular motion.'[11]

Intelligent and independent, Coalby was not bowed by the newcomers. He observed them, rejected them when necessary, and used them when they had some value. When Tench left the settlement in 1792, he wrote, 'The natives of NSW possess a considerable portion of that acumen or sharpness of intellect which bespeaks genius. On subjects in any degree familiarised to their ideas, they generally testified not only acuteness of discernment, but a large portion of good sense. I have always thought that the distinctions they showed in their estimate of us, on first entering our society, strongly displayed the latter quality.'[12]

A lookout was set up on the South Head in January, 1790. The track to the lookout took advantage of the well-worn Cadigal pathways through the elevated heath country on the ridge. [Old South Head Road] This was the first time that the land had been opened up to the east. 'A party of seamen were fixed on a high bluff called the South Head at the entrance to the Harbour, on which a flag was ordered to be hoisted whenever a ship might appear.'[13] There was a four month wait till the first of the second fleet arrived.

It was to be more than ten years before any other Europeans settled in Cadigal land to the east. Land grants to the west, near Paramatta, were much more desirable than the rocky, sandy hills to the east. Agriculture was a priority in the early years and free settlers and soldiers wanted to become pastoralists, 'landed gentry', using cheap convict labour to develop the land. The plains to the west and beyond the mountains, crossed for the first time in 1813, were the world of the 'exclusives', of John Macarthur, an ex-officer of the New South Wales Corps, and other free settlers.

The gentry did not 'trade', and the first people to move to the rocky hills to the east were men and women who lived by their own standards, rather than those set by the more conservative members of the new settlement. These men and women were ex-convicts, (emancipists) outsiders, and native born, (currency lads and lasses), and lived their lives against the backdrop of the harbour and ocean.

These self made men and their families lived to the east of Wolloomooloo

Hill, and many converted their punishment of transportation to their advantage, finding opportunities for upward social mobility. Some developed a ruthless business sense, others had rare and useful skills. As rewards for their merit they were given grants of land which they developed in a variety of ways ranging from marine villas and country estates, to light industrial uses. They were friends and business partners, or fierce rivals. Their exploits were followed in the press and their large estates, out of town, ensured privacy. They fought for equal civil rights with the exclusives.

Prominent emancipists who owned property to the east at various periods before 1830, were Sir Henry Brown Hayes, Thomas West, William Thomas, James Underwood, Robert Cooper, Francis Ewin Forbes, and Daniel Cooper. Of the two members of the NSW Corps who owned land in the area, Thomas Laycock's career ended in drunken disarray, and Captain John Piper married Mary Anne Shears, the daughter of a convict, renouncing his commission after she had borne him several sons. William Wentworth was a currency lad, whose mother had been transported for seven years, and whose father D'Arcy came to Australia after being acquitted of several charges of highway robbery.

In spite of their differing backgrounds, these family groups worked and socialised together. Thomas West employed William Wentworth to defend a land dispute, Robert Cooper's son, John, married Thomas West's daughter, Naomi. James Underwood raced horses against John Piper at the first race meeting in Hyde Park in October 1810, and William Wentworth rode his father's horse at the same meeting. Simeon Lord, a prominent emancipist businessman, acted as John Piper's agent and was James Underwood's partner in sealing and trading for some years. John Piper's daughter, Sarah, spent her honeymoon at The Retreat, the house built by Sir Henry Brown Hayes. Her father subsequently bought it, and later sold it to William Wentworth. When John Piper got into financial difficulties and attempted suicide, it was Daniel Cooper who lent him money, and bought Henrietta Villa, Piper's mansion. Daniel was a witness at Robert and Sarah Cooper's wedding, and Daniel Cooper and James Underwood were both appointed to the Standing Committee of Emancipists in 1821, when they petitioned the Governor regarding emancipist's rights. They identified themselves as a distinct group and at the meeting of emancipists held on 23 January 1821, the first resolution stated, 'The emancipist colonists of the Territory … are now possessed of the larger amount of the property of the colony and have become the *middle class* [our italics] of society therein.'[14] Members of this new *middle class* class were frequent guests at Governor Maquarie's table, who took up his position in 1810.

Everyone in Sydney was dependent on the commands of the Governor. Only the Governor could make Land Grants. Only the Governor could grant Pardons. The fortunes of the convicts and emancipists depended on his moral philosophy. Macquarie wrote, 'My principle is, that when once a man is free, his former state should no longer be remembered, or allowed to act against him; let him feel himself eligible for any situation which he has, by a long term of upright conduct, proved himself worthy of filling. What can be so great a stimulus to a man of respectable family and education, who has fallen to the lowest state of degradation, as to know, that it is still in his power to recover what he has lost, and not only to become a worthy member of society, but to be treated as such?'[15]

Thomas West was one such man. Six months after Governor Macquarie's arrival, he was granted land between 'Mr. Palmer's estate at Woolloomooloo and the South Head Road, about a mile and a half from the township of Sydney.'[16] Thomas was twenty-six when he arrived in Sydney in 1801, having been transported for burglary. He had left a wife and child in England and because he was a carpenter, he was immediately put to work in the lumberyard.[17] At this time many freedoms were open to convicts. The sentence that most had received was transportation, and they were free to move about the town unless they had a sentence for hard labour or had re-offended. They were responsible for their own accommodation, but food and some other necessities were supplied through the Government stores. In return for working for the Crown they were able to earn money through their own labours, or by trade after the set hours of work.

Thomas lived with Mary Rugg. She had been transported for seven years for stealing cloth, and in the Muster of 1806 was registered as Ticket of Leave, which was granted after a convict had lived an exemplary life of conduct and industry. By 1807, the West's had two children, Naomi and Obed, and in 1810, Thomas was ready to establish his own business. He had been in the lumberyard for nine years and had been promoted to overseer. The yard was a very large walled area in George Street, and blacksmiths, coopers, sawyers, iron and brass founders, harness and collarmakers, tailors and shoe makers, carpenters and joiners worked there. A separate overseer superintended each class of labourer.[18]

The Wests moved on to the land and Obed, in his memoirs, described his new home. 'At that time, the place had the appearance of a dark and dense forest, immense mahogany trees, blackbutt, and other of the eucalyptus species growing in great profusion, while in the glen leading up to the house, a number of large cabbage trees used to grow, and for many years the stems of these palms, quite two feet in diameter at the base, were to be standing. About 200 yards from the mill a large swamp commenced. It swarmed with aquatic birds of every description — redbills, water hens, bitterns, quail, frequently all kinds of ducks, and when in season, snipe, landrails, and at all times, bronze winged pigeons could be had in abundance. Brush wallabies were also very numerous in the vicinity, and many scores of them I have shot. It may seem strange to hear that within the memory of any person living, the head of the swamp was a great resort for dingoes. I have killed numbers of them, and often in daylight, when the day was dull, I have seen them come up to my very door and take the poultry.

The mill was a single motion one, having one pair of stones and an overshop wheel about 24 feet in diameter. Near the creek was a large dam in which was stored the water for the working.'[19] Work on the mill took more than two years to complete, while Thomas continued in his job as an overseer at the lumberyard. He was still a convict, as he had never applied for a Ticket of Leave, and so could remain on the Government Stores and guarantee a living for his family.

Lady Macquarie was very happy to open the mill, even though Thomas had been unable to heed the directive of Macquarie for couples to marry, and end 'the scandalous and pernicious custom... of persons of different sexes co-habiting together unsanctioned by the legal ties of marriage.'[20]

An emancipist, William Thomas, was granted forty acres of land on the east side of Rush Cutting Bay in 1817 but sold the land almost immediately, by-passing the normal legal channels of the Land Titles Office to avoid the conditions of the grant, which required him to undertake cultivation of a proportion of his land and not to sell for seven years. He had been given the land, possibly as recompense for the death of his son in an accident involving Lady Macquarie. This accident was described by Governor Macquarie in a letter to Under Secretary Goulburn on December 15 1817. His wife had been traumatised by the child's death, running with him in her arms into his mother's house after he had fallen under the wheels of her carriage. Charles Thomas, 'having blinded himself by throwing sand over his head, a common amusement of the children here, left his companions and ran under the near side horse.'[21] Lady Macquarie's own son was only seven months old at the time, having been born after she had suffered six miscarriages, and her distress was apparent.

James Underwood was happy to celebrate the arrival of Governor Macquarie after the colony had experienced a period of near anarchy and uncertainty. On January 26 1808, some 400 soldiers of the NSW Corps, followed by settlers, had marched on Government House and arrested Governor Bligh, whose investigations into the sometimes dubious business practices of the colony had been a continuous source of frustration and was bad for business. Underwood had arrived in the colony aged twenty, in 1791, and within ten years was well established as a boat builder and trader. His young mistress, Phyllis, had been assigned to him as a servant. She had been transported for theft, and in September 1803, a daughter Charlotte was born. However a month later, Underwood was described in the Sydney Gazette of October 16 1803 as a 'respectable inhabitant', who ordered his horse and cart to assist the work of filling the new bridge over the Tank Stream. He and his partner, Henry Kable, transported in the first fleet, expanded their boat building business rapidly, as trade between Sydney and the lower Hawkesbury developed via Broken Bay.

However, their expansion was limited through trade restrictions imposed on the colony by the East India Company, which disallowed the building of boats capable of international trade, so they developed an extremely profitable sealing business with Simeon Lord, who had been transported in 1791, and had begun operating as a broker soon after his arrival. He found an ingenious solution to access the overseas market. In 1806, he had his London brokers, Plummers, buy the Sydney Cove for Lord, Kable and Underwood, for 2,200 pounds, which, after an expensive refit, cost 7363 pounds. Plummers could not advance the cost of cargo, so they hired her to the Government as a convict transport. Plummers were the registered owners as they had a mortgage on her, so the Transport Board may never have known that they were shipping convicts on a vessel owned by three ex-convicts living in Sydney.[22]

By 1810, the traders were aware of the difficulties of foreign ownership of ships and there were problems in calculating ahead because of time and distance. So Lord and Underwood began to invest more of their capital in manufacturing and processing. Underwood was building and selling whale and flat-sterned boats and replacing and maintaining others, and in 1812 he opened a Coffee House in George Street, which sold 'a quantity of choice spirits and wines.'[23] Some years later, with Robert Cooper and Francis Ewin Forbes, he saw the potential of using the clear water in the creeks on the steep slopes to the east of Sydney for the establishment of a distillery.

By 1812, the road to the South Head was a popular excursion, but was being cut up by carts cutting timber for firewood. The road had been built by subscription and the Governor set up a toll gate at the South East extremity of Hyde Park. However, no tolls were to be paid or demanded at the new gate for private carriages, gigs or riding horses.[24]

Further down the harbour, Captain John Piper was given a grant of land in 1816, bounded on one side by Point Piper Road. He married Mary Anne Shears, the daughter of a convict, in February 1816, and laid the foundation stone for the new house in that year.[25] They held the most spectacular parties in Sydney at Henrietta Villa, but they were not entirely accepted socially. Deputy Assistant Commissary General George Thomas Blaney Boyes, reported to his wife, 'Captain Piper is the naval officer here, a situation that has given him four or five thousand a year — and I suspect he spends every farthing of it. He lives in a beautiful house just after you enter Port Jackson… He has laid out immense sums upon it and in making roads to it… He sends carriages and four and boats for those who like the water… he keeps a band of music and they have quadrilles every evening under the spacious verandas. At the table there is a vast profusion of every luxury that the four quarters of the globe can supply, for you must know that this pick-pocket quarter contributes nothing of itself…I was invited but declined, for there is no honour in dining with Piper, for he invites everybody who comes here indiscriminately.'[26.]

In a few years Piper's career as a high flyer was over, and Simeon Lord and Daniel Cooper helped with loans to pay his debts. However his properties had to be sold, and Daniel Cooper bought Henrietta Villa. Daniel had arrived in Sydney in 1816, having been transported for life. He, like so many others, immediately developed a series of business interests and was spectacularly successful.

These emancipists were successful businessmen but some of those who had been set free by a pardon, thought themselves superior to those who had served out their time or had re-offended. 'At one of the public dinners of the emancipists 'pure', (as have neither been punished nor convicted of any offences in the colony) some years back, a terrible fracas ensued from one of the proscribed inadvertently gaining admittance (impure), who being assailed with a universal shout of, "Turn him out, turn him out", forthwith squatted himself at the end of the table and commenced upon his soup, skillfully entrenching his position by rolling the corner of the tablecloth round his hand, with a view of pulling the whole of the smoking pageantry off the table in case of molestation.'[27]

A major crisis affected all the transportees in 1820. Edward Eager, a pious, rich emancipist, and the largest shareholder in the Bank of NSW, sued Mr. Justice Field for defamation. 'Justice Field rejected the suit with reference to a case heard in England, in which it was decided that a Governor's pardon as distinct from a Royal pardon did not restore a convict to any civil rights whatever save the right to remain on the earth.'[28] The implications of Field's verdict went far beyond the case. If a Governor's pardon had no status then a sizeable proportion of the colony's population also had no rights. Business in the colony could not run if this were the case.

Macquarie himself had granted 352 free pardons and 1164 conditional pardons. The emancipists rushed to protect themselves and drafted a petition to the King, signed by '1368 of those persons, by whose labour and industry, this your Majesty's colony has been cleared and cultivated, its towns built, its woods felled, its agriculture and commerce carried on.'[29] Simeon Lord, James Underwood and Daniel Cooper were on the standing committee.

Mr. Eager was deputed to carry the petition to England in his defence, which was successful. Macquarie had fully supported the campaign and a crisis was averted.

In 1823, James Underwood and two other emancipists, Robert Cooper and Francis Ewin Forbes, were granted land between the holdings of Thomas West, William Thomas and Captain John Piper, for the purpose of building a distillery. It was a deep valley called Frog Hollow, beside a fast flowing stream that could be easily dammed, and extended up to the South Head Road.

'On Monday last the 19th instant, the Proprietors of the Sydney Distillery, the first and only one established in NSW, laid the first stone of their building in the presence of a great concourse of people consisting chiefly of mechanics who all seemed to feel a peculiar interest in the prospect before them. Mr. Robert Cooper addressed them in a very appropriate speech, in which he adverted to the agricultural interests of the colony as dependant upon establishments of this nature for its prosperity, and hoped that the settlers would find New Holland's gin as palatable as Bengal Rum. The families of the proprietors together with a few of the HOPS and PRIDE of Australasia, partook of the plenty provided for the occasion and spent the day in youthful hilarity, assisted by the enchantments of music. The mechanics, labourers and other spectators, had the whole carcass of a sheep roasted for them, and of their own accord employed a bagpipe as the cheapest and best music with which they could amuse themselves.'[30]

However the partnership was short-lived. Mr. Forbes's share was bought by Underwood almost immediately, because Forbes found himself in financial trouble when his firm, Eager and Forbes was dissolved. By 1825 he was in trouble again, 'having fraudulently and surreptitiously possessed himself and others of a herd of cattle'.[31]

A disagreement between Cooper and Underwood was caused by Underwood buying out Forbes' share of the partnership. Underwood now had the majority of the holding and control of the business. Ill feeling between the two broke up this uneven partnership, and by July 1824, Cooper retained only three acres on the South Head Road where he built Juniper Hall.

Robert Cooper, who had arrived in 1813, was sentenced to fourteen years for receiving stolen goods. 'To support his contention that he had believed the goods merely smuggled, not stolen, Cooper produced witnesses who testified that he had frequently been prosecuted for smuggling. The judge commented on the extraordinary nature of his defense, proof or guilt of one sort of crime being offered as proof of innocence of another.'[32] He married three times, his first wife dying before he came to Sydney. His third wife Sarah, a currency lass, presented him with fourteen children, and it was for her that he built Juniper Hall, the large house on the South Head Road, opposite the Sydney Common. It was completed in 1824.

'While perhaps not the finest house in Sydney, Juniper Hall was certainly a large and comfortable Colonial Georgian dwelling of two storeys with a basement, and four large rooms on each floor. The rooms were located about a general stair and by closing two doors in the foyer, it could be divided into two distinct houses. The kitchen was in the sandstone basement and bathing facilities were located in an outhouse. A coach house, stables and servants' quarters were also built, and the garden well stocked with fruit trees. The house featured stuccoed-brick walls, small-paned, shuttered windows, and a semicircular fanlight over the front door. It commanded an impressive view, standing 200 feet above Sydney Harbour, looking out to Botany Bay.'[33]

Finally, with another great party, the Sydney Distillery was opened. 'The

King of Spirits was drawn in a carriage flanked by courtiers and accompanied by a 300 gallon keg of the new local rum. There was a band of tambourines and throngs of people dancing in the street, leading to Underwood's warehouses and the promised sumptuous feast. We can't pretend to describe the liveliness of the company, many of whom unconsciously acknowledged the rums full proof before they departed, while the unbounded joy of the host may be better imagined than related.'[34]

But Cooper was not to be outdone. A week before the opening of Underwood's distillery, Cooper obtained a site from the Government at Blackwattle Swamp, where he intended to build one of his own.[35] He was living in style. The Australian of July 19 1826, reported a christening party for one of Robert's twenty-eight children. 'Mr. and Mrs. R. Cooper celebrated on Monday evening, by a spirited ball and sumptuous supper. The ladies who were nearly all 'currency lasses' who equalled if not excelled in number the other sex. Emblematical figures of peace and plenty, encircled by the olive and cornucopia were designed in chalks on the ballroom floor in a very tasteful way. Plenty exhibited herself under the most tempting forms in fruits and wines and pastries during the night and Tuesday morning dawned before the merry group had quitted the pleasures of the ballroom'.

The Cooper's were in a prime position to observe and be observed by society because the South Head Road had become by then 'the grand equestrian resort, along which gigs with well dressed people and spruce dandies à cheval may be daily seen careering. Sunday is here, as everywhere else, the great gala day, when all the various equipages are most profusely shown off — when the animating bustle here displayed, the clouds of starting dust scattering abroad from behind the carriage wheels and heels of horses, and the passing smiles and coughs of the different groups hurrying backwards and forwards, present a very lively picture. The road terminates at the tall and airy lighthouse perched on the bold headland and forming the southern entrance to the harbour and overlooking the whole southern ocean. An abundance of gigs may be hired in Sydney at 15/– a day and riding horses at 10/–.'[36]

In 1830, Thomas West, the oldest resident to the east of the town, needed the help of one of the newest, William Wentworth, who had bought Captain Piper's property, The Retreat, at Vaucluse several years before. Gangs from the Public Works Department had begun to quarry stone from West's land for the new gaol. He had never received a title deed for the land, but knew his request in 1810 had been to the South Head Road and he claimed the land. So he simply ran his fences up to the corner which the new gaol made with the South Head Road. On January 21 1830, John Busby reported to the Colonial Secretary, 'I sent yesterday to remove a number of these stones and the party was met by Mr. West, his son, and several other men, who with threats of violence, prevented them from approaching the quarry for such a purpose.'[37]

West was defended by Wentworth. Evidence was given in the case that a path called the Maroo was the shortest walking route to the South Head and because the path skirted Palmer's grant at Woolloomooloo, travellers on foot had to skirt round his property to the south and then turn north east to rejoin the Maroo. One had to pass Mr. West's house on the way to the stepping stones at Rushcutter's Bay and the land bounded by the path had always been his land.[38]

The Australian Newspaper reported on 14 October 1831, 'The King vs West. This action being one of intrusion raised to eject the defendant from certain land on the South Head Road of which he has been in possession upwards of sixteen years, was brought on for the third time on Wednesday last, before Mr. Justice Stephen and a Special Jury, who, to the infinite delight of a crowded court and as we prognosticated twelve month ago, gave a verdict FOR THE DEFENDANT(!!!) thereby foiling Mr. McLeay and his favourites, who no doubt strained every nerve to get so tempting a spot into their clutches. Happily, this time, to the credit of a Jury, the sharks are outwitted!!' Mr. William Wentworth owned the newspaper.

The two Governors who followed Macquarie were Governor Brisbane and Governor Darling. Both these men were under the orders of the Home Secretary to toughen the convict system following Bigge's report criticising Governor Macquarie's lenient attitude towards the emancipist class. Orders included a drastic reduction in the granting of pardons and a purging from the colonial bureaucracy of emancipated convicts. This was done as the British Government was concerned that transportation was losing value as a deterrent. They may have been right.

However, Peter Cunningham, who spent two years in the colony and published his journal in 1827, wrote, 'Our emancipist body, in honest truth, forms the most useful and enterprising portion of our community; all the distillers, nearly all the breweries and the greater portion of the mills and various manufactories, being owned by them, while they have never so far as I can learn, disgraced themselves in any of the smuggling transactions whereby many of those who came out under the proud title of free men have tarnished their reputation. Several of our most respectable merchants have told me that in numerous matters of business when they have been concerned with the emancipists, their conduct has always proved most honourable.'[39]

When Governor Darling left on October 22 1831, there was an enormous celebration.

The Australian reported, 'Upward of four thousand persons assembled at Vaucluse to partake of Mr. Wentworth's hospitality and to evince joy at the approaching departure. The scene of the fete was on the lawn in front of Mr. Wentworth's villa, which was thrown open for the reception of all respectable visitants, while a marquee filled with piles of loaves and casks of Cooper's gin and Wright's strong beer, was pitched a short way off. On an immense spit a bullock was roasted entire. Twelve sheep were also roasted in succession and 4000 loaves completed the enormous banquet. By 7 p.m. two immense bonfires were lighted on the highest hill. Rustic sports, speeches etc. whiled away the night and morning dawned before the hospitable mansion was quitted by all its guests.'[40]

This event was reported quite differently in the Sydney Gazette, the pro-Darling newspaper. 'The roaring, bawling, screeching, blaspheming, thumping, bumping, kicking, licking, tricking, cheating, beating, stealing, reeling, breaking of heads, bleeding of noses, blackening of eyes, picking of pockets, and what not... The orgies of the lowest rabble of Botany Bay, congregated in the open air, shrouded by the curtain of night, released from the eyes of the police, and helewated by the fumes of Cooper's Gin, have excited universal disgust and abhorrence among decent people.'[41]

It was the end of an era.

By 1828 the population of New South Wales had increased to 36,598. Governor Darling had granted land to Government officials on Woolloomooloo Hill, and four-acre lots were for sale in the Valley of Lacrozia in 1831, on Crown Land between West's, Underwood's and Thomas's grants.

The people who had settled the area initially, had the drive and skills to succeed in the early turbulent years of Sydney. They could look towards the city that had given them remarkable opportunities, for they had been able to transform themselves into a new middle class. They were a small group, but had large families. James Underwood had eleven children, Robert Cooper twenty-eight, and Thomas West four, a total of forty-three. These children born in Australia were known by the name of 'currency, as distinct from sterling, or those born in the mother country. The name was originally given by a facetious paymaster of the 73rd regiment quartered here — the pound currency being at that time inferior to the pound sterling. It is laughable to see some of the capers some of our drunken old sterling madonnas will occasionally cut over their currency adversaries in a quarrel. It is then, "You saucy baggage, how dare you set up your currency crest at me? I'm sterling, that I'll let you know". A currency lass, asked how she would like to go to England, replied with great naivety, "I should be afraid to go, from the number of thieves there."[42]

By the end of the decade the area that was to become Paddington had changed. The first of the estates had been built, but it would remain 'the bush', for many years to come.

And what of the Cadigal people? The initial devastation of the European invasion was one that the Cadigal tribe could never recover from. The smallpox epidemic decimated their population and their land was progressively occupied. Their hunting and fishing grounds were heavily taxed by the needs of the settlement, their culture and traditions were disrupted. The distinct Cadigal culture was eroded by other tribes attracted to Sydney, and as the years progressed, the people from different tribal groups were perceived as 'the same', and thus, individual aboriginal cultures and traditions were ignored. In 1827 Cunningham wrote, 'The women everywhere wrap themselves in some species of cloak made of opossum skins or else in a blanket, but the men walk carelessly about, quite naked, without betraying the least shame; even many at this day parading the streets in natural costume, or with a pair of breeches probably dangling round their necks, which the modest-meaning donor intended to be applied elsewhere.'[43]

Obed West recounted a devastating incident from his childhood. 'One day some of the blacks, in walking over the south-east corner of the estate, discovered a plant of spirits which it is supposed had been manufactured at an illicit still in Middle Harbour. A day of wild dissipation followed, and while they were in a state of intoxication a fire occurred, by which a number were burnt to death and others severely injured. One of the injured ones was called 'Pussy Cat'. Through the effects of the fire she was bent almost double, and had to make her way by the aid of two sticks. The blacks managed to provide for a measure of their wants by fishing, and the scene in and about the bay was rendered peculiar by seeing blacks in their frail canoes as they floated about, engaged in this work. Among the best known of the aboriginals was Major White, who must have been 70 years of age, and well remembered the arrival of the first ship and white men into Port Jackson; then there were Marroot, Crangerang, Cullabar, Tommera, Blueit, Dulnuke and Boolmena (all spelt phonetically), but who, with all their descendants, have long passed away, and left the territory to the pioneer colonists.'[44]

Chapter Two
Paddington Hill

By the end of 1831, the beautiful valleys descending to Rushcutters Bay were no longer the domain of the emancipist merchants. The wilderness to the east was becoming fashionable.

NSW's population was now more than 50,000, and buildings were extending beyond the town boundaries. The Valley of Lacrozia had been surveyed, and four acre allotments were for sale. This was an extension of the Woolloomooloo plan, which made land on the hill available to government officials to build villas 'that looked as though they had just arrived from England and had been set up for sale as an experiment. They were painted white, with shady verandas and green Venetian blinds.'[1]

The aborigines who called Rushcutters Bay, Kogarah 'had a lingering fondness for their old camping ground'[2] on its western slopes, camping there intermittently until the 1860's. The increasingly popular walking track, the Maroo, wound down past Mr. West's 'fine fruit trees and cultivated land'[3] to White Conduit House, a hotel on the eastern side of the creek. 'The large grassy flat at the rear of the building was used on holiday occasions for many old fashioned amusements, and was the scene of many a merry gathering. Its English prototype has been described as 'a celebrated place of cockney amusement' and there is no doubt that the heart and the footsteps of many a cockney dwelling in Sydney turned lovingly in the direction of Rushcutters Bay.'[4]

Bentley's Bridge, built of stone, with a single arch, replaced the stepping stones across the creek. A resident who spent his childhood there, remembered that 'this was a regular rendezvous for a host of young Sydney desperados, bushrangers in embryo, who used to locate themselves in force at this point and 'stick-up' the lads who had been on a wild berry gathering expedition. The wild bushland abounded in the summer season with 'gee bungs and 'five corners'* and when the boys who were a long morning tramp from the city, and running risk of sunstroke and snake bite, were returning with well filled bags, they were stopped at this bridge (the only available crossing place), with cries of "Bail up". Sometimes the returning berry hunters would amalgamate into parties of sufficient strength to resist this 'blackmailing' and many a desperate 'five corner' fight ensued. These juvenile robbers went by the name of 'spicers.' Another resident, recollected that the boys also used to collect shrimps from the head of the bay and set up poles 'covered with snares made of horse hair and used for the purpose of collecting Rosella parrots, (pretty Joeys). I used to go to school somewhere about the middle of the flat, the master's name was Hogg, and on my way I had to pass over a plank that bridged the creek. The flat at that time was covered with a prickly bush bearing a yellow flower somewhat akin to the gorse species.'[6]

There was a second bridge across the creek at the head of the valley on the South Head Road, where there were several airshafts that were part of a water tunnel from the Lachlan Swamps to an outlet in Hyde Park. This extraordinary project which began in 1827 and was supervised at first by Colonel Busby, was 'a meandering construction ranging in dimension from small shafts to caves three meters high.'[7] Water was desperately needed in the town, and was sold from carriers or collected by individuals. 'I had to go with a hoop and two buckets for water, that trickled from a spring in the rocks into a deep basin that had been hewn out of the solid rock by the inmates of the Darlinghurst Gaol, and let me tell you that water in those days was a rather scarce commodity, as Mr. Craddock and other purveyors of the fluid with their carts could not always be relied upon, and the price was 3p a bucket.[8]

The pipe, which was in the north west corner of Hyde Park, began to flow ten years later, and initially was a great success with plenty of water moving by gravity along the tunnel. Major Barney, who had taken over construction after Colonel Busby, stated that there was 'sufficient water in the tunnel to last for twelve months without a single shower of rain falling.' However Chambers Encyclopaedia states that from July 1838 to August 1839 not a drop of rain fell in Sydney'[9], and within a few years the supply was totally inadequate.

Further along the South Head Road, Reverend Hill had a house and land adjacent to Thomas West. He was one of the founding members of the Australian Subscription Library and in 1826, Governor Darling granted 6 acres of land to it, in aid of the building fund, on the other side of Reverend Hill's property. He was a Church of England clergyman, and was the regular minister at St. James when it was consecrated in 1824. He was secretary of the Benevolent Society for 16 years, was an advocate of free public schools, and the founder of the NSW Society to promote Christian knowledge among aborigines. His house was a half hour's walk from the church and the convict

Reverend Hill, Mitchell Library, State Library of New South Wales.

barracks at Hyde Park, which he visited regularly. He died of an attack of apoplexy in the vestry at St. James in 1836. A tablet in his memory extols his virtues. 'In affectionate remembrance of his unwearied labours of seventeen years, his serene resignation under no ordinary trials, his blameless and useful life, his prompt attention to every call of distress, his faithful and fearless reproof of the sinner.'

Those who were Grantees, or were wealthy enough to buy 4 acre blocks, built large houses in the valley. One of them, Engehurst, designed by John Verge, was built for Mr. Hely, the Superintendent of Convicts, and was below Juniper Hall. Judge Therry, who was the legal officer for the Legislative Council built Flinton. He was a forthright man and was known to have felt that Governor Gipps, who arrived in 1838, talked too much for his own good. In Therry's view, sincerity was one thing, but it was hardly dignified to tell the Council that he didn't care one farthing, whether they passed a particular measure or not.[10] Flinton, completed in 1834, was also on the northern side of the South Head Road, and had 'verandas surrounding the stone house of fourteen rooms. The grounds included a coach house, stables, outbuildings and a cottage. Joseph Maiden, director of the Botanical Gardens, laid out the grounds.'[11]

By the end of the decade James Underwood was going 'home' to Surrey, a wealthy and successful man. He had leased the distillery in 1836 with a farmhouse and garden attached, to Abercrombie and Mackay, and decided to subdivide some of his land, as the demand was rising.

Allotments were advertised in October 1839. 'Such a choice spot for health and extensive scenery cannot be outvied as it has a perfect view of the best parts of Sydney, Darlinghurst, Port Jackson Harbour, the South and North Heads, Waverly Village, the Surry Hills gardens, Botany Bay, New Town and other suburban parts. Consequently to what ever point of the compass the eye turns, it is certain of not only pleasing the imagination, but also of enlivening the spirits of even the most abject—for here they might have all the comforts of a quiet country life.'

Stone for building was available on the land and there were four streets named; Paddington, Underwood, William (after his son) and Elizabeth (after his wife).

Developers bought up to 12 lots each, and only 7 were sold individually. The cost was approximately 360 pounds per acre. A year later 3 lots were sold for double the price.[12] Paddington speculation had begun.

Governor Bourke had established a system of bounties in 1835, to encourage emigration, but the system was seen in England to be one where the poorest, least useful people were encouraged to apply and some parishes made it very hard for some to refuse. The emigration authorities stipulated that a minimum of clothing and bedding be bought for the journey, nothing but bare boards being supplied on the ship. Some emigrants lacked even the mattresses and blankets needed, and these were sometimes provided by the parish.[13]

A young arrival, after his ship had arrived in the harbour, and was anchored north off Pinchgut Island, wrote, 'I put off on a boat about 9 o'clock, leaving Sarah on board the vessel until I could find a nest for my little bird — as we drew near I thought of the dangers we had escaped and the distance we were from our friends, and the feeling that I was among a nation of strangers having to seek for my living came over me very strong.'[14]

The NSW Calendar and Directory of 1834, advised emigrants that 'houses may be built on the outskirts of town for thirty five pounds each, on ground of nearly the same value. The rent of a house so constructed is from eight to ten shillings a week.' Building regulations allowed that shingles of hardwood were as safe a covering as people could afford, but they insisted that if houses were conjoined, an 18 inch party wall was the minimum thickness allowable. Robert Taylor, bricklayer and carpenter, had thirteen cottages in hand along South Head Road, nine feet high, twenty four feet by twenty feet. He claimed he could only afford nine inch walls. The space and money lost by thickening the walls would force him, he said, to a second storey and of course to a higher rental.[15]

There was little permanent work for mechanics, and wages were low for common labourers. In 1834, common labourers could expect 14/– a week without board and lodging, so the rent of a cottage of two or three rooms would be prohibitive. Stonecutters/setters did better at 4/6 to 8/6 per day.[16] Emigrants were advised that, 'the most economical and safest, as well as the most comfortable mode for mechanics, is for several families to hire a house jointly, and to live in common, not to board, otherwise they run the risk of being pilfered and injured in a thousand ways.'[17]

With only casual work available and high rents, it was very difficult for emigrants without capital to cope, and 82 per cent of the population in 1841 were mechanics, labourers or servants.[18] Apart from the problems of housing, food was expensive and of a poor quality. A Mr. Pughe writing in the early 1840's reported, 'Imagine a composition of water, whitening and milk brought to your door every morning, and sold at the rate of 16p a quart as milk, suspicious looking eggs, one third of which are possibly rotten, 4p to 6p each; bread 9p the 2lb loaf; cabbages and cauliflowers 6p to 1/–, fowls and ducks 5/–to 7/– shillings a pair, and beef and mutton in every respect inferior to Indian fed meat at 9p and 10p a pound; washing such as it is 5/– or 6/– a dozen; servants 25 to 30 pounds a year and their food; all this with the thermometer occasionally at 112 in the shade, and always extremely hot in the summer season, you will then be able to form some calculation as to how far income would go.[19]

Charlotte Godley, writing to a friend in New Zealand, described another torment. 'The mosquitoes completed the picture, and left us very little peace after the candles were lighted. My husband wore gloves and a pocket handkerchief over his head and even then could hardly sit still to write or read, and though he slept in them, it was of little or no use. I was at last so sleepy from continual short nights that I could scarcely keep awake if I sat down anywhere for half an hour.'[20]

In August, 1840, a decision was made to move the Barracks from George Street to Paddington Hill, on land that had been part of the Sydney Common. There was a hotel, The Union, and a grocer's shop on part of the Subscription Library Grant site. The rest was subdivided and sold. Again speculators bought up several blocks at a time, but the boom was to be short lived, as a devastating drought in country areas caused prices to drop and some blocks were left undeveloped for years.

The construction company for the Barracks was Brodie and Craig, Royal Engineers. The site was a most uninviting sandhill. The larger trees had been carted away for firewood, and 'woodcutters had even begun digging up and making use of the roots of the old trees for the same purpose.'[21] Building of the officer's quarters began at the eastern end, and the stone was quarried on site. Convict labourers were accommodated at the western end in a stockade, 'under the control of a very big man called 'The Boomer'. I think his name was Green and he opened a hotel called the Green Gate or Golden Gate. This man had been a sculptor's model. I recollect having been shown some original drawings of muscular arms and limbs executed by the artist.'[22] The prisoners were soon replaced by a party of stone masons, who were free immigrants brought from England to erect the Customs House and other buildings in Sydney. They also erected a number of houses in the immediate vicinity, [Paddington Village] some of wood, others of stone, to accommodate the influx of new civilian residents.

The other public buildings in the area were the new gaol and courthouse at Darlinghurst. There was room for 3000 prisoners and in the late 1840's the gallows were erected over the main entrance. 'The condemned man's body, when the bolt was drawn, fell dangling on the outside of the gaol wall on the street. In the forties, the public hangman was named Green and he lived in a hut in the centre of what is now known as Green's Park.'[23]

There was a third large building on the South Head Road. Joseph Marshall had married Obed West's niece, Louisa. He was the son of a physician, who, arriving in Sydney in 1840, and finding a lack of many medicines, decided to manufacture them. He bought a property, Belmont Villa, which included the spring feeding Rushcutters Creek, and a garden sloping down to the corner of Dowling and Oxford Streets, and got to work. An abundant supply of pure water was necessary for the preparation of medicines, and it also proved to be ideal for home brewed beer, which the doctor made for his family and a few friends. Persuaded that the quality of the beer merited large scale production, he set up Marshall's Co-operative Brewery Ltd., and began winning medals and certificates for his beverages.[24]

Frederick Garling, Old South Head Road, 1842, Mitchell Library, State Library of New South Wales.

John Hardwick, View from my bedroom window, 1853,
Mitchell Library, State Library of New South Wales.

John Hardwick, Panorama of Paddington, 1853, Mitchell Library,
State Library of New South Wales.

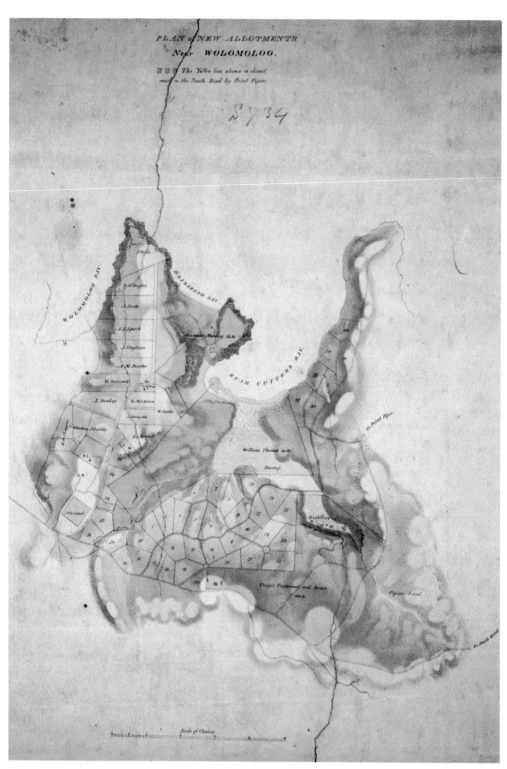

Plan of New Allotments Near Wolomoloo, 1828, State Archives Department

By 1846, the population in NSW had almost doubled again to 197,000 and the village opposite the new barracks was well established. Further up the hill were cottages and larger houses on the Paddington Estate and more villas were being built. John Gurner had commissioned John Verge to submit plans for Duxford, and W. T. Cape opened his school in Elfred House, on a four acre grant on the Glenmore Road, having resigned from Sydney College over a dispute regarding money being spent on buildings rather than teacher's wages. Obed West had completed his new house, Barcom Glen, beside his large dairy in 1845. 'It stood in a large excavation in the solid rock, which looked like a dry moat around the house. The basement containing the kitchen, pantry, store-room and cellar, was below ground level but had windows opening into the 'area' for light and air. This 'area' or dry moat was wide enough for the domestic washing to be done there and there was a laundry copper and set of wooden tubs which stood outside the kitchen and were filled with water from the natural springs at two corners of the moat. Entrance into the house was by means of an elegant little bridge spanning the moat and leading into the hall on the ground floor. Here stood one of two grandfather clocks. Obed would not allow them to be set at the same time as he liked to hear the chimes separately. In the entrance hall there was also a cedar cabinet containing the service lift or 'dumb waiter', which connected with the kitchen below, and narrow flights of stairs leading upstairs and downstairs. All of the doors, stairs, trims, and joinery were of cedar.

On the left as you entered the hall, was the breakfast room built straight above the kitchen with its fuel stove. Adjoining it was the dining room, and a door led from here to the drawing room with an Italian marble fireplace. The remaining corner of the ground floor was filled by a narrow passage and two small bedrooms. Upstairs there were just three large bedrooms and a hall running from the front of the house to the back. The master bedroom occupied one end of the floor and had windows opening onto three sides, and the other half of the floor must have been a dormitory for boys and girls. There was no bathroom to begin with. At some stage a veranda was built around three sides and covering the moat. The veranda was open at the front, but enclosed at the two ends, providing for an office/bedroom and carpenter's shop at one end and a large bathroom and sewing room at the other. There were two privies back to back at the bottom of the garden. In front of the house stood two big Norfolk pines with staghorns. Two immense Moreton Bay figs shaded all the space on the NW side of the house. Up the hillside was the remains of a vegetable garden, a glass house and a green house. The whole garden was enclosed by a wooden fence with a small gate leading out into paddocks lying towards Rushcutter's Bay.'[25]

Thomas Broughton had bought part of Gurner's 1830's grant, and built Bradley Hall, before he became Mayor of Sydney in 1847, and Thomas Ridley had done sufficiently well in his market garden, leased from Obed on the flats at Rushcutter's Bay, to build Lohort. Judge Kinchela, after renting Juniper Hall, built his own home, The Terraces.

Rich and poor lived alongside each other in Paddington, the rich surrounded by gardens and orchards, the poor confined to wooden cottages and small two storied stone houses, often conjoined, in the village, and on the hill above the Barracks.

Eight years after construction began, the 11th Devon regiment arrived at the new Queen Victoria Barracks in 1848, led by Colonel Bloomfield. They marched to their new quarters on August 6, but they were not pleased. 'From city life they were removed to suburban and as they marched out the gate they gave vent to their displeasure in groans and hoots — very unsoldierly-like conduct but perhaps excusable under the circumstances.'[26] Colonel Mundy wrote of the new Victoria Barracks. 'Gentlemen of my profession, liable to service in this colony, will not be glad perhaps to learn that the Barracks have been removed from George Street in the midst of the city, to the top of a suburban sandhill about a mile and a half from the central thoroughfare'.[27] There were several major disadvantages. Firstly, the westerly winds whipped sand off the sandhill across the parade ground. Soldier's eyes became red and swollen and 'discharge a glutinous sort of matter, which seals the eyelids together. This disease is attended also with an itching sensation. It is generally remediable by shading from the sun and washing the eyes with a little weak goulard water.[28] Secondly, the barrack square itself was a sandheap, especially the eastern portion of it, and the soldiers were required to level it, by handtrucking sand to the rear where it was used to fill up stagnant water holes.[29] Thirdly, it was a good half hour's walk to town.

Some civilians were sympathetic. 'The band on a Tuesday afternoon, played in front of Richmond Terrace in the Domain, and I used to pity some of the rank and file as they carried the ponderous green painted music stands from and back to the Barracks — rather trying on a warm summer afternoon. Trams were not thought of in those days, nor was an omnibus engaged to make the journey less wearisome — totally unlike some of the regimental bands that came after, an omnibus being always requisitioned for their convenience.'[30]

From 1849 the 11th was the only guard over convicts in NSW. They also took responsibility for the NSW Mounted Police, helped with firefighting and with any civil uprisings. 'For this the soldiers received no more than 3/6 per week'[31], and they supplemented their income by tailoring, bootmaking and making cabbage tree hats. The wives assisted their husbands in their manufacture and in the afternoon 'women and children could be seen sitting on the veranda of the new barracks, cutting and plaiting the straw.'[32] The hats were made by opening out cabbage palm fronds, boiling, then hanging them out to dry. The spine of each frond was removed and the leaf split into strands for plaiting into a flat braid. By the 1850's, pay had increased to 1/– a day and 6p for food and keep, which was a ration of meat, a pound of bread, and anything else that could be scrounged. Some soldiers grew vegetables, and they had to do their own cooking. They wore white calico trousers, and scarlet jackets with high collars. Their equipment consisted of crossed-over breast straps, on the left supporting a bayonet and on the right, an ammunition pouch. On the back, a knapsack, which contained a blanket roll and any other equipment they may have been ordered to carry. If outside the barracks on work detail, they carried a linen bag for food and a water bottle. Their headwear was known as a shako. It had a light pom pon and a silk tassel.[33]

The residents of the village quickly became used to the sounds of activity, the music of the band before the officers' quarters in the evening, and the tattoo as the day's work ended. A Paddington resident remembered how he 'stood as a lad at the main gate to see the regiment leaving the barracks for the grand parade in the Domain on May 24th, Queen's Birthday, making one of a large crowd that not only assembled there but lined the road down to the pump that stood in front of the Courthouse at Darlinghurst. It was a boy's ambition in those days to get near the Drum Major Campbell but, at the same time to keep a safe distance from his staff, that was used occasionally to tap the head of some adventurous lad, just as a reminder that his presence near proved distasteful to the majestic wearer of the huge bearskin cap. Then came the pioneers with their leather aprons and battle-axes followed by the band, then the jolly old Colonel on his charger, ready for a sly glance at a well-dressed female on the road, the sight of such generally commanding his attention. When the review was over, the band and the grenadier company marched to Government House, the grenadiers as a guard of honour for the levee. Taken on the whole, the 11th were a good stamp of men, from the Colonel down to the youngest drummer boy. Of course some tippling was indulged in. 'Tooth's Tanglefoot' or 'Soldiers Joy' were the favourite beverages, while some patronised what the soldiers called 'calamity', and today call colonial rum, but the great majority of the men were steady. A few of them were seriously inclined and spent their Sabbath afternoons in teaching young children in the Bourke Street Wesleyan Sunday School. There were some very good cricketers among the officers. Many a time have I watched them practising on the garrison ground at the rear of the Barracks — next to Billy Goat Swamp.'[34]

The 11th became heroes after they attended a serious fire on January 16 1853, at the Kent Brewery. 'The engines of the fire brigade and the insurance companies were quickly on the scene but had great difficulty obtaining water. They did not start working until three hours later, and then made little impression on the fire because of insufficient water pressure. Before the 11th arrived, 'a number of persons had made their way into the cellars — an extensive range of which runs under the building where the fire was going, and had drunk to excess of whatever they could, and this outrageous conduct was soon put a stop to. But it was not until 1am that the fire was under control. General Wynyard commended the troops, who in addition received monetary rewards from Tooth's.'[35]

However it seems there were some renegades. 'The late Sir Thomas L. Mitchell, Surveyor General, was waylaid and robbed by some of the soldiers of that regiment [the 11th] on the Glenmore Road when returning from the Barracks after dining with the officers of that regiment. Sir Thomas was in plain clothes and not recognised. Being an old soldier himself and a Peninsular man, he would not or could not identify the assailants. A walk to my domicile from the city at night was often a danger — many residents at Surry Hills, including Majors Christy and Smith, Captain Westmacott and others were sworn in as special constables. On one occasion with a friend, we rescued a young sailor from two ruffians.'[36]

The officers' balls held at the Barracks were affairs of unusual splendour attended by up to four hundred of the elite of the colony, and at Christmas time all the windows were illuminated with candles.

'The Regiment's departure for Britain in October, 1857, was a memorable occasion. On the afternoon of Friday 23rd, the men were mustered on the parade ground at Victoria Barracks. The band had struck up the inevitable, 'The girl I left behind me', and the regiment marched down to the Exchange building in Macquarie Place. Countless flags and banners hung from buildings. At times during the march it was a matter of difficulty to get along, from the number of acquaintances who were constantly running up to grasp the hand of red-coated friends whom they were about to lose, perhaps for ever. At the Exchange building, Sir Alfred Stephen, presented Colonel Bloomfield with an address signed by 3000 Sydney residents and a testimonial of several hundred pounds. The huge crowd cheered loudly and the Regiment then marched down to Circular Quay.

Some soldiers remained behind and took up residence in the village. Sergeant Major Thomas Haynes opened a public house on the corner of the Glenmore and the Old South Head Roads within a few yards of the Barrack gates. This he named in honour of his commander, The Colonel Bloomfield Hotel. I believe he changed it afterwards to the Hero of Waterloo. Sergeant Lees, established himself as a hotel keeper on the South Head Road, at The Eagle Tavern, and afterwards he joined the local forces. Samuel Curry who was 18 years a Colour Sergeant, established himself as a grocer and druggist on the Old South Head Road in 1862. Then there was big Sebastian Hodge, who had been a boy in the band. He left with the regiment but came back to Sydney on gaining his discharge. He was janitor and drill sergeant at Sydney Grammar School.'[37]

By the 1850's there was a whole generation of young people who had been born in Australia, the currency lads and lasses. The girls who threw flowers at members of the 11th Regiment as they marched down to the quay, were described by a visitor to Australia, Mr. Frank Fowler. 'The young ladies are in many respects remarkable. At thirteen years of age they have more ribbons, jewels and lovers than perhaps any other young ladies of the same age in the universe. They prattle, and very insipidly too, from morning to night. They rush to the Botanical Gardens twice a week, to hear the band play. The first time I visited the theatre, I sat near a young lady who wore at least a half-a-dozen rings over her white gloves, and who, if bare mosquito-bitten shoulders may be deemed beautiful, showed more beauty than I ever saw a young lady display before. Mr. Fowler also describes the young men. 'The Australian boy is a slim dark-eyed, olive complexioned young rascal, fond of Cavendish, cricket and chuckpenny and systematically insolent to all servant girls, policemen and new chums. His hair is shiny with grease, as are the knees of his breeches and the elbows of his jacket. He wears a cabbage tree hat, with a dissipated wisp of black ribbon dangling behind, and loves to walk meditatively with his hands in his pockets, and if cigarless, to chew a bit of straw in the extreme corner of his mouth.'[38] Von Hugel, however, gave a different impression. 'They are an educated, powerfully built and fine looking race of men, open hearted and clear-headed, friendly, good-natured, modest, yet vigorous in word and deed. It may be that I met only the best of them but I shall never forget the months I spent in their company. The native born are more than a match for the immigrants in integrity, sound views and physical stature.[39]

Their prowess at swimming was much admired. 'There are many young men who think no more of swimming out a mile or more or back, than a stranger would of taking a walk that distance. From habit, the exertion is not fatigue to them. Men and women, boys and girls, all more or less indulge in this healthy enjoyment; and so much indeed was bathing in fashion at one time, that it was impossible to walk about any time of day, by the waterside about Sydney without being annoyed by bathers in all directions.'[40]

Peter Cunningham spoke of their accent. 'The London mode of pronunciation has been duly engrafted on the colloquial dialect of our currency youths and even the better sort of them are apt to meet your observation of 'A fine day', with their improving response, 'Wery fine indeed.'[41]

Shops on the South Head Road were increasing and there was plenty to gossip about. One evening a bootmaker, William Stock was fitting some Adelaide boots on a Miss Annie Murphy, when Timothy Callagan entered and asked the price of Wellington boots. Without waiting to try them on he grabbed them and bolted. Unfortunately for Timothy the boots were odd sizes, and Mr. Stock was a faster runner than he was. The boots were valued at one pound, the equivalent of more than a week's pay for a labourer. On another occasion, 'Harriet, a dark haired, sprightly eyed, pretty faced wife of a fancy baker who makes batches, twists, crackers, turnovers, etc on the South Head Road' was in

John Hardwick, Ormond House, 1853, Mitchell Library, State Library of New South Wales.

court accusing Alice Gray, her ladies' maid, of stealing a chemise worth 4/6. Poor Alice's only defense consisted of a 'flood of tears'. She was sentenced to seven days of hard labour at the Darlinghurst Gaol.[42]

A third incident is reported in full. 'Thomas O'Connell, alias Captain Connelly, was placed at the bar, charged with performing various eccentric

Robert Cooper Esq.

gyrations on the South Head Road, during Sunday afternoon, to the infringement of the Queen's peace and to the infinite astonishment of the natives, male and female. The prisoner is a hale uproarious old fellow, as drunk as he could stand in the dock, so much so that Dr. Rutter remarked that he was still under the potent influence of the jolly divinity. He shouted out, "I'll be damned if my name's O'Connell; I've been many years in Her Majesty's service and I wish I'd been shot before I'd come to this country."

Constable Whale; "He was very drunk, dancing, shouting and staggering on the South Head Road."

Prisoner; "That's very like a whale; I was not drunk; I was a full corporal or an general, or a ral of some sort or other, in the Spanish war and my name's Captain Connelly" (Here he doubled his two hands to his mouth and imitated the trumpet reveille).

Mr. Moffat; "The mud on the South Head Road is enough to make anyone stagger." (Laughter)

Mr. Egan JP; "You must pay ten shillings or spend a night and a day in gaol."

Prisoner; "What! Send me to gaol! Oh Moses! I am the son of an Irish King."'[43]

Many people were getting tired of the dissolute ways of many of the residents of Sydney and soon after he arrived in 1838, Governor Gipps became patron of the newly formed Temperance Society. He spoke of legislation to prohibit wages being paid in alcohol and to license all wholesale dealing in spirits.

Robert Cooper however was incensed that local distilleries were to be closed down and made an impassioned, if somewhat incoherent, appeal against the Prohibition of Colonial Distillation in August 1839. 'I do most urgently and with becoming respect, entreat of you to pause ere you stultify the policy of the local government hitherto as well as destroy utterly all future confidence on the part of individuals and the public in respect of the government. As to the morality of the proposed prohibition, it would be difficult to imagine how any morality could be discovered from a measure which involves in it a breach of faith, not merely towards an individual but to the public. While on a further consideration of the subject, the possibility of the mere prohibition of colonial distillation working any good moral effect, or to produce any reduction in the amount of intemperance [is unreasonable], while the importation of spirits is to be continued.'[44]

In June, 1843, Robert Cooper had decided to stand for the New Legislative Council against William Wentworth, and Captain John Piper's son-in-law, Mr. O'Connell. He harangued the mob from an omnibus, and his supporters from Blackwattle Swamp 'fell upon all who expressed dissent in so vigorous a manner, that Cooper was able to talk away for some time without interruption.'[45] He was not elected and by August he had been declared bankrupt and was forced to rent out Juniper Hall.[46]

There were already a number of hotels on the South Head Road. They provided food drink, shelter, warmth, light, lavatories, sometimes a bed and above all, company, to the many left homeless by itinerant work and lack of family. Even those with a home met in the public houses to talk, sing, dance, dice, play cards and plan activities. Not only horse and foot racing, cricket matches, regattas, wrestling, dog fights and cock fights were arranged but also Friendly Societies, Masonic Lodges, trades unions, and debating societies, held meetings there.[47]

One of the most popular was the Paddington Inn. 'A globetrotter of 1853 wrote thus; One Sunday afternoon I paid my fare, 6p, and took an outside seat for a short drive to the country. At the end of two miles we reached a coy little inn which was our destination. Jane Beard was painted on the sign in large capitals, and on entering the house, I found Jane Beard to be a handsome young widow about 25 years of age, rather stout and with such a thoroughly good-natured, pretty English face that I thought she was well worth going two miles to see. We remained nearly an hour — no one seemed inclined to leave, and the bus had to wait beyond its time to get a return cargo. The house was crowded with people, and the pretty widow had a smile and a joke for everyone. I got into a little parlor in which were a chimney sweep, his wife, his wife's sister and two children, who had come on the same errand as myself, and they had all partaken so freely of the widow's good cheer to be nearly speechless.'[48]

But all was not revelry and high times. The Temperance Movement was gathering momentum and during the 1840's and 1850's 'the bourgeois family was propagated as the most suitable form of social organization for the new nation. Its general prescription was that women, as wives of men and mothers of children, were entrusted with the moral guardianship of society. They were expected to curb restlessness and rebelliousness in men and instill virtues of civic submission in children.'[49]

Paddington was about to become respectable.

Chapter 3
Cast Iron Morality

In 1853, a young man, John Hardwick, arrived in Sydney, which was described at the time as being very like an English seaport town. 'The same kind of butcher boys and baker men, cab drivers and bus conductors, even the constables who quietly pace the pavement.'[1] John documented his travels in letters to his mother, brothers, and sisters, and after spending a few days being splendidly looked after at Petty's Hotel in the city, he began to look for permanent accommodation. He went with his friend Arthur W. to meet Mr. and Mrs. Stamper and their three children in Paddington, and decided to lodge with the family for one pound a week. His letters reflect the views of an educated, temperate, young man.

The house adjoined Ormond House and was opposite Juniper Hall, 'a noble looking mansion surrounded with picturesque grounds and gardens. This estate belongs to our next door neighbour, an old Australian of the name of Cooper, and a genuine specimen of his class. He came out here many years ago 'at this country's expense', and amassed an immense fortune as a distiller. His wife is a big, masculine woman using her authority pretty freely … It appears that some years ago they lived a while in France. There is a large family upgrown and largely dispersed, one daughter married to a count they say. Old Cooper seems to have lost the greater part of his property through his children's imprudent extravagance. I can't tell why they left Juniper Hall for the smaller house adjoining alongside, except it were for economy's sake.

Rents are so expensive and houses so greatly in demand that the covetous landlords are careless of finish and comfort. Old Cooper leaves the property arrangements to his wife, and this managing old lady is by no means pliable as far as the comfort and convenience of the house is concerned. Every morning

I have to roll up the blind and afterwards lift the window and prop it with a piece of chip. But the bedroom is roomy and neat and looks out towards Paddington. My bedstead is iron and quite big enough for two. The woodwork (as usual here) is of polished cedar and looks very handsome.'² He decorated his room with vases of flowers that he had collected on his rambles and soon became fond of his companions. 'The Stampers are kind hearted and sensible people. Mr. Stamper, a solicitor from Liverpool, is rather deaf and defers in minor matters to his wife's judgement. He is an enthusiast in drawing and has a wonderful talent for design and decoration. Mrs. S., who has a cast in one eye, has three little children, one called Malanethon — they buried a child who they had called Avise — wasn't it singular? ... She exhausts her ingenuity in the cooking line, but now has a new stove and makes pudding brimming with treacle.'³ They had porridge for breakfast and John took sandwiches with him for lunch. In the town, two miles down the South Head Road, John could have also bought double and single Gloucester cheese, York and Westphalian hams, Indian guava jelly, Indian curry powder, Turkey figs, Normandy pippins, and even Fry's chocolate.⁴

There were seven people living in the house, and John spent most of his time in a rocky nook where he read, sketched, and was occasionally bothered by bull ants, or was out exploring the area. 'Last Saturday I had the most delightful walk in the immediate neighbourhood — at the back the ground falls away suddenly to Rushcutters Bay and the valley in the bottom is the most delicious scenery you can imagine — I can make a short cut to this paradise in a few minutes by a footpath through a craggy wood which clothes the Paddington declivity. On the opposite side the ground rises very steep and this hill is traversed by several serpentine roads and adorably elegant villas...Towards the city this lovely vale is closed in by the heights of Woolloomooloo which are surmounted by three windmills, and these add greatly to the whole.'⁵

Sometimes he was hampered by the weather. After some days of heavy rain he did 'manage a walk about a mile up the road beyond Paddington. In this direction the country presents nothing but an immense tract of moorland, covered in furze and heather. Goats are extremely numerous but they have scanty herbage. In the afternoon I had a ramble in Paddington Wood. I discovered the principal waterfall, and proceeded some distance down this descent of rocks. I did not however, reach more than half the distance to the distillery in the valley, the ground being very swampy. The opposite heights looked exceedingly fine, presenting an immense amphitheatre clothed from top to bottom with luxuriant gum trees.'⁶

John attended the Wesleyan chapel in Bourke Street, where some members of the 11th Devon were also teaching Sunday school, and was asked to run the second Methodist Sunday school in Underwood Street. He shared his duties with Mr. Tempest who was a wholesale ironmonger and local preacher. He lived further up the South Head Road where he shared a house with three other young men.

A few months later John reported to his mother that the school was becoming popular and the 'children are getting to love it, and love us.'[7] In September they gave the children a tea. They met at the school about three, recited pieces and sang hymns and Mr. Turner talked to them for an hour. 'We then turned out for a scamper and romp — then tea and buns, and finished up singing, 'Oh that'll be joyful'. The children dispersed with cheers and clapping.'[8] The teachers and friends adjourned to tea at Mr. Turner's house, with singing in the drawing room.

Two years later, children were able to go to the new Paddington school, where 227 of them learnt to read, often using the New Testament as their text. They learnt writing in three stages; in large hand on slates, in large hand on paper, and in small hand on paper. They also learnt arithmetic.[9] Teachers received a halfpenny a day per child, and were paid a small salary.

John became more friendly with the Coopers' and the whole household was invited to dinner on Mrs. Cooper's birthday. She also invited them to Juniper Hall, which had been renamed Ormond House. 'This fine house is very extensive and roomy and is surrounded by a noble balcony. It is now let to the conductors of a Benevolent Institution — an Asylum for Orphans and Destitute Children. I peeped into the schoolroom and saw the youngsters busy with their lessons. The view from the upper regions is certainly most extensive in every direction. I was not aware, until Mrs. Cooper explained, from the balcony, how adjacent to Paddington is the nearest point of the ocean — I was astonished to remark going to bed on Monday evening that I could hear the breakers as they dashed against a cliff in heavy surf. This fact I verified next day as I stood near Paddington Mill, when I not only distantly perceived the successive waves, but a lady residing close by assured me they were readily audible when there was a heavy sea.'[10]

After several months he was getting anxious about a job. 'I fear Ma will be discouraged when she finds I am still doing nothing, but the fact is, every place is crowded and overstocked with newcomers. If you think of commencing on your own account there are swarms in the field already, and as to situations, clerks are a redundancy and there is no choice of occupation. I really am puzzled what to do — I fear it will have to come to a situation on the long term, and I will have to content myself with something ordinary, for I am not yet known. I have been very desirous to start storekeeping but can't tell where to look out for a position.'[11] John eventually found a clerk's position through a friend, with Merchants and Importers. He worked six days a week, and was pleased that on Saturdays he could leave the office early, about 2 or 3 o'clock. But he had to work extremely long hours, sometimes not leaving until 11.30 on Saturday night.

Lack of work was a common problem. 'There are many persons of better education and social habits, who are reduced to so much suffering for want of any kind of employment for which they are fitted, and who make their distress the more severe by their struggles to conceal it. And of this class there appear to be competent clerks and accountants who cannot obtain situations. There are many men, both mechanics and labourers of good character and sober habits able and willing to work for their daily bread, who nevertheless cannot obtain employment.'[12]

John had sent some of his sketches to his mother in February 1854. He commented, 'The Panorama of Paddington, is to the life. Oft it has gladdened my eyes as I returned from a country stroll to view this identical scene. I also like the view of the Paddington Barracks from Darlinghurst. It is soft and harmonious. I know every land mark, house and tree from my frequent peregrinations in this, the most beautiful suburb in Sydney.'[13]

John Hardwick was a typical member of the educated, conservative, temperate, middle class. Although he could see the Paddington Inn from his bedroom window across the open paddocks, he never mentioned visiting a hotel except for Petty's, where he stayed for a few days after his arrival. By 1860, there were considerable congregations of Methodists in Surry Hills and Paddington, Presbyterians at St. Johns, Anglicans at St. Matthias and even Congregationalists in Paddington Street. Although Mass was said as early as 1866, regular attendance for Catholics was not possible until 1879 when St. Francis Church was built.[14] The Methodist Church on Oxford Street was not completed until 1877. Respectable new immigrants carried radical ideas of self-restraint and moral improvement. But there were plenty of others who all too frequently lived in a muddle of alcohol, street brawling and irresponsibility. And almost none wanted to go to the country. They found it a silent and slightly menacing place and they preferred the conviviality of city life.[15]

In 1854, there was a Committee of Enquiry into the increasing evidence of intemperance. In the twelve months ending June 1854, 660,360 gallons of spirits, 296,142 gallons of rum, and 364,218 of gin and brandy were released from bond in Sydney. This did not include spirits made in the colony, and the annual consumption of spirits amounted to more than two and a half gallons per head.[16] The consequences of widespread and excessive drinking were a nuisance to the rich, and a burden on the public purse. John mentioned peeping through the window at the children in the Asylum for Orphaned and Destitute Children, many of whom were the victims of alcoholic parents. The Asylum was run by the Benevolent Society, which had leased Ormond House from Sarah Cooper in 1852. Five hundred pounds was set aside by the Legislative Council for the conversion of the house into an orphanage, and 89 children were accepted in the first year. Nineteen children were under five. Three years later a report was commissioned by the Governor to investigate whether the government was getting value for money for its donations to charitable organisations. Mayne and Merewether, the commissioners, were condemning of many of the services, including the Orphan Asylum. It was claimed that the building was 'old, out of repair, damp, dirty and unwholesome, from want of due attention to ventilation and cleanliness. The arrangements for washing children were slovenly and imperfect — the offices, filthy in the extreme.'[17]

In Paddington, and in fact the whole of Sydney, there was very little water for drinking, let alone bathing. The situation had become so desperate, there was a story, possibly an urban myth, of a person who was charged with being intoxicated. When he was asked how he became so, he replied that he had nothing else to drink, so he drank beer. The case was dismissed.[18] In Paddington there was only one pump in front of the courthouse at Darlinghurst,[19] and another at the corner of Burton and Oxford Streets, which were fed from Busby's Bore. The water quality was very poor, and in 1850, George Brown was convicted of dumping 200 tons of nightsoil at its source.[20] The Professor of Chemistry at the new University of Sydney, opened in 1852, began a campaign against the use of lead piping and also warned of pollution from abattoirs, wool washing facilities and cemeteries. Much of Sydney's night soil was deposited in an area in front of the cricket ground and drained into the water supply.[21] People in the Paddington village relied on the generosity of Mrs. Campbell who had a large paddock near the intersection of Glenmore and Oxford Streets. There was a copious spring on the estate and she permitted local people to use it for many years.[22] When Thomas and Obed West built cottages to rent in the 1850's, Thomas set up a trust to maintain a waterhole on their property, and erected a paling fence and wicket gate to keep out cattle and goats. Only tenants and occupiers of the estate were permitted to use it.[23] Those living in the villas on the slopes were often able to dig wells, but for people like the Stampers, their nearest source of supply would be Campbell's at the bottom of the hill, or a water carrier whose water was not only expensive, but of dubious quality.

Paddington continued to expand. An enterprising gentleman, Mr. Downey, saw some portable cottages at a Dublin exhibition and had four of them imported and erected in Magenta Place, off Oxford and Dowling Streets. 'The door and window frames were of cast iron, grooved to receive the woodwork. The veranda posts were of cast iron and the timber cut to size.'[24] Mr. Downey was returning after a second trip on the sailing ship, Dunbar, and drowned when it was wrecked on the South Head in 1857. Local residents were horrified as they watched 'the dead and mutilated bodies, as they were thrown upon the rocks.'[25] There was only one survivor who later became the lighthouse keeper of the new light on the South Head.

In the new subdivisons in the 1860's, where several sections of the Sydney Common had been made available for sale, developers were not responsible for

Oxford Street, Paddington, looking east from Regent Street, Mitchell Library, State Library of New South Wales.

street maintenance. They were often undrained, unlevelled, and inaccessible to wheeled vehicles. Something had to be done, so in September 1859, a petition for a new municipality, independent of the Sydney City Council, which had been incorporated in 1842, was signed by 172 persons residing in Paddington. Its boundaries were to be the Point Piper Road down to Double Bay, west to the city boundary and south to the Old South Head Road, but there were strong objections. Many residents didn't want to associate with the wealthier residents of Darling Point and 'an excited orator at a meeting held in connection with the movement for incorporation, declared that he didn't want them big bugs in his municipality.'[26] A majority agreed with him. The petition was successful and in 1860 the boundaries were shifted so that the southern boundary was the Sydney Common and the northern the New South Head Road. Paddington never extended beyond Point Piper Road. Municipal Councillors were elected by owners of property, many of whom were members of the local churches and regarded themselves as temperate, respectable citizens. They were interested in furthering their education through public libraries and mechanics institutes.

Local councils were given an extraordinary variety of tasks by the State government, including the building and improvement of roads, traffic regulation, toll roads and bridges, public lighting, licensing of public vehicles and carters, establishment of Council quarries and sale of gravel, paving of footpaths, fencing of dangerous areas, watering and scavenging of roadways and so on. On water supply, urban councils were supposed to provide watering places and public baths, administer the Public Health Act, prevent people

Oxford Street, Paddington looking west from Point Piper Road, Mitchell Library, State Library of New South Wales.

spitting in the street, dispose of night soil and kitchen rubbish, build and maintain drains and sewers, and establish mortuaries and cemeteries. Libraries, bands, parks and gardens were to be established and maintained.[27]

The first meetings of the Paddington Council were held at the Paddington Inn. Thomas, the son of James Underwood, was rejected as Chairman in favour of Mr. Perry, and a month later Underwood's position was declared vacant as he was bankrupt. The Council was given 400 pounds credit from the Government. Underwood Street was repaired, followed by Elizabeth and Victoria Streets, then the Council received its first complaint. A Mr. Stewart wrote about dangerous holes in front of his residence in Gordon Street. The Council 'resolved to inform him that on examination of the government plans of the municipality they couldn't find any Gordon Street and so work would not be done.'[28] In the same year, sections of Busby's Bore collapsed near the barracks and was never repaired, but the water found its own course and began running again.[29]

By 1862, the first rate collector of the new Council had resigned and the position was advertised at 60 pounds a year, with a house and three and a half per cent commission on the rates. Seventy-seven applications were received. In the following year, from rates collected, the Council allocated 22 pounds for works and 1,400 pounds for other expenses.[30]

There were 535 dwelling houses, with 2,800 residents and one foot constable servicing the area. 60 per cent of the houses were wooden, stone, or brick 2 roomed cottages with a skillion at the back for a kitchen and storeroom, and shingled roof. Thirty per cent were 4 roomed stone houses, 'finished in a very superior style and in every respect adapted to the purposes of a small respectable family. Cellars were commonly attached and the front elevation generally sheltered by a veranda. The kitchen and storerooms were detached.'[31] The remaining 10 per cent were villas and large houses. Rents were 7/– for three rooms and detached kitchens, or 13/– for a two- storied brick or stone house. Carpenters earned 2 pounds 14/–, stone masons 3 pounds.[32]

After a few years, the ratepayers were disillusioned by their newly elected Council and in 1864 a petition was presented. 'We, the undersigned rate payers of this municipality, hereby express our unqualified disapproval of the course being taken by you as a majority at the present Council in your intended purpose to expend the *entire municipal revenue* upon the erection of a most expensive Council Chambers for which there is no immediate or present necessity, while the most important requirements of the municipality still remain unprovided for, such as a full supply of water for all public and domestic purposes, the further extension of street lamps, and the completion of all those street improvements still remaining... We desire particularly to call your attention to the public pledges given by you at your election with regard to water supply in particular, which you are now about to violate most shamefully, and we now call upon you to either relinquish your present project, or to resign your seats and give place to those who will carry out the wishes of the majority of the rate payers'. It was signed by 226 Paddington residents. It seems there was some coercion, as a second petition was published, signed by 35 rate payers. 'We the undersigned ... do hereby protest against our names being appended to the request published in the Sydney Morning Herald on 12 March 1864. We were told and believed it was a petition for a supply of water, and under that impression we sanctioned our signatures. We still retain great confidence in the present Council.'[33]

The Council Chambers were duly erected in spite of the protest. Mr. Humphrey, who was elected at the head of the poll for the first Council, campaigned strongly against the new building, but was not re-elected. As a result the Council decided they were entitled to proceed, and bought land on the South Head Road [Women's Hospital] in 1866. The Council also paid Randwick Council 500 pounds, for the triangular portion of land around St. Matthias Church, Paddington. The expenditure would be more than offset by the revenue from rates on the new Sydney Common sub-divisions which had 292 lots for sale by the end of the decade.[34]

Ormond House had become an exclusive Boarding School for girls, run by a Miss Blaxland, then in 1868 the Benevolent Society leased it again. This time it was a Home for Deaf and Dumb children. Down in the valley, Eugene Dominic Nicholls had begun experiments in a one story stone cottage in Boundary Street, constructing ice-making machines, [Ice Street] which could make blocks from ten pounds to one ton. Thomas Sutcliffe Mort became interested and invested money in the project. Together they formed the NSW Fresh Food and Ice Company, with chilling works in the Blue Mountains, a cold store at Darling Harbour and refrigerated railway vans for meat and milk.[35] A tannery was using water from the other creek in the valley after James Elly Begg bought Underwood's distillery. He also bought Engehurst, while he built his new house, Olive Bank Villa, further down the hill away from the subdivisons on the other side of the South Head Road. His son bought Ormond House and part of William Cape's Elfred Estate and put a road through to Glenmore Road, calling it after himself. Later the Council saw fit to change the name from Begg to Ormond. Street.[36]

Horse omnibuses ran along the South Head Road, and often the buses were almost up to their axles in clay and mud. The passengers would have to get out and walk for the rest of the journey. At the top of the hill the bus proprietors had petitioned for a stand near the Point Piper Road with a shelter and watering for the horses.[37] In his reminiscences, G.V. Portus remembered the buses which 'took my infant fancy, especially those with four or even five horses — doubledeckers upon whose top story I was never allowed to go. The outside passengers, exclusively males, climbed up at the back by a series of spider steps, hand over hand and sat back to back with their feet braced against a rail. My bus travel was mostly on single deckers and always on the inside, which was reached by two broad steps. They were furnished with two carpet-cushioned seats facing each other along the length of the bus, and there was straw on the floor. These interiors were lighted at night by a flickering candle behind a little glass door that seldom kept shut, and swung to and fro with the motion of the bus. You paid your fare through an ingenious partition of glass, behind which appeared the driver's left hand to give you change. You rang a bell to tell him you were passing your money up, and he rang the bell vigorously if any dilatory passenger neglected to pay the fare.'[37] James Lees, a former member of the 11th Devons, who lived on Glenmore Road, ran outrigger cars to Waverley. They had two wheels, were driven by two horses and held about ten persons.[38]

The number of houses had almost doubled to 864 by 1873 and ten years later there were 2,347. It was impossible to provide adequate water and sewerage for such a large number of dwellings. In 1868, a pump had been installed outside the Barrack wall at Glenmore Road, and in 1869, 34 rate payers had been so disgruntled by the inactivity of the Council that they petitioned for inclusion in the city again.[39]

Max Kelly in his book, A Paddock Full of Houses, gives a detailed history of the transformation of Paddington, from a village into a suburb of Victorian terraces. Subdivision was neither simple nor rapid. As a general rule it was rare for any large estate in Paddington to be subdivided into its final form at the outset. The characteristic process was for an estate to be divided into smaller land parcels, (say into allotments of 60 foot frontages to the proposed street), themselves to be subdivided into smaller areas again, (say 30 ft. frontages), and finally when building was to commence, were often re-subdivided to allow a 30 foot street frontage to take two 15 foot wide houses. Nor were the large estates of Paddington sold in their entirety. In most cases they were sold off, over a period of time, in parcels of various sizes. One example of this was the Underwood Estate. After the initial sales as the Paddington Estate in 1839, the lots for sale in 1872 consisted of a section of the Old South Head Road, Albert Street, and a section of Underwood Street (12 lots with 20 foot frontages). In 1875, the largest number of lots were sold — 606 lots of mainly 20 foot frontages. The third parcel was sold as a block of six acres in 1876, and the final 214 lots were sold in 1886. Land was divided and sold for a variety of reasons, and rates increased fourfold on the Underwood Estate between 1863 and 1873. Some landholders, however, like Obed West, were reluctant to sell, and this prolonged the process of subdivision for more than 50 years. The land was advertised in much the same way in 1875 as it had been in 1839. A section of the advertisement in the Sydney Morning Herald for the Goodhope Estate, to be auctioned in 1875, described the area. 'One enjoys uninterrupted views of unsurpassed grandeur ... grassy slopes and oceans of woodlands, the ornate grounds of the neighbourhood properties and the villas of Darling Point — while the background is relieved by the waters of the lovely harbour, with its bold rocky headlands, all of which lend enchantment to the view, and form a picture of artistic beauty rarely if ever excelled'.

Some speculators sold the land as they had bought it, unimproved. George Davidson, however, by trade a stonemason, but working as a contractor-builder, bought two lots from the land speculator, John Cole in 1879. Davidson built one 16 foot wide house and the family moved in. They occupied the house for three years. By this time Davidson had completed the building of the second (identical) house, as well as a more modest third house adjoining. The third was 'hung' from the external side wall of his second house, affording him significant savings on construction costs. Upon the completion of this, his last house, the family, which included five daughters, moved in, enabling him to rent the more imposing pair of houses next door. This he did for seven years, until 1889, when he moved into what is now 75 Goodhope Street, the only one of his three houses that he had not lived in.[40]

The eleven year cycle of development of George Davidson's three terraces is also an excellent example of how terraces were financed. It was better for the owner builder to live on site and it was often necessary to complete one house and then to consolidate finance, before another was built. Davidson, and most other builders, constructed their properties in order to let them, rather than sell them.

Terraces were divided up into living areas downstairs and bedrooms upstairs. The ground floor consisted of a front parlour and back parlour. The front room could also be used as a bedroom if the families grew too large.

Originally the kitchen was built separately to reduce fire risks, but later was incorporated in the main body of the house. The water closet was situated outside near a back lane. Two to three bedrooms were situated upstairs. Interiors included pressed tin ceilings, picture rails, cornices and skirting boards. The houses had fireplaces in the front and back parlour of the ground floor, one in the kitchen and in the main bedroom upstairs. Most fireplaces were cast iron and coal burning. The houses had polished wood floors. The most significant external decorative feature of the architecture was the cast iron work. It was mass-produced both overseas and in Sydney. Some patterns were imported and later copied with or without the permission of the original manufacturers, and the same designs might have been seen in Paddington, Parkville, and Paris. The nature of the mass-production of the material led to a unity of style in public taste. It was the architecture of confidence and prosperity that only fell from favour during the depression of the 1890's.

The funding for the building and purchasing of houses often came from building societies that concentrated on investing in the district. One such society that was particularly active in Paddington, was the St. Joseph's Investment and Benefit Building Society. One hundred and seventeen loans were granted for Paddington properties by the Society between 1870 and 1890. In newspaper advertisements, St Joseph's encouraged thrift and saving. One paragraph, headed, 'The Value of Small Savings', illustrated its message with an anecdote.'The celebrated Benjamin Franklin said that a man who uselessly spent five pound a year, threw away the means of purchasing the use of one hundred pounds', and the Society's Saving Book was peppered with phrases such as, 'Pennies Become Shillings; Shillings Pounds; Pounds Hundreds', 'Who Nothing Save Shall Nothing Have' and 'As you Sow, so Shall you Reap'. Two thirds of the Society's clients came from working or semi-professional people wishing to use the society to buy or build their own house.

Paddington was rapidly becoming a suburb for both the middle and working class.[41] This is evident from the statistics for Paddington residents in 1871. Twenty five per cent were professional/commercial (superior), 25 per cent domestics, 3 per cent petty bourgeois, clerical, semi professional, 40 per cent skilled artisans/apprentices/hired hands, 6 per cent unskilled, 1 per cent non-urban occupations.[42] Many more terraces were built over the next twenty years. The Towers, a mansion, built in 1885, by Herr Rassmussen, in Gordon Street, was an exception. There were also some small industrial uses of the land such as Marshall's brewery, and Begg's tannery, and the Old South Head Road had a nucleus of clothing firms offering cheaper goods than the city. Some people made goods on the premises although much work was carried out in workers' homes.[43] The lack of steady employment led people to start businesses of their own, including renting horses and carts and using them for selling vegetables, carting water, and collecting scrap.

Only 26 per cent of Paddington residents were home owners,[44] and there were problems regarding payment of rent because work was often casual, or part time, with long hours and poor conditions. However skilled workers were joining unions, which promoted temperance, and encouraged self-improvement. Paddington Council considered its library to be one of its most successful ventures and it qualified easily for the Government subsidy of 200 pounds because they had more than a thousand readers.[45] The Paddington Wesleyan Mutual Improvement Society explained that its purpose was to enable its members to acquire The Art of Public Speaking, an attainment worthy of every young man's serious consideration. 'A very important feature of these societies is the fact that they lead to study, induce the members to read the various debatable subjects and to consult the different authorities who have written articles with reference to the matters in dispute and thus gain knowledge of subjects which they otherwise would not have troubled themselves with at all.' The Programme included Impromptu Speeches, An Evening with Shakespeare, Reading Exercises, Elocution, and Debates.[46]

At home, for the ladies, there was the piano. It was the pinnacle of working class aspirations. In 1892, the young radical critic, Francis Adams, observed that the urban tradesman generally owned a small iron framed time payment piano, on which his daughters, returning well shod and too well clothed from the local public school, discoursed popular airs with a powerful manual execution. If one had to sell the piano it was all over.[47]

Children were required to attend school between the ages of seven and fourteen. Fees were 3p a week, and a family attending the Glenmore Road School who were suffering financial hardship, wrote complaining that their child had been sent home with 3 written on his hand. The Glenmore Road School had opened in 1883, with more than 400 children enrolled. The Paddington School had a large enrolment as well and little Ethel Turner, aged 11, who lived just up the road at 485 Oxford Street, had her first day there in 1881.[48] She went on to complete her education at Sydney Girls' High School, but many girls did not stay long. They were given exemptions because they were needed at home. Coles Funny Picture Book was one of the most popular children's books of the time, and was full of stories about both good and bad children.

Children were often too sick to go to school. In the twenty years between 1870 and 1890, living conditions deteriorated because the government and local municipalities couldn't keep up with providing services for the exploding population.[49] When the Paddington School opened in 1856, there were 227 children enrolled, by 1896, there were more than 1500. In 1871, Paddington's population density was 10.2 people per acre and by 1891 it was 44.1. There were an average of 5.3 persons per inhabited dwelling.[50] Busby's Bore could no longer provide an adequate water supply, so water was piped from Botany

Swamps and was stored in the Paddington Reservoir before being distributed. By 1875, Paddington's water supply was the most grossly contaminated with fecal matter in Sydney.[51] 'Monstrous accumulations of night soil and rubbish were dumped behind the Victoria Barracks. An official explanation was that it was done to get rid of large, unsightly or dangerous holes. Complaints were made about rubbish not being collected for days, and gutters which 'often contain putrefying filth of all descriptions.'[52] Municipal councils were held responsible.

During the summer of 1884–5 typhoid fever was more prevalent than usual, and by February hospitals could take no more cases.[53] Women were advised to prepare dry earth for use in dustbins and lavatories. 'Choose suitable earth, charcoal and street dust, make a sieve of fine wire netting to remove stones and trash, and manufacture copious amounts.'[54] Water and sewerage drains were combined, so the outlets round the city had become gravely polluted and many foreshores were foul with putrescent slime. Obed West described Rushcutters Bay as a Slough of Despond, and Lady Martin, wife of the Chief Justice, 'brought to the end of her tether by the "nauseous and toxic smells emanating from Rushcutter's Bay", walked out of their grand mansion at Potts Point and refused to return.'[55]

Babies drank contaminated or watered down milk, causing diarrhea and dehydration and in 1887, there was a severe outbreak of diphtheria. This often fatal infection was sometimes diagnosed by doctors as severe croup, as a membrane formed across the throat making breathing difficult. Doctors prescribed sulphur. Home remedies of kerosene or eucalyptus, as well as sulphur, were used for sore throats, which was the first symptom of many illnesses. Children particularly disliked having sulphur powder blown down their throats. 'Mother made a small paper funnel or perhaps used a reed from a nearby creek and placed the narrow end in the child's mouth. When all was ready, the mother put a pinch of sulphur powder in the wide end of the funnel and gently blew it into the child's throat. Alas! Wicked children had the habit of beating their mother to the draw; a quick blow from the child, and mother had her face and clothes covered in sulphur powder.'[56]

There was even advice for canaries with sore throats. 'It is said that a little cake dipped in sherry wine will restore the lost voice of a canary bird.'[57]

Mr. Perry, the first Mayor of Paddington, willed his land on the corner of Elizabeth and Oxford Street, to be used as a dispensary 'for the relief of the suffering who are unable to pay for medical treatment.' It was staffed from Sydney Hospital and opened in 1882.[58] Further down the road, a chemist carefully recorded all his prescriptions. In 1887, the average price for medicine was between 2/– and 2/6, but after hours the price went up to 4/–. An analysis of one page every month over four years, showed that the most common requests were for painkillers, and help with sleeping, as well as diarrhea, coughs, mouth ulcers, (caused by lack of vitamin C — the diet of most people was based on a heavy consumption of meat), indigestion, constipation, rashes (with lots of lotions and dressings), and bronchitis. Quassia chips were used as an enema for threadworm, Glycerine and borax as an antiseptic for throats. On 24 June 1889, there was an entry for Potassium permanganate. 8 Condy's Crystals pills, sugar coated, 2 to be taken each day.[59] This was highly dangerous and may have been used to induce abortion. It was sometimes injected into the vagina for the same purpose. There had been a report, too, of the body of a new born baby being found in Moore Park by a boy, James Alt, who lived in Dowling Street. It was wrapped in a piece of new grey flannel, a piece of new white calico, and was tied up in a piece of brown paper. The body, seen by Dr. Egan, was that of a fully developed female and appeared dead about two days.[60]

The Sydney Morning Herald of May 27 1882, reported 210 suburban deaths for the month of April, which were 61 above the average for the previous five years. Causes of death were listed as cephalitis 10, convulsions 7, bronchitis 11, congestion of the lungs 5, enteritis 5, typhoid fever 10, diarrhea 26, premature birth 6, paramenia 2, child birth 1, old age 5, atrophy and debility 12, dropsy 5, tabes mesenterica 9, phthisis 22. There were eight accidents including a fatal fall from a cliff at South Head, tetanus 1, burns 1, poison 2, (children internally and externally by carbolic acid), drowning 1, suffocation 1 (an infant), injuries received from a fall of clay, 1. James Troughton, aged 12, who lived on the South Head Road near Marshall's Brewery, died whilst playing with a number of other boys on some planks near Billy Goat Swamp in Moore Park. 'He turned a somersault into the water, and not being able to swim, drowned. He was got out of the water and Dr Bohrdt of Botany Street, [Flinders St.] was sent for; but after every effort had been made to restore animation, life was found to be extinct.'[61]

Life expectancy was 47 for males, and 50 for females in 1890. The Nepean Scheme was supplying cleaner water to Sydney, and two huge sewerage mains were built — one discharging into the Cooks River, the other at Ben Buckler at Bondi. By 1900, 70,000 houses had been connected to them for an average expenditure of 10/– to 12/– per house, and the bays around the city gradually cleansed themselves and became usable again.

In the 1870's, bathrooms began to be built in the houses, but public baths of various kinds enabled anyone who was interested, to experience the novel sensation of having his skin cleansed all over. A Mr. Wigzell opened five new bathrooms for gentlemen and two for ladies in Oxford Street, allowing half an hour's scrubbing upon payment of 1/–.[62]

The diversity of Paddington residents is revealed by these examples of occupations, taken from a random page of the Sands Directory 1888. They included constable, tanner, merchant, gardener, cab proprietor, bootmaker, clerk, dressmaker, stonemason, produce and fuel merchant, grocer, draper, quarryman, blacksmith, tailor, greengrocer, printer, upholsterer, carpenter, warder, plumber, photographer, master mariner, painter, packer, coppersmith, saddler, chemist, plumber, hatter, watchmaker, manager ESA Bank, coachbuilder and wheelwright, architect, commercial traveller, inspector of conditional purchases, bookbinder, accountant, surgeon, school teacher, draftsman, furniture broker, butcher, builder and contractor, compositor, plasterer, French polisher, photographer, brass moulder, weed presser, marble mason, pattern maker, professor of music, bricklayer, and wool sorter.

These industrious, respectable people occasionally let their hair down. For special occasions, ladies had abandoned their crinolines and coal scuttle bonnets for tight lacing and bustles. Clothing was still largely home made, although factories were beginning to turn out mass produced garments. More and more women were entering the paid work force in new industries in factories, as shop assistants and in clerical roles. The typewriter was providing opportunities for clerical work and some women were entering the professions. People flocked to the exhibitions at the Garden Palace in the Botanical Gardens in 1879, and the streets of Sydney on Saturday night were bright with the lights of hundreds of shops. Every busy street had at least one open air coffee stall, ranging from charcoal heated, square boxes with funnels sticking out the top, to a marvellous steam machine with lacquered boiler and funnels of brass. Coffee varied from a penny to 3p a cup, depending on how much chicory and burnt sugar had been added to make it dark and strong.[63] Paddington had no less than eight oyster bars operating. Not all grand parlours, these bars offered a tempting range of seafood and ale in a basic setting.[64]

There were weekend bicycling excursions that women enjoyed, and the men played cricket and rugby, or went to the races at Randwick. G.V. Portus described the four-horse buses that took the footballers to the Union ground in Moore Park. Each had their colours on a flagstaff, floating over them. 'I liked the Pirates, black with skull and crossbones. It was no mean cavalcade and it mightily impressed us boys. Hansom cabs did not impress me so much. They were gloomy things of black or dark blue, while the buses were always painted a brilliant yellow. There was not much to see from inside a cab except the horse's tail and hind quarters. But I can remember how exciting it was when the cabs, coming back from the races, used to race each other along Botany Street, [Flinders Street] where I lived, especially if the hirers had backed a winner.'[65]

Moore Park had been laid out between 1867 and 1869. 'A portion, once a swampy piece of ground, is devoted to the purposes of a zoological garden, and the pit of the old morass is now a little lake with an island in its centre on which palms, willows and ferns display their graceful foliage. Animals from various climes are suitably housed and provided for. Young broods of lions and tigers are here, elephants with their howdahs frequently packed with many

Officers of the 50th Regiment in front of the Officer's Quarters, Victoria Barracks 1870, Government

children and in addition to camels, bears, leopards and other ordinary occupants of a menagerie, there is a fine collection of birds and beasts of Australasia.'[66]

The Royal Agricultural Society was also given 16 acres of land on the Common. It was worth very little, being a desert of rocks and swamps with some holes 15 feet deep. In 1882, the opening of the Royal Agricultural Show was postponed, after nearly four inches of rain fell in nine days, but when it did, it was an exciting outing. Ring events included horse jumping, trotting, sheep dog trials, and bicycles races.[67]

A little further afield, there was another menagerie at the Sir Joseph Banks Hotel, which could be reached by road or by steamer. On March 24 1882, the annual Grocer's Picnic was held there, attended by more than 600 people. They had oysters on their arrival, and danced to the Young Australian Band before luncheon. In the afternoon there were athletic sports. It was, at times, a rather wild place. On one occasion, a gentleman rode one of the elephants from the gate of the menagerie out into the waters of Botany Bay. If one was not eligible to attend the Grocer's Picnic, Mechanic's Institutes used to organize 1/– subscription balls, where young, working class people could meet each other.

For young, middle class people like Ethel Turner, author of Seven Little Australians, the Barracks down the road provided plenty of social opportunities, ranging from balls at the officer's mess, to tennis parties, and theatricals. She organised excursions, and on one spring day 20 of them caught the 2.30 boat to Watson's Bay, and walked from there to Bondi, arriving at 5 pm. They had tea, strolled, and sat in the moonlight.[68] There were musical evenings, with supper, and G. V. Portus described his mother's At Homes in Botany Street [Flinders Street] on the first Wednesday of every month. There was a continuous concert from 8pm to 11pm, and jelly, to be served for supper, was made by placing one chair on another with the legs of the top one sticking up in the air supporting a flannel cloth, through which the jelly slowly dropped into a mould.[69]

In March 1885, the Barracks was the scene of a tumultuous farewell of volunteers leaving for the war in the Soudan. 'From early morning, on the 3rd March, the Victoria Barracks presented a scene of activity and excitement. Soldiers, volunteers, and friends thronged the place. Those destined for the Soudan were in the highest spirits, and those who were left behind were filled with such military ardour, that if one 'Soudan man' had remained behind, a hundred were ready on the spot to fill the vacancy… From crowded balconies, parapets and thronged pathways, went up a great shout, as the procession with difficulty, owing to the density of the crowd, moved on. The scene in Oxford Street was bewildering. Long lines of flags intersected the street, and every coigne of vantage was packed with spectators, many of whom cast bouquets of flowers on the moving column. The Soudan boys were especially marked in the matter of floral favours, and touching scenes of parting were visible on all sides.'[70]

After the Centennial Act was passed in 1887, a decision was made to create a Centennial Park that would surround a State House, on the suggestion of Sir Henry Parkes. He wanted a focus to be fixed on NSW as Australia's centre, and the Great Hall within the State House would be the location of national assemblies. It was also to contain a mausoleum for people such as himself, who would be honoured by a state funeral. 'If our scheme is carried out, it will convert that particular portion of the surroundings of Sydney into one of the most coveted, the most fashionable and the most healthy suburbs of Sydney.'[71] A competition was held, the winner submitted a design massively over budget, and the project was abandoned, but plans for the park continued.

Mr. Charles Moore, the Director of the Botanic Gardens, and Frederick Augustus Franklin, were both involved in the designs. Mr. Moore's were more formal, Mr. Franklin's adhered more to 'picturesque' principles. Mr. James Jones, the head gardener of the Botanical Gardens, was in charge of the works, and came into conflict with Mr. Moore. He wanted to retain native flora but he was ignored, and the land was divided into halfacre blocks, cleared by gangs totalling over four hundred men. The land was then manured, turfed and levelled.[72] The sandy soil caused problems with land stabilisation, as well as making it difficult to plant some types of trees, but the park was opened in January 1888. The Paddington entrance to the park was decorated with a splendid arch of evergreens (the main gate not being completed until the end of the year) and an estimated 40,000 attended the opening. The actual site for the opening was enclosed with a brush fence, to which only the aristocracy was admitted. Moore was determined to discourage 'loafers and wasters' so very few pedestrian gates were built. Moore considered his park a place of passive recreation for the upper classes. The main drive was to be a carriageway and genteel horse riding was encouraged, while the predominantly working class sport of bicycle riding was prohibited. There were draconian by-laws. It was forbidden, among other things, 'to climb trees or fences; lie on seats; walk on the grass bordering any path; engage in any game, train for any race, or throw any stone or missile; light fires or annoy visitors; conduct any performances or entertainment of any kind; or to gather or meet publicly together in any way in a group consisting of more than nineteen persons.' Drunks or people of bad character were also forbidden to enter the gardens ,and perambulators were not allowed since they disfigured the walks. As a concession to the disabled, those confined to wheelchairs who successfully applied for 'a special order' could enter the gardens when the walks were dry. When the Paddington Council organised a public demonstration in the Park, to aid flood victims, Moore only reluctantly, granted permission. Picnics were only allowed in the park from 1894, and they were subject to the same rule.[73]

Soldiers leaving for the Soudan, Oxford Street, 1885, Mitchell Library, State Library of New South Wale

Federation Celebration, Centennial Park, 1901, Mitchell Library, State Library of New South Wales.

The Town Hall was completed in 1891, and was opened on October 3. Fifteen hundred people were present. The Governor and Lady Jersey arrived at 4 o'clock, to the strains of the Paddington Band and a chorus of welcome was sung by the pupils of the Paddington Superior School. The Mayor gave full particulars relating to the building, and Lord Jersey formally declared it open. 'It is to be hoped that the building will always be the abode of harmony and the scene of friendly debate and wise criticisms.' The Town Hall was used for balls, and various Lodges and Friendly Societies in the suburb moved from their meeting rooms in the hotels.[74]

Paddington was now being described as a business suburb,[75] but there were cases of extreme hardship during a depression that lasted several years. Wool prices had been slipping and there was a huge foreign debt. There was a run on the banks in 1892. At one bank, a crowd, mainly women, struggled and fought their way to the bank building and then perched themselves on the coping, clinging to the iron railings with one hand and clasping their bankbook with the other until they could force their way to the counters. Altogether the bank paid out over 50,000 pounds in gold during the day.[76]

James Dillon was the Mayor in 1893. The Council rented a house in Glenmore Road and the aldermen and others worked assiduously in collecting food, which was cooked by their wives and other ladies, and distributed to the poor.[77] Unemployment rose dramatically, and for the unskilled there was still only casual seasonal labour. Young men banded together in pushes that were known from the localities in which they lived, such as the Woolloomooloo and Gipps Street Pushes. These larrikins had a language, manners and dress peculiarly their own. 'How and where these larrikins are bred it is impossible to tell, for many of them seem at some remote period to have been born to better things. These idle dissolute youths — they are mostly young, consort together for the purpose of waging war upon society.'[78] 'Larrikin trousers flared at the bottoms into a bell-shape and extraordinary attention was paid to shoes, the heels of which grew higher as the decade went on — some with enamel work on the toe caps, even mirrors, probably of Californian /Mexican derivation. Girlfriends were called donahs and liked violent colours, velvet jackets and ostrich feathers.'[79]

In 1886, a sixteen year old girl had been waylaid by a cab driver, and he and a group of young men took her to a small mound called Mount Rennie in the middle of Moore Park and raped her repeatedly. There was a huge public outcry and eleven youths were arrested. Four were hanged in January 1887, at the Darlinghurst Gaol.[80] The Women's Christian Temperance movement became more vocal. Masculinity had to be tamed of its selfish, aggressive qualities.[81]

By 1894, the depression had eased and the building continued in Paddington. Frances Adams, writing in 1893, was disparaging. 'Newtown, Enmore, Paddington, and the Glebe are simply that congerie of bare brick habitations, it is just as much an arid and desolate waste as the mid — desert.

They oppress the soul and shrivel up every poor little instinct and aspiration towards a natural purity and beauty in man woman and child. The shoddy contractor resides here in his vilest and most hateful shape.'[82]

Paddington residents did not agree, and spoke of their suburb with pride. George Walker was the mayor in 1894, when the Bellevue Hill cable tram line was officially opened. The Minister was presented with a gold pair of scissors which was used to cut the ribbon stretched across the road at Boundary Street, and the tram entered the municipality.[83] This new line was an added convenience for those who lived between the Old and the New South Head Roads and trams were operated by massive drive belts in the Rushcutters Bay engine house. The Council also took responsibility for the South Head Road, which had previously been maintained badly by a trust, and improvements began. The Council worked to get more recreational space for cricket and football and had been given some swampy land by the government in the valley. In some places it had taken thirteen feet of filling with refuse, before the Council could make anything of its surface, but Hampden Park [Trumper] was opened in 1897. 'Two distinct groups of residents attended. Donations of free beer from Marshall's and Tooth's breweries were most welcome for some of the residents, but the committee, finding that many were inclined to consume more than was necessary for their welfare, stopped the supply and allowed the remainder to run to waste. Produce merchants gave bags of potatoes etc, all the butchers of the district gave a sheep each, the bakers, bread, and the grocers, jams, tea etc, besides many other useful articles of consumption. Thousands of people assembled, and a bullock was roasted whole. Sports were carried on, including the old fashioned games of catching the pig by the tail and climbing the greasy pole and a fancy dress match was played on the oval with great enjoyment to the multitude assembled.'[84] The traditions of the earliest settlers continued.

Chapter Four
The Renters

In the first decade of the twentieth century, Paddington was in its prime. The population had reached 26,000, and there were 4,800 houses. Only West's and Brown's estates were still to be sold, with provision for 200 more houses.[1] The general health of residents was improving now that the area was sewered, and more people were using ice chests to preserve food. Refrigerated milk was coming from the country for sale, thus reducing the risk of contamination that often affected city dairies.[2] The Benevolent Society had bought the Flinton estate for a women's hospital, which was opened in 1904, and lit by electricity, with fireplaces, lifts and sixty beds. The poor received free care, the well-to-do paid fees, and the middle class had Aid Societies, Lodges and Friendly Societies. The Outpatients Department, in the former Council Chambers on Oxford Street, was dark and cramped, and all the instruments had to be brought in from the hospital every day.[3] By 1909, there were over 1000 outpatients a year. The hospital treated an average of 142 patients per month. Of 870 births in one year, there were only 31 deaths.[4]

The Council was taking its responsibilities seriously. Health inspectors found only 7 out of 103 local shops to be selling adulterated food.[5] Garbage was being collected twice a week. Baby health centres were established in 1914,[6] and families were having fewer children, more widely spaced. The Paddington Library was the largest of all the local government libraries.[7]

Oxford Street had been woodblocked, (a process of paving the street with wooden blocks covered in tar and gravel) and one of the Councillors commented that all they needed now was carpet. After rain, however, the blocks would swell and become uneven, while in winter the horses slipped on the greasy blocks. The Council sent out small loads of sand to give the horses a better grip on the roads

Oxford Street, 1925, Mitchell Library, State Library of New South Wales.

when it was raining. One cause of resentment was that the length of road outside the Victoria Barracks was not rateable. Several Councillors wanted the Barracks to be sold and demolished, so that they could be developed for more housing. Almost all the rest of the streets had been asphalted.[8]

Trams had seen the demise of the horse omnibus. Trams were so efficient, that by 1930 they could move 92,300 people in half an hour from the Showground on a special line along Greens Road, which was also used during major sporting events.[9] At peak hour, during the week, trams coming from the city were severely overcrowded, and commuters resented the penny fare ending at Darlinghurst and not continuing up the hill to the Town Hall.

When there was a major outbreak of bubonic plague in Sydney in 1900, Paddington emerged relatively unscathed, with fewer than twenty cases.

Council exhorted people to remove garbage. However major dumping was still happening in parklands although there was a tip in the old quarry. Billy Hughes described the trauma of disinfecting houses where plague victims lived. 'A body of desperados, fortified by strong drink, carried on a veritable orgy of destruction. One lady assured me tearfully, they had whitewashed her piano. Some of the fellows made a little by catching rats, for which the health department paid a penny a scalp. "It's a great game. You arm yourself with a stick, tuck your trousers into your socks and sail in." '[10]

The Factories and Shops Act of 1912 provided for the sanitation of factories, safeguarding machinery, and restrictions on overtime,[11] with one third of employees belonging to a union. A basic wage had been introduced in 1908, along with the old-age pension in 1909. But permanent work was for the lucky ones. For others, the strain of finding work was a continual worry, particularly for Paddington residents because 89 per cent of them rented and only 11 per cent were home owners.[12]

Jim was born in 1910 and his parents were dealers. 'They went round and he had a horse and cart and they got bags and mended them. He'd bring home a cartload of bags and they had sewing needles, bag needles they called them and they'd mend 'em and take 'em back and get so much for 'em.'

Maisie was born in 1916 and her father had various jobs, including bricklaying. 'There was no wet weather money or special benefits then.'

Dolly was born in 1917 and her mother worked in a shop in Oxford Street. 'They used to say she was the prettiest girl who ever walked down that way. My Dad got work where he could get it. He worked for a furniture place, and used to pick things up off the wharves and he finally ended up working for the Paddington Council. When I was young I used to say he was a dirtman, but by the time I got old enough, I said my father was working in the cleansing department. We'd meet him over at the corner of the Barracks and the horse would have a drink at the horse trough there, and he'd put us in his cart and take us back to the stables. They were in Little Napier Street, and he rented them. He'd take the horse and give it some feed and water, and every so often he would give the horse a billycan of Epsom Salts and molasses, and then we'd walk home.'

Albert was the second youngest of a family of nine when he was born in 1928. His Dad had spent most of his life on his horse and cart. 'He bought bottles on Mondays, Tuesdays he sold fruit and vegetables, and then he sold fish on Fridays, he was a bottlo, and on Saturday he sold fruit and vegetables again.' They moved regularly, but always in Paddington, usually because they couldn't pay the rent. 'At the time I was born we were livin' down what they call the flat, round Hamden Oval. We lived in one in Glenmore Road, the top end near Edgecliff, we lived in the bottom end of Cambridge Street in a big house there, and we lived in one in Lawson Street and one in Alma Street. Where else did we go? And another one in Gurner Street.'

Albert used to go out with his father selling fruit and vegetables on a Saturday afternoon to get his money to go to the pictures. 'More times than not you didn't get it, because he never sold anything to get a profit. You'd start at six o'clock and sometimes we'd go down the markets with him, and then we'd kick off at Glenmore Road and Oxford Street and go all round Paddington. We rented a stable across the road on the corner of a lane. I never got around horses much. They were there to do a job and that was it. My father sold rabbits too and we'd come home from school and we'd skin the rabbits, and hang the rabbit skins up and dry them out, and the next time he went to the market he took them to the market, and he'd get 18 pence a pound of rabbit skins, because that was sold to the hat manufacturers in those days. The cart was an ordinary dray, a two wheeler.'

Brodie Sreet. 1920's, Mitchell Library, State Library of New South Wales.

James was born in 1926 and his father was one of the lucky ones. He had a permanent job as the head storeman at Wolloomooloo for the Sydney Morning Herald. He walked down the hill to work every morning for forty years.

At Easter hundreds of men would flock to the docks to have the opportunity to lead a cow to the Royal Agricultural Showgrounds for a few shillings. In 1910, those who missed out formed a blockade, which in turn caused a cattle stampede through the streets.[13]

However, in spite of the scarcity of work, Paddington and its residents were described with pride in Paddington, Its History, Trade and Industries. 'There is no suburb around Sydney that is more popular than Paddington. Its streets and footpaths are well made and well kept and efficiently lighted at night time. The houses are compact, well designed and as a rule possess every modern convenience. On all sides terraces of houses and cottages are to be found, all of which seem to be occupied by a good class of people, paying substantial rents, and consequently, the municipality bears a good name in regard to the class of population which reside there.'[14]

Paddington's favourable location was noted in The Globe Residential Guide to Sydney (1915): 'It is a healthy suburb within twelve minutes of the city and

The Burns, Johnson Fight, Sydney Stadium 1909, Mitchell Library, State Library of New South Wales.

conveniently situated to famous surfing beaches of Bondi and Coogee. Trams run frequently from Central Railway and Circular Quay.'

In 1910, The Paddington Superior School was exemplary. 'One was struck by the result of the strict discipline of the scholars, their well- dressed condition and their attentive demeanour. A large number of the boys are given manual training, and 80 of them are equipped with tools valued at 70 pounds, and are taught in relays. Others study elementary physics and chemistry. There are 300 volumes in the excellent school library. Students have football, swimming, and cricket clubs and physical drill. The girls are taught both plain and fancy needlework. Fifty-four attend domestic cookery classes daily in the cookery centre, and 12 attend from Glenmore Road and 24 from Albion Street School.[15] There were more than 1500 children attending the school which educated students to the age of 14.

For the privileged, there was an exclusive school in Glenmore Road. 'Glen Ayr Collegiate School is a Boarding and Day school for girls, run by Anglican

sisters of the Church. It is a splendid, large building in a high and healthy part of Paddington overlooking Rushcutters Bay.[16]

Others were not so lucky. By 1905, children between the ages of 5 and 16 could be charged with neglect, no fixed abode, loitering, begging, sleeping in public places, or soliciting.[17] A Children's Court was established at Ormond House [Juniper Hall] in a small front room on the ground floor. The remainder of the building provided a shelter for girls who had been arrested and were under temporary care. Dormitory accommodation was supervised by female officers. It was overcrowded and children were sometimes kept there for many days, as bail provisions were not available. The vast majority were not virgins. Examining doctors pronounced on the frequency of intercourse and venereal disease. Many of the girls had been found wandering the streets of Sydney in bad company or in houses of ill repute. Some had been habitually in the company of larrikins and were declared uncontrollable. One girl was found bathing naked in the river in the company of men and boys. Some were living

White City Scenic Railway 1913, Mitchell Library, State Library of New South Wales.

in unsuitable premises where they shared accommodation with family males. Incest was common. Some of the girls had escaped from another institution or had run away from home, but most were designated as having lapsed into a career of vice and crime.[18] It was a far cry from the report of the Cooper's christening party, in the 1820s.

Down in the valley at Rushcutters Bay was 'The House of Stoush'. (Sydney Stadium) It was established by Hugh D. 'Huge Deal' McIntosh in 1908, as a venue for boxing, and later wrestling. McIntosh was 32, and had had a successful career as a pie seller and promoter of bicycle races. He rented the 'out of town paddock' at Rushcutters Bay for 2 pounds a week from a Kings Cross ironmonger, and erected an unroofed wooden stadium at a cost of 2000 pounds. The stadium instantly went into profit when a capacity crowd paid 13,000 pounds to see South African, Tommy Burns, knock out the Australian, Bill Squires, and later fight the American, Jack Johnson.[19] Boxing had been banned temporarily in the eastern states of the United States. The Stadium was built in the year of the visit of the Great White Fleet, a huge contingent of the American armed forces. There was a spectacular parade of both American and Australian soldiery in August in Centennial Park.

In 1912, the stadium was roofed, and by 1913 a group of businessmen, headed by Snowy Baker, had bought McIntosh out. Baker was aloof, autocratic, and authoritarian and dominated the Australian boxing scene for many years.

Boxers were the heroes of the working class. It was a sport that all boys were encouraged to learn, and was part of physical education programs in public and private schools. For the poorer working classes, it was a way to improve their lot in life and earn extra money. Attendance by women at boxing was not encouraged by Snowy Baker until the 1920s, when a band played between bouts, and afternoon tea was served at weekday matinees. The brutality of the spectacle was not softened when 'blind' fights were held between young boys during the Thursday afternoon weigh-ins and medical inspections. About eight boys at a time were bundled into the ring, equipped with gloves and blinded by a chaff bag pulled over their heads and tied tightly around their necks. They fought until only one boy was left standing. [20]

The most famous of the Australian stars was Les Darcy, who combined his boxing career with an apprenticeship in black-smithing in his home town of Maitland, where his talent was recognised early. His Irish ancestry was shared by a fair proportion of the local Paddington population, and he was incredibly popular because of his personality as well as his talent.

There was a famous bout between Darcy and Fritz Holland in July 1914, at the House of Stoush. The match went for twenty rounds and was decided on points, with Holland the victor. Maurice O'Sullivan reported that,'Referee Harold Baker, without hesitation, crowned the weary Holland victor. He was quite right, but then came the raging aftermath, the boiling over of all those heated fans who had followed every punch of that epic fight. Holland ambled across the ring and shook the hand of the smiling boy. Then pandemonium broke out and I copped a flying bottle beneath the shoulder blades.'[21]

The love of Darcy's life was Winifred O'Sullivan, the daughter of Maurice O'Sullivan, the publican of the Lord Dudley, on the corner of Quarry Street and Jersey Road. Though Les didn't drink he often served behind the bar, and it was a popular place to be. He and Winnie used to go to dances at the Paddington Town Hall every Friday night. 'If Les wasn't boxing on the Saturday night we'd go then, too. He really didn't know how strong he was, or rather, how fragile the rest of us were. My word, if I hadn't kept reminding him, my feet wouldn't have touched the floor all night.'[22] (Winnie)

Les Darcy died on the 10 May 1917, of blood poisoning, in Memphis, Tennessee, before his full potential was realised. His funeral procession passed from St Joseph's Church, Woollahra, up Jersey Road and down Oxford Street on the way to his final resting place at Maitland. Two hundred professional boxers marched as part of the funeral cortege. Among them were the champions, Jimmy Clabby, Dave Smith, Harold Hardwick, and Les O'Donnell. 'Each one of these four champions had been flattened at some time or another by Darcy. There were so many cauliflower ears you couldn't count 'em. We had no trouble with the crowd. They were as respectful as if in the church. They let out a cheer when they saw Darcy's Buick loaded with dozens of wreaths, and they cheered old Starlight, an aboriginal boxer, the champion of Australasia. He was dressed up to the nines. A proud man, Starlight. The men in uniform marching in the procession got a cheer, too. But nice and respectful. The whole route, every balcony and rooftop was crowded with people. Trams had stopped, of course.' (Acting Superintendant Brodie, traffic controller)[23] It was estimated that a quarter of a million people lined the funeral procession.

Another sporting hero at the time was Victor Trumper. He grew up in Surry Hills but later moved to Paddington. He scored 11 centuries in the 1902 Tour of England with the Australian Cricket team, but the moment which made Trumper a local legend was when he scored 335 in 180 minutes for Paddington, at the Redfern Oval on 31 January 1903. 'Trumper was cricket's supreme batting stylist, timeless and unassailable in his symmetry, artistry, and elegance.'[24] He was a tea-totaller, non-smoker and an Anglican. Trumper died on the 28 June 1915, of kidney disease.

For others, White City in the valley at Rushcutter's Bay next to the Stadium, was a place for thrills. It opened in November 1913. 'Conspicuous against the sky line is a range of artificial Alps over whose glacial contours cars packed with joyous white citizens speed continuously. In the midst of the grounds a tall fountain dominates a little lake and round this in every direction rise edifices of all descriptions. Merry whirls, joy wheels, a Palace of Folly, a spectral windmill and the Japanese village with its bridges, tea houses and indisputable jinricksha.

Funeral Procession Oxford Street, "Everyone takes off their hat when a hearse passes by."
Maisie

Entrance to the White City Amusement Park 1917, Mitchell Library, State Library of New South Wales.

Maisie and her brother

Mary aged 6

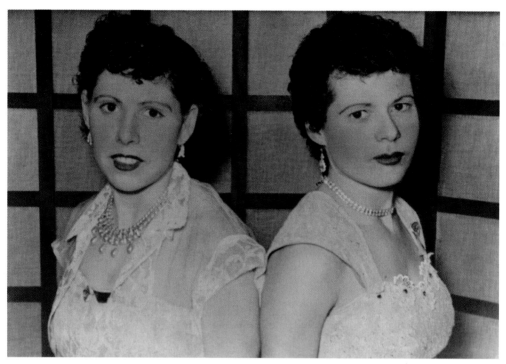

Nicolina and her sister

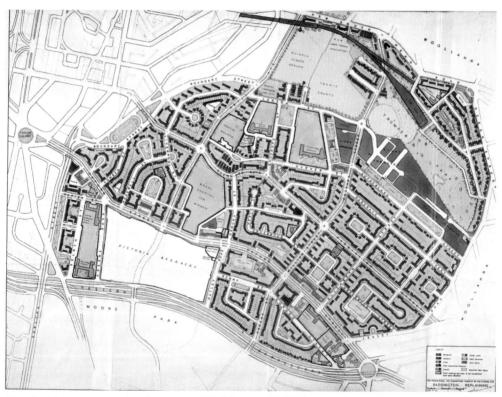

Map for the proposed development of Paddington 1947. Proposed was the complete demolition of all Victorian and Georgian houses to be replaced by blocks of flats. The alignment of the streets was also to change. Sydney City Council Archives

In one corner, some of the visitors are performing an involuntary cake-walk; one simply enters the contrivance and it does the rest. A few yards away one perceives a stream of bewildered people vainly endeavouring to escape from a glass maze in which they are imprisoned like flies in a tumbler. Every foot of the ten acres of park is occupied with some form of entertainment devices. Band music is also provided.'[25] A resident of Paddington remembered that 'they had one of the best ballrooms I've ever seen. The ballroom was on the right and they used to play the turkey trot and the bunny hug. You'd go in this big entrance, all fancy work and plaster and that, and when you came in the main gate Houdini was doing a stunt there, strapped to a board.' In 1919 it had vanished, destroyed by a huge storm. 'We didn't go to school that day.'[26]

During the years of the First World War times were hard. Women entered the workforce in increasing numbers in offices and factories, and as shop assistants and teachers.[27] Most, however, stayed at home to cope with large families, and very little income, varying amounts of which went to the publican. Church groups were campaigning for early closing of hotels, and one petition was presented to Parliament in the form of a beer barrel and accompanied by a brass band, with 150,000 names on a continuous reel of paper more than three kilometers long. A referendum was held in June 1916 and six o'clock closing was introduced.[28]

At the end of the First World War the people of Paddington went to a memorial service in Centennial Park. It was a sombre occasion as many young men from the area had died.[29] The war left a legacy of social problems, tensions and alcohol abuse. *Mary* was born in 1922, but she was told that her father had never really recovered from the war. He travelled a lot, working as a Post Master General's Department linesman, and drank heavily. Everyone had hoped that life would return to normal, but on 24 January 1919, a man died of influenza, the first of 6000 victims of an epidemic that was to sweep over New South Wales.[30] By the last three weeks of June more than 1000 cases per week were being admitted to hospitals. Paddington suffered death rates greater than 5 per 1000 residents. It was a social disaster of considerable magnitude, decimating the work force, closing schools, and causing the suspension of sports meetings. The Showground became an emergency hospital for up to 500 patients at a time, and the Hall of Industries was converted into a morgue.[31] Paddington Council set up a fund to help those laid off work during the epidemic, and money was raised from a concert held at the Five Ways Picture Palace, with the sale of raffle tickets, buttons, ribbons and donations.[32]

Maisie's little sister Gwennie died of the flu at the age of 18 months. 'My mother was in bed with the flu. I can remember some lady with my mother. It was my grandmother and she also died. She was nice to me. We had to wear white masks, and I can see my little sister on a wash stand, laid out on a wash stand. You got buried from the house then, because I know my brother Maxie

Nurses at the Riley Street Depot during the 1919 influenza epidemic, Government Printing Office C

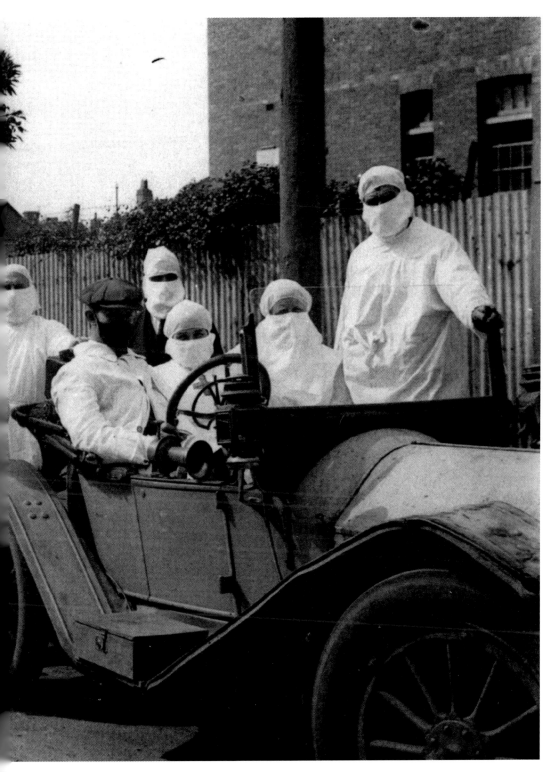

The Neighbours-"My first camera", *Maisie* 1929

got buried from here when he was 12. They had a horse-drawn carriage, or a hearse. They would take the coffin out and put it in a carriage type of thing. You didn't walk behind it, you had horse drawn things to go in. Anyone that saw one coming, they'd all lift their hats and stop.'

Developers were disparaging about densely populated areas like Paddington, describing them as unhealthy, and promoted sanitised garden suburbs such as Haberfield. After White City blew down, a design competition was held for a Rushcutters Bay Estate. Scott Griffiths was the prize winner, but the project didn't proceed.[33] Those who could afford to spend money on public transport or cars were able to move out of the inner city, away from their work place. Those who could not, were happy that they were close to the city, the beaches, the racecourse, and sporting grounds. Cars were a dangerous luxury. *Maisie* described the neighbour's reactions to the two cars in the street. 'People used to say, "Oh that's Cecil driving around." He had a red car and he'd tear round Gipps Street at a speed to work, where they had their catering part up in Brodie Street. They used to cater for balls and that up at the Town Hall. So you'd have Cec tearing around in this red car. And then the Colley's, they got a car. I was about 11, I think. Everybody was coming to see their car, it had a running board. We had skipping ropes, and hopscotch on the street because the only thing that came up here was Cec Bray's red car. You'd draw your hopscotch on the thing, like one, two, three and then the wings, and I'd play hopscotch there practically all day. You'd look out if this Cec was coming. I remember him giving me a lift home once. Mum used to send me to visit anyone that she couldn't get to visit in hospital, and I was at Randwick somewhere, and coming up was Cec, and "Oh, you live up in Paddington don't you? I'll give you a lift home." So I get in the car, but he had to go to another half a dozen shops to collect the trays, you see. He'd deliver a big tray of cakes and then he'd go back in the afternoon to collect them. Well, I got home real late, and my mother said, "Where've you been?", and when I told her I came home with Cec, oh my poor mother, "Don't you ever do that again, don't you ever get in a car like that again."'

At the Royal Easter Show in 1900 'an object of curious interest in the parade ring was the Thomson motor car. Unfortunately this car did not come under any classification provided in the programme, but the judges of the horse vehicles yesterday expressed their opinion that it should be highly recommended for a prize. This car is a purely Australian production and was driven by Messrs H. Thomson, the inventor, and E. L. Holmes, several times around the track, and an exhibition of trick driving and steering was given.'[34]

Children loved the Show. Companies started placing samples of products in labelled bags and the show bag was born. Sideshow alley got bigger, and among the attractions by 1920, was the Tallest Man at eight foot six inches, the Handcuff King, and the Pinhead Chinaman whose head was only as big as an orange. *Dolly* went twice a day, and often got in for nothing. 'We used to stand outside and watch them singing out for Sharman's, the fighting and that you know, just like a big canvas tent with drawings on the canvas of the fighters, and then the fighters would come out and you'd see them, and people from the crowd would go in if they wanted to challenge them and they got paid or something if they won. We used to watch on the outside. We'd never go in.' *Albert* also used to get in for nothing. 'You'd take a milk can over with you, and you'd get all the free milk. All the cows that was milked in the show in those days gave milk away. And I had a brother who used to work over there and he used to milk the cows and all that.'

Bridie O'Shaunessey was born in 1929, and her Dad picked up some casual work at the show shovelling up manure and leading cattle in the Grand Parade. 'Dad used to get free tickets and the show bags were really sample bags. You'd get a little packet of self-raising flour about this big, Vegemite, peanut butter, little bottles of sauce, some chocolates, but mainly they were groceries. Dad would take us into the ring and we watched woodchopping, horse jumping, rodeos. At night they'd have the fireworks, then they'd have the rodeo.'

There was excitement for *Maisie* the night the electric lights went on in Oxford Street. 'It was called the Great White Way. Everyone was going to see, they put these great white globes in the Town Hall.' *Jim* remembered the lamplighters. 'They'd come around of a night and he'd have a stick and it was an up and down thing and you'd pull one and they'd come around again around daylight and they'd pull it off. We used lamps in our house, kerosene lamps'. *Dolly* had gas lights and took candles upstairs to bed. There were other new inventions too. With the coming of the wireless, *Dolly's* family went up to Oxford Street and listened to the cricket on a radio in a shop, but before that, they had walked down to Hyde Park where there was a telegraph, and they sat and watched the scoreboard. 'Not that us kids were interested in the cricket'.

After the First World War, food was expensive, so the Paddington Council set up an open-air market in 1920 on the Barrack reserve next to the Town Hall. It was open twice a week, and a year later a market hall was built in Oatley Road below the houses, where many of the army officers lived. But it was not profitable and was closed by 1922.[35] The war and the influenza had taken its toll on the Council's finances. In less than ten years Paddington's liabilities exceeded its assets by almost 50,000 pounds, and 67,000 pounds was urgently needed to repair its neglected streets. Labor was investigating ways of increasing its vote on the City Council, which it had taken over in 1918, and proposed Paddington's amalgamation with the City of Sydney. The Labor Party did not succeed.[36]

Jim's first job in 1924 was at Anderson's hat factory doing piece work as a blocker. He got out of it. 'It was too hard. I was standin' over boilin' steam all day and I finished up like a skeleton.' He finally got a permanent job with the Woollahra Council. He was a ganger. 'We used horse and cart, draught horses and what they call tip dray. They load them up with stone and they come to the job and they pull a lever and it tipped up, and you'd click him on, he knows straight away, he was educated and he'd pull the dray up. Out at Rose Bay was a big metal wharf, you wanted metal, three quarter, half inch or two inch metal, they used to pull underneath a hopper and there were sections, there was a fella there all the time and he'd pull a lever and it would drop down into the cart and when you got your issue he'd shut the lever off. You'd take it back to the job, and you put your ballast in first, the big rocks and you'd have to pack 'em in and then the little stones, and you put the metal on and you put your tar on and you roll it.'

Others found what they could.

The Rabbito: 'There was the rabbito, Harry Paine. He came from down Comber Street. All the pussies used to follow and he'd clean and skin the rabbits while all the people would get their plates. "Rabbito, Rabbito, 1/6 a pair." He had a blue and white apron.' (*Maisie*) *Dolly's* Mum 'used to cook them lovely.'

There was a new rabbit recipe in the Labor Daily[37] 'The rabbit is boiled till tender, then all the meat is removed from the bones, cut up and mixed with cooked macaroni, grated cheese and seasoning and liquid. A dish is lined with short pastry, filled with the rabbit mixture and covered with paste. Pie should be baked in a moderate oven for half an hour'. *Maisie* never had rabbit, and couldn't even handle it to cook it. She said it looked too much like cat to her.

The Iceman: 'You'd see people, if he was a bit late on a Saturday, people'd be running around saying "Where's the ice man?" People would be getting all their meat in, and if your ice was getting a little bit low you'd be worried. Sometimes it would be nearly 1 o'clock and he'd be up at the top of the street, and people would be coming out with their towel. They'd bring your block of ice right into your house and put it in the ice chest. If they were very low on ice they'd go and get it themselves while they were waiting. (*Maisie*) *James'* Dad used to get into trouble if he forgot to empty the ice tray from under the ice chest and in the morning the floor would be nicely washed.

The Chinaman: 'This poor old Chinaman used to come around, because later on there was a horse and cart, but this Chinaman, he used to have two baskets as big as the copper, and a stick across his shoulder, poor old man. And he'd waddle down. And people around here used to buy off him, I think they called him Charlie. But these two big baskets full. You can imagine they were heavy, and a stick across his shoulder.' (*Maisie*)

The Travelling Salesman: 'Tommy Healy had the shop on the corner of Shadforth and Gipps and you could just buy tea and sugar there. He used to get the tea in big cases and then make up pound bags and go round.' (*Maisie*) 'Another chap who used to come around was the Indian chap, who had a long coat that went to the ground like a bus coat, and if you opened it up, it had about 100 pockets! And he used to carry around all tea and coffees. We used to buy a bit from him.' (*O'Shaunessey sisters*)

Gipps Street 1929 *Maisie*

The Milkman: 'We used to have a milkman call, they used to have a tap on the back of the milk cart and fill a little ladle thing up and we used to leave the billy-can on the ledge. My brother used to drink half the milk and put water in it. My mother caught him one day.' (*Dolly*)

The Coalman: 'The coal man used to have a black leather hat. His face was black from the coal, he was covered in black. He never dressed in anything different, he was always the same. See, everybody used to buy a lot of coal, and then you'd have the open fire place, and we used to all congregate around that of a night time. And we'd be listening to the wireless and reading Nancy's Witches Tales.' (*O'Shaunessey sisters*)

The Coffinmaker: 'There used to be a lane there that ran through from Napier Street to Selwyn Street and that was called Dead Man's Lane, on the bottom there they used to make the coffins for Kinselas and everybody called it Dead Man's Lane.' (*Dolly*)

The Clothesprop Man: 'We had lines, everybody had lines. No washing machines in those days. And you had to have a prop to hold your lines up. He used to come around on a horse and dray yelling "Props, props for sale". All the kids used to take their mother's props to use as hockey sticks! So he did really good.' (*O'Shaunessey sisters*)

The Bottle-o: 'He used to collect your empty bottles. He paid you whatever it was. You used to sell him all your bottles. You know the bottle yard up in Elizabeth Street and Underwood. It was at the back of that restaurant in Elizabeth Street. 6p a dozen.' (*O'Shaunessey sisters*)

The Man from The Water Board: 'He'd probably come about once every month I'd say. And he would open up the drain down outside 25 Prospect Street, and everybody would be notified to shut off their taps and then the water would flow. All the rusty water would flow and we wouldn't be allowed to use our taps till he was finished. Then they'd come along and they'd tell you to turn their taps on. Everybody would turn on all the taps in the house and all this rusty water would all run away. And boy, it was rusty. It was black…until it run white and clear. Much clearer than what it is today.' (*Mary*)

The Racehorse Owner: 'The horses used to be stabled at the Paddington tip which was from Quarry Street, Harris Street to Cecil Street, up the Trumper Park boundary to Bowes Avenue, back to the Lord Dudley Hotel on the top, and there was a big incinerator worked there. They were horse and drays up until then. The people stabled their horses, in fact a bloke called Kelso used to stable a racehorse there called Masterpiece, and he'd pick it up about every October and as sure as Christ wore knickerbockers, it'd win the Welter at Randwick the week before Christmas with all Paddo on it, because it used to be… they'd say to me, "Sonny take this bet and give it to Masterpiece", and everybody used to take him, he was as fat as a fool. Lumley's livery stables were in Forbes Street. There were six horses in there permanent, and that was at the back of the Lord Dudley Hotel.' (*Bert*)

"Dolly Bible, my Mum and the neighbours" *Maisie* 1929

The Tram Conductor: 'There'd be five seated on each side, and then I think five standing. The poor conductor, he was the one worst off, hanging on there, trying to pull tickets, especially in wet weather, he'd pull tickets and he had nothing to hold on to, till the corridor ones came.' (*Maisie*)

The Music Teacher: 'Miss Bloomfield, she was an old Tivoli player, she's been dead for years, a great teacher, and they taught every instrument known to man, because they were all Sydney Symphony violinists, but the old lady who taught me was on the Tivoli for years playing mandolins.' (*Bert*)

For the kids there were one or two special days to look forward to, Cracker night, and Christmas Day. Cracker night took a lot of preparation. 'Out the back used to be a block of vacant land, and all through the year, the kids who lived around the place, used to gather and put it on the end of the terrace of houses in Elizabeth Place there, and build up a big bonfire, and the night before the bonfire, the larrikins who used to come from the picture show, they set fire to it. But it didn't make no difference because when bonfire night come again, there was a bigger pile of junk.' (*Albert*) 'The Fire Brigade used to come round if it got too dangerous, and they used to put it out. But it didn't get too dangerous. It was only a couple of times that they put the water on it. Everybody from around the area used to come and watch it. I can remember bringing kiddies there in my arms watching the flames. It was good.

There used to be a tile place down here in Elizabeth Street, called Wilson's Tile Works. And he had a show of crackers in his window. And one of the fellows that we used to knock around with, had the bright old idea of putting his magnifying glass onto the thing, and it started a fire in the tile shop. And they didn't put any more crackers in the windows then! It never caused much damage, but it broke the window.' (*Bill*)

Christmas Day was memorable. 'Actually, my uncle and my father cooked Christmas dinner on quite a few occasions, because at the time Mum had just had *Vera*, and then two years later he did it again because she'd just had *Johnny*, and two years later she'd just had *Lizzie*. And she was busy, so they cooked beautiful Christmas dinners, and always had this big mixture of nuts, and you'd get outside cracking the nuts. They were always so crisp. The adults used to fall asleep after a big hot meal, and all the kids would be out there cracking nuts. It was the same in every house. We'd go into each other's houses, and the adults in every house would all be asleep.' (*O'Shaunessey sisters*)

Mary loved Tiger Timms. 'Tiger Timms. Now there's a book. Tiger Timms, like you see the Ginger Meggs books. Tiger Timms Annual used to come out once a year. And the Fitzgerald kids, they were a little bit better off than others, and they used to get this Annual every year. It was a beautiful book, but you never see them today. Oh, they'd show it to you on Christmas Day. But you see, on Christmas Day all the kids would get out in the street. And you wouldn't have a mile of toys. You'd have your doll or your little tea set or whatever the

Nana Newton and friends

kids had. And the boys were the same, their bow and arrows and their cowboy things or whatever. I think kids in those days didn't ask for a lot.'

Maisie remembered getting a baby doll. 'They were celluloid and the legs were only together with elastic, and the two arms. And then Dolly Bible, she lived in Prospect Street, she wanted to have a go and she pulled it, and its arms and legs fell off, and I was broken hearted about that on Christmas Day. I can't remember having a great deal of toys. I had a little pygmie gramophone. It was a little tiny gramophone. I remember having a little brooch with my name on it, and that chap in number 3, Jackie Perrin, he came up. It was when I was seven you know, and he said, 'That's a lovely brooch, I think I'll take that.' It had *Maisie* written across it. And I cried my eyes out. It was as big as a shilling with *Maisie* written across it. It was lovely. He didn't take it, he was only playing with me. He was a nice boy, Jackie Perrin.'

Sometimes the whole family would go to the beach. One of *Maisie's* neighbours had his horse and cart in the stables behind 21 Gipps Street. 'He took us all to Bondi Beach in that once. On a Sunday morning. That was really funny. He took us out sitting up in the back of this cart, horse and cart, but no one took any notice. And Bondi Beach, all it was just a mass of sand, no buildings or anything.'

Bill's family went by tram. 'We used to go out on a Sunday and we'd have a picnic out there, and I used to get up at 5 o'clock, get out there at 6 and try to get a cubby house for the day, because my mother didn't want to sit in the sun. I'd plant myself in this thing until my mother and her friends got down there. There used to be about three families I suppose, and they used to all sit in the cubby house out of the sun, and it was good. But I think everybody, you know, that was an accepted thing for them. They used to do it. It used to stop them going to church, which I didn't like to do. I wasn't keen on church at all.'

Mary went to Bondi with Nana Newton. 'She would pack all this wonderful ham for all of us. She'd make potato salad, and she'd have radishes, and she'd have celery and she'd have cold meat, and she'd have made cakes. And she would take all this out there to Bondi, we'd traipse out there in the tram. And there'd be a ton of us. And then we'd all get in our cossies and off down to the beach, and come back again and eat. And she'd wait on us. She was the most wonderful woman. Really marvellous. And so that was picnics.'

People started to buy radios. *James* received a cheerio on his birthday. 'I think everyone who had a radio was right into Uncle Bimbo or whatever the bloke's name was. And you know, at 5 o'clock they'd say, "*Jamie* if you follow the string from the road over there, if you look underneath the chair in the lounge room, there's a big surprise for you!". It was a Hornsby train set.' For most of the other kids in Paddo, presents were few and far between, but everyone had a cake. There was no such thing as a holiday. However, one was arranged for *Bill*. 'There used to be a Sydney City Mission on the corner of

Underwood Street and William Street where those big blocks of units are. And they used to have things every year, they used to take a lot of boys away, and I went to a place called Shelley Beach. I don't know where it was. We got into a train for it. I think it was the first time. My mother packed up a dilly bag for me. I was only going to stay a week. They said, "Don't worry, we'll look after him". The first day I was up there they fed me tripe, and I'd never eaten tripe in my life. And I said, "Oh I've got to go from here". And I just left. Me and another fellow we just left. And we just came back. I couldn't stand that. They put you into a dormitory. As soon as they put the lights out I said, "That's it, I'm going back to the station", which was walking distance. I don't remember if we had any money to get on the train or not, but we got on it somehow. And we walked from Central Railway back to Dudley Street.

Boy playing cricket, Mary Place

Chapter Five
We Done it Hard

Australia had borrowed heavily in the 1920's and embarked on a dash for growth that relied heavily on favourable external circumstances and increased the country's vulnerability. Early in 1929, sharp falls in the prices of wool and wheat, the withdrawal of English capital, and the fall in export prices by 50 per cent caused a severe financial crisis. Labor took office the week Wall Street crashed, and was unable to protect the jobs and the jobless, which at the height of the Depression was over 30 per cent.[1] Paddington, where most of the population were either employed as unskilled labour or in trades, and who rented their accommodation, was hit very hard.

'To obtain food relief an applicant must be registered at the State Labour Exchange for at least seven days, and he must make a declaration that he has been unemployed for at least fourteen days and is without resources which he might use for his support. If he possesses any property (with the exception of a house) which he might realise, he cannot obtain relief until all his resources are exhausted.'[2]

'Dad was out of work for two years. The Lord Mayor's Fund, they'd give them one Sunday night every so often, I think they'd get a pound. They'd go sweeping the streets from midnight until 6 in the morning. That kept them going a little, it was gas money and things like that. And bottles, they'd sell little bottles. My brother and I would find little bottles and you'd sell six little bottles for a penny. You'd just have to look around and find them. You'd find one here and there. I remember there was Mum's wooden veranda and there was cracks in it. And where they'd drop money from time to time, we'd put a stick down the crack with a bit of soap, and get the penny up and get another penny for the gas. They were hard times. Well, Dad, he used to borrow his brother's bike and he used to ride around looking for jobs, and occasionally you would get a couple of hours somewhere. A lot of people too, in Liverpool Street, they had their possessions put out on the street. It wasn't until Jack Lang bought in the Moratorium Act that they stopped doing that. A lot of people around here lost their homes. There was a Mrs. Simmons down in Glenmore Road. She had to get out and they were on their way to what they call Happy Valley at La Perouse and people went out there and just built little humpies. And Mrs. Simmons was on her way and she met with an accident in a tram. Anyway she was compensated and she was able to come back and pay her rent. There's a lot of funny stories like that. It was very bad, very bad.' (*Maisie*)

Others were living wherever they could. An elderly couple had to be rescued on more than one occasion by the Fire Brigade from their house in Glen Street, which was entered through a wilderness at the foot of the Scottish Hospital, because there was a culvert at the bottom of the street that could not cope after excessive rain, and the gully filled with water.[3]

The *O'Shaunessey's* Dad was in a dole queue. 'They actually used to go to the Post Office and they'd get vouchers for meat and bread. And my Gran helped out a lot because she had a book shop and so she supplemented. She would come up here on a Wednesday and she got a pension, and we'd have a party type thing. She'd bring things we didn't normally have. Dad would get work wherever he could. He'd walk and get work. And when we were all in hospital he'd walk to visit us. He was a resilient sort of a bloke.'

Mary's Dad used to have to get in the queue at the Paddington Town Hall. 'You would have coupons and you would get rice, and plum jam and you'd get ginger and melon or something like that, you know, jam. I don't ever remember him getting meat. 'Cause I think my grandfather supplied the meat in the house and any vegies and that type of thing. And then once a month, I'm not sure whether it was once a month, but I think it was, when your name came round, I s'pose they worked it out alphabetically, you got a turn on the pond. And believe you me, that was a dirty job. They used to wear these boots up to their knees, the men. Not women, men. The water lily pond up there in Centennial Park. And they'd get a guinea for that. 21/–. Well they had to do their share of whatever it was. I don't know how many worked on it, but I can always remember that this was a godsend to get this guinea, because things were really tough. And so they were pretty rough old days.'

Bert lived in Sutherland Street. His Dad was a gambler. 'Never drunk. You see, you'd come home and the old man would have sold the furniture. There'd be no beds, there'd be nothing. Gambled. He could go like the hammers of Hell. I had two brothers, one died. I was the eldest.'

People were angry and frustrated. 'There was a horse trough there, opposite the Rose and Crown in Gipps Street, and that's where the politicians used to stand. Well, the politicians, this was a very strong Labor suburb and when the

Dolly on the right, with her brothers and sister

Liberals would come around, everybody would throw tomatoes at them. That was a night out, because of the Depression you see. No one had anywhere to go, and they'd go around to listen. One night he got hit with an egg and I often think, that poor thing. He was standing up on that horse trough, making this speech. "Oh, the Liberals are talking here tonight, we'll go and listen to them." That was a funny thing. There were some funny things that happened around here.' (*Maisie*)

Meals were always there and that was what was important for the kids. 'You didn't have the nice things that you would have later on when the money was coming in. We didn't have any sweets at night. You'd be having something else. Probably some bread and jam. Mum and Dad did all the worrying. Sometimes some poor fellow would pull up. "Can you give me a cup of tea?" And Mum would always give them a cup of tea. Someone said, "You can't be giving your stuff away, it's the ration". My Mum said, "While ever there's tea in that cupboard and a bit of sugar, I'll never knock anyone back for a cup of tea".(*Maisie*)

Dolly used to go to the local shops and ask for 'sunburnt chocolates — the chocolates were in the window and they'd get sunburnt and they couldn't sell them. And we'd go to the fruit shop and ask of there were any 'specks' — fruit

Our First Communion *O'Shaunessy sisters*

'My sister and me' *O'Shaunessy sisters*

that was going brown, and then to the grocery shop to see if they had any broken biscuits, and then to the fish shop to ask if they had any scraps that came off the chips, there was no cholesterol then. And my brother, down the lane there used to be choko vines, and we used to pinch them and sell them to the fruit shop.'

The *O'Shaunessey's* could get broken toffee at Selfridges for a penny. Their Mum used to make a lot of stews. 'We used to make dumplings, and lovely jam tarts, and lemon sago puddings. We had a lot of stewed fruit because stewed fruit was cheap. My grandmother had a couple of peach trees in her back yard, and she'd bring the peaches up and Mum would stew them for us. Mum would make lots of biscuits, tarts, scones, pies and pastries. See, you'd always have the oven going. After school we'd have bread and dripping. And we used to have bread and condensed milk. They used to save the dripping from the meat that was had, and use it later. See, you don't do that these days.'

Bill got tuppence to take to school. 'I used to get a pennyworth of chips off Mr. Beveridge and a Chester bun off the Panford's, which was so thick and about three inches square and it was a meal in a penny.'

Shoes were more of a problem. 'Dad used to be getting up and he'd mend our shoes. Like a cobbler, he'd have to resole our shoes. He'd get up and he'd make you a cup of tea and a bit of toast, and you'd sit there and watch him while he was mending the shoes.' (*O'Shaunessey sisters*) *Bill* was always barefoot, but got a pair of shoes when he went to Super Primary at the Paddington School. 'I got a pair of shoes and socks and Mother said, "Now you're in bigger school you'll have to wear socks and shoes". I remember getting stone bruises. You used to step on a stone on your heel and you used to get a bruise. You couldn't put your heel to the ground. Every second kid had no shoes.' *Bert* had shoes with cardboard soles.

Clothes would be passed down from one child to another. 'And even in the neighbourhood, a lot of people, if they had children, they'd pass the clothes on to others. You often had to rely on the generosity of other people. But Dad was a beautiful sewer. My school uniforms, I can remember playing games and that you'd get them caught, and I'd have a big corner tear there. And he'd impeccably mend them. He was very good.' (*O'Shaunessey sisters*)

'In those days people were pretty straight. Pretty honest. For instance, the clothes men would come round. Old Mr. Agrinoff had a shop up in Oxford Street, and he and his wife were a terrific old couple. They carried Paddo on their back during the Depression because Mother would go and get your school clothes to start you off, because the old man wouldn't give you any money. A shilling a week they used to pay Mr. Agrinoff, and every Saturday afternoon he'd walk around Paddo collecting his 1/– from all his customers. Nobody welshed, there was no welshing, no bad accounts.' (*Bert*)

Bill remembered his corner shop on the corner of Paddington and Cascade Street. 'Mum used to deal there because we were living in Dudley Street at the time. They used to allow her to stock up and fix up at the end of the week when she got some money. But also they used to say to us, if we brought back the paper bags and they were neatly folded, they would give us some lollies.'

The lady in *James'* corner shop across the road, said that his mother kept the shop going, because she had cash. 'Often the shopkeepers didn't have enough money to buy stock. The shelves always seemed to be half empty. Probably they only had enough money to buy six half-pound packets of tea or something.'

The boys were always scrounging for work after school and at weekends. *Bill* would go up to Cook's Bakery in Victoria Street. 'We used to have trolleys and they'd turn the straw once a week and sweep the manure out, and you'd go round with it on your trolley, three sugar bags full and you might find some one who wanted manure for the garden. We used to sell it for 6p a bag.' He also used to go down to a boat builder and pick up offcuts of timber and sell them. Kids used to get a penny if they ran messages for neighbours, but *Mary's* grandfather was very proud. She was not to take money. 'Some one might give you an apple or an orange. They'd offer you a penny. "Don't take it!"'

Bert was selling papers. 'I fell off the bloody tram and went under it. I was eleven months in hospital. Every rib in me body broken. I didn't remember much from the minute I hit the deck. I was about 14 or 15. It was leaving from beside Brownie's butcher shop, beside the Royal, at Five Ways. I got on it there and I must have moved me foot on the one behind me, and away I went, straight under the tram. The only thing that saved me, it was a corridor tram and the centre board held me strap. Otherwise I would have gone right under, and it would have cut me in half. It was common for paper boys. A bloke called Meredith lost his leg, old Kevin Ross who lived in Forbes Street, he lost his leg on papers. Lightning Jack got killed up at Darlinghurst. He was probably the best ever. He could go between two trams passing each other, he done it on a wet night one night and he never made it, cut him to pieces.' When he got older *Bert* would get paid to cut a quarter of wood down at a coal and coke yard on the corner of Roylston and Hampden Streets. 'Me and Chika, we used a cross cut saw an we'd get ten bob and we thought we were bloody princes.'(*Bert*)

Sometimes the kids got sick, very sick. *Jeannie's* nephew died from a germ from the cow's milk. *Maisie* and *James* got diphtheria, the *O'Shaunesseys* scarlet fever, and *Bert* and his brothers pneumonia. Sometimes they got all three.

Bridie O'Shaunessey was in for scarlet fever. 'I was nine and I can remember Sister Dundas and Gerald Crigg from up the road who was in at the same time and was the same age as us. And *Vera* was in the same room as me. *Vera* went in on the Wednesday and I came in on the Friday. *Johnny* came in the following Monday. But *Vera* and I were in the same ward, and no visitors could come in. They could talk to you or look at you through the windows. They were quite long wards, there'd be about twenty beds. What we used to do, as soon as the sisters went out and the lights were out, we'd get out of bed and run up the wards, and as soon as you'd hear the sister coming, you'd run and jump back into bed…I remember coming home from hospital. We had a relative that was staying with us and she knitted me a blue twin set and made a little cream pleated skirt.' (*O'Shaunessey sisters*)

James had diphtheria when he was five. 'I was rushed from this house to the Children's Hospital at Camperdown and then after a couple of days, was transferred to Prince Henry Hospital. I was that sick that the doctor called an ambulance, a motor ambulance. I was in isolation, which diphtheria called for in those days, but my mother and father would come out and see me. We were probably ten or fifteen feet away from one another. You would wave at one another.'

Maisie's minor ailments were treated at home. 'If you got something like a little cut that looked a bit bad they used to make poultices. Bread dipped in really boiling water and castor oil on it, and that would be put on, or another poultice would be a soap with sugar, made soft. That's what we used to have put on us. Or a boil, if you got a boil or something. Of course they had Bate's Salve then. That was black stuff. What they'd do, cut a piece of cloth and make a little hole in the middle and put all the Bate's Salve around, and that would get the boil going. And if you had an earache, you'd put a bag of hot salt on your ear. A bag of salt. Headaches, some brown paper with vinegar on your forehead for a headache. I remember always getting my mother soaking the brown paper in vinegar and I'd lay down for a while. That was better than having all those tablets you have now. I'm living proof of it.'

Maisie couldn't go to the opening of the Sydney Harbour Bridge, because she had the toothache, and a few days later she went to the dentist. 'Before he started to pull my tooth out, he got his wife and son in to hold me by the shoulders. And I'm kicking my legs up and saying, "Let go, let go, let go". He didn't let go. And everyone was saying, "Oh Fitzy, he's always harmful." He had a picture in front of you, where you sat in the chair. He was a dentist in the war. It was a photo of him in his uniform, it wasn't real, but it was him in a uniform with all the blood dripping down. When you went to get your tooth out, you looked up and saw it. Up in Hopewell Street. So that's where you went for 1/–, you could get your tooth out. He said, "I brought Leo and my wife in because I knew the injection wasn't taking." And someone said, "Don't be silly. Fitzy's never got any money to buy any injections, he only put the needle in with probably water in it." But oh, it hurt. Dear, it hurt. My mother was with me, but she was nursing a little baby because she was minding Sylvia Ross. See you didn't have the money to get fillings in those days. You didn't have money so you just went and got your tooth out.'

Dolly's Mum was into preventive medicine. 'I used to get rubbed with eucalyptus and camphorated oil, and you got done regardless of whether you had a cold or not, and you'd start, you'd be lying on the table, and you'd be giggling like mad, and Mother would say, "Be quiet, I haven't touched you yet," and every change of season we'd get a dose of rhubarb magnesia, it's like powder, and we'd go, "Ugh it's just like cement."

If anyone was very ill, the family would tie a piece of red cloth round the telegraph pole and the children had to be very quiet. There was always someone to help, to knock on the door, take a cup of tea and bath the children at night. And there were always the Salvos. 'It was funny Saturday nights at the Rose and Crown when they'd all come out, the men had had a few drinks, and the Salvation Army would be there, and they would line them all up and then march them around to a soup kitchen in Glenmore Road. They'd be marching around singing, 'Glory Glory Alleluia', or something. The Salvation Army used to have the War Cry because they don't believe in drink and that. I s'pose that's why they kept going, to sober them all up. As they come out, Archie Hill would be saying, "Righto gents, all out please, all out gents". And they'd stagger out one after the other. And the Salvation Army would be saying, "Come on, come on". And they'd be marching.'(*Maisie*)

Brigadier Broadbent, a Salvationist, came to Paddington in 1929. Her father had been a jockey before he was converted. 'You just go to the place where you are appointed whether you like it or not. Everybody was welcome at the Church, there's no discrimination, colour or creed, it doesn't matter, and William Booth, he felt the door should be open to everybody. In the Church there is music and freedom. They had a very nice hall right in Glenmore Road, but our quarters, we used to call it quarters, military term see, it was underneath, mind you it was very nice, beautifully furnished, you came off the street into the Hall. That meant you had to come down steps to get down into our home, and it wasn't a very nice area in those days, and the officer before us had a big, tin shed built into a soup kitchen, and these men used to hang around there and all down the side, and I nearly had a nervous breakdown there. The quarters were nice but living underneath, it wasn't a very nice area at all. We were there just one year. Over at Moore Park there used to be a hostel, it's a beautiful building at Moore Park, it's still there and we used to take in girls there. They'd come to the city to work and nowhere to live. A respectable place, they used to go and live there, and go to work from there and they came to Paddington, that was their church, and only for them, we would have found it very hard. They formed mostly our congregation.'

Brigadier Broadbent and her husband went to Taylor Square every Friday night. 'It was all open then and there was a palm tree and we used to stand round there, and my husband had the piano accordion. We were heckled there and it was hard going, but we had a little bellow organ and I used to play and we used to hold a service with about three or four of us.

I had my second baby at home with a midwife. I had a lady, a nurse and she was up in Hornsby, and I had to contact her of course. My husband had a motor bike and he had to meet her in the city and rush her out to Paddington, but I had no trouble. The Women's Hospital was just opposite, and that took up quite a bit of visitation. We had a few folk what we call 'became converted' and they were a tower of strength to us. They were very encouraging.'

Every week they went to the hotels. 'I used to like that. It was a real avenue of service. Some people used to find it hard, but they got to know you, and I never found anything nasty in a hotel. They would always respect you and always looked for you and looked for the War Cry. We called it the White Wing Messenger and lots of folk have become Christians after reading that, they've been led to a Church from the War Cry. You have the box and the money, that's not it at all, because many a time I folded it up, and I put it in their pocket and I said, "You take it home", especially when I knew there was children, we had one for children, The Young Soldier. The saddest thing was a man sitting a child on the counter giving them drink and you'd see them there. "Oh" I said, "Look, no". Of course then I'd give 'em a lecture. I think it was so sad to see that, a little child sitting on the counter and giving him the glass. They'd look for you and say, "Any tickets today? I wouldn't dare go home without them", and so that's an avenue and the message gets through, and we've seen the result from the War Cry in the hotels.'

They had three weeks holiday per year, the rest was seven days a week. 'We said, "Now we're down here we're going to have Monday off, and we'll take the children down to the beach." We took them down to Bondi, only once, never again. We could never afford the time, every day was taken.' (*Brigadier Broadbent*)

Later, in the thirties, there was a band that played on Sundays. *Maisie's* Mum used to give the Salvation Army a 3p for playing. 'She was funny, my Mum, she used to love one song. "Can you play 'Nearer my God to Me?'". That all died out you know, it's a shame. The Paddington band fizzled out. People were very good to Sallys'.

After six o'clock closing was introduced, people would sell alcohol from private homes at inflated prices to those who wanted to drink after hours. In Sydney there were some large scale operations in this illegal trade, but also many small dealers who would sell their grog to the locals. *Bert* explained where sly groggers got their supply from. 'All that grog that they were getting, was from the hotels in Paddo, the Four in Hand, the Light Brigade, Woollahra, Fred Kay's Imperial, and the Canberra, he owned both at the time, he was the dual middle and light heavy, Fred Kay. I think that Irish girl [Kitty O'Shea] has got one of his hotels now, that would be the Canberra she's got, and they used to give us all their bottled beer and that would be taken then by this other fella and me. The publican would tell the poor bastards that would come there after work, "Oh sorry mate, our beer delivery hasn't arrived, can't give you a bottle of beer," because it was six o'clock closing in those days, and that, with cigarettes, were sold on the black market. The bloke I was working for would take it straight to the distributor. We were the carters, that's all. My role was insignificant, I was only the strong arm. They used to get a pound for it when it was about 2/6 a bottle. He was up in Caledonia Street beside the ice works. The little stone cottage is still there right on the corner of Taylor Lane and Caledonia Street, and it was taken to them where it was sold. Now the last cab off the rank on Sunday mornin' when you were sellin' it, was the police car that got loaded.'

Maisie described how a sly grogger in Bethal Lane, off Gipps Street, used to sleep in the back room with all his money in his trousers while drinkers were in the front room. One night someone with a long stick managed to hook his trousers, and the money, and because he didn't have his pants he couldn't chase them. 'All the neighbourhood heard him yelling, "Me trousers, give me back me trousers."'

Sometimes there were fights. 'It could be brutal, you'd see two blokes punch hell out of each other. I watched a fight out side the Dudley one night between Nick and a bloke that had a gun shop at Bondi. Both men could handle themselves. They fought for three-quarters of an hour. They couldn't get a winner and they decided to call it off and went to have a beer. And that's how it was. There was none of that business, "I'm calling the police I've been assaulted". None of that crap. Sort it out. The fight was over. There was no grudges carried and there was a lot of good men around Paddington. We turned out some good fighters. There was Jimmy Reeves, and he was the original Pride of Paddo, he was the lightweight contender. He was trained by his father who held the lightweight title in 1918.' (*Bert*)

The two main forms of gambling in the 1930's were SP [Starting Price] Bookmaking and Two-up schools. There were SP bookmakers all over Paddington, one in every pub and many working out of private households. Starting Price Bookmaking was illegal but occupied the place of the TAB in the society of the time. It was made profitable by the fact that it was the only form of off-course betting. It was illegal and untaxed. The Two-up school was run up at Arnold's Quarry. 'Cockatoos were at the game. The leads were run out from Hardy's Rubber Factory for the lights, and supplied courtesy of Hardy's Rubber and their workmen. The police couldn't get you there at that game, because the cockatoos are up the top of the tip with binoculars. They're looking up Elizabeth Street, they're looking up Jersey Road, and the minute the filth come into view, up go the flags, and away go the players, and by the time the coppers get there, there's no point raiding.'(*Bert*)

In Paddington there were not only small time villains but also violent criminals. Guido Calletti was born in 1902, in Paddington. He was described as a gunman and a gangster, frequently in the company of prostitutes and women of notoriously bad character, of drunken and untidy habits, and violent disposition.[4] George Blaikie, author of Wild Women of Sydney, wrote that Calletti 'owned' famous 1930's prostitute, Nellie Cameron, and at various times fought major underworld figures such as Frank Green with razor, gun, and boot to retain her possession. Calletti put a high value on mobility, making liberal use of the Sydney taxi service, for which according to Blaikie, he never paid. 'Drivers who kicked up a fuss, were invited to take a close look at the Bengal blade razor Guido produced, and demands for payment quickly died away.'[5] Guido Calletti and Nellie Cameron opened a fruit and vegetable shop on the corner of Jersey Road and Oxford Street across the road from the Light Brigade Hotel, and about 30 metres from the Paddington Police Station and Court House. This was to be a start of a career away from crime, but soon after, the fruit shop became the front for a brothel.

The Darlinghurst Push, of which Calletti was the leader, was one of many larrikin pushes in Sydney, all of which controlled the crime in each area. However, as well as controlling crime, they acted like a vigilante group protecting the interests of locals. 'Nobody would touch you in Paddo in those days. You'd get your bloody legs broken. Look you've got no burglary, you've got no gangs as such. Well, you might have a few.' (*Bert*)

Bill explained how his sister was protected. 'I can always remember my sister *Nancy*, she was coming home from work one night, she was working late, and she was trying to be picked up by a couple of fellows. Anyhow, one of the neighbours from down the street, I didn't know him at the time, he just walked over and his name was Vic, and he said to her, "What's the matter *Nancy*?" And she said, "Oh these blokes are having a go at me." And he just walked over and pulled them into gear. And he said, "If you do it again I'll belt the hell out of you." And see it was like that. Everybody would look after every body. They were good neighbours to each other. There was one mob I was scared of. They had a reputation of just giving you a belt at times. It was the *Brown's* gang up here. That was the fellow that run it, *Brown*. His mother used to have a shop across the corner here, corner of Underwood and George Streets. And his mother had that shop. There used to be about five or six things, and he used to be the boss of them. They did what he wanted and everything like that.' He explained that it was easier to avoid them. 'Discretion is the better part of valour. They'd give you a whack. They'd jostle you and push you out of the road. You weren't supposed to walk on their territory. But they soon stopped that, because the coppers down here at the time used to come down and check them out. They said, "Any more of that and action will be taken." You could leave your front door open and your back door and you could go out and nothing would ever happen.'

Crime in Paddington was not undercover. Everyone in the community knew where the local SP bookies and sly groggers were. Members of a push would not have a full time job or collect the dole. They wanted little detail of their lives recorded. Instead they relied for an income on the odd casual jobs and petty crime, tea leafing (thieving), rolling drunks, conning mugs and pulling lurks. Guido Calletti's and Nellie Cameron's lurks included 'the badger game', a form of blackmail based on the arrival of an angry cuckolded husband. 'Nellie would select a client suitable for the 'badger treament', and secretly signal to Guido, who would stand by until the appropriate moment, and then rush into the chambre de l'amour, catching the couple in flagrante delicto. Guido would declare himself cruelly wronged and demand compensation. The 'pigeon' could well be a married man who was treating himself to a little bit on the side, or a boy from the bush who was terrified at what Mum, Dad and Mabel back home would say when his lapse was reported in the newspapers.'[6]

Another scam they carried out was snowdropping, which was the theft of clothes. Guido was a man who appreciated a good cut of a suit, and as a professional criminal he needed many to avoid identification by the police. 'Nellie and Guido would steal clothes from the Domain Baths. Both would wait outside the baths and identify the 'pigeon' that they would steal from. They would enter the baths separately. The 'pigeon' would carefully wrap up his clothes in his towel, and place them somewhere where he could keep an eye on them while swimming. When he had got in the pool, Guido would engage him in conversation. Nellie would walk over to the unfortunate man's bundle, and place her towel over it and say to those nearby, 'I think I had better put my husband's clothes with my own.' She would put the stolen clothes in a suitcase, and leave the baths and go home, while an angry business man stomped around the baths in his bathing suit.'[7]

Frankie 'Little Gunner' Green, was another local criminal. He had been involved in similar scams to Guido, and the two had duelled for ascendency in the underworld. Both had 'owned ' Nellie Cameron at one stage. He was a vicious criminal who ended his career in crime as a stand over man extorting money from other SP bookies in Kings Cross, while working as an SP bookie himself. He also was a pimp, and lived with and made money from, a string of younger girls. Green carried four bullets in his body, one at the base of his spine that caused him a great deal of pain, and another in his stomach, which caused a cyst to form. He became frail but was still vicious. Near midnight on Thursday 26 April 1956, police were called to Green's house in Cooper Street, Paddington. They found him slumped over with a big carving knife driven into his chest near the collarbone, and piercing his heart. A bottle of beer was on the table in front of him and a glass of beer in his hand. One of the most vicious men ever to put his boots on was dead.[8] Guido Calletti also died as he had lived, violently, in Kings Cross in 1939. He was 37 years old. He had tried to take over the territory of the Kings Cross Push, by intimidation of gang members at a party in Brougham Street. He was shot three times. Strangely no one saw who fired the fatal shots.

Accident site: Fiveways Paddington. Government Printing Office Collection, State Library of New Sout

The kids were aware of these things but were more interested in their own activities, often down in Centennial Park. There were reports of boys swimming nude in the lake opposite Randwick Racecourse, and tram passengers complained. The Ranger made a half-hearted effort to catch them, but, 'maybe he slows down on purpose because he remembers he was a boy himself once.'[9] *Albert* stole goldfish from the lakes in the park. *Maisie* remembered that there were only four swings and she had to wait too long to have a turn, and *Mary* and her friends hired horses and went riding. *Bill* used to race boats. 'Little boats. I used to have a model boat, fully equipped with sails and everything. They used to set it up on a time trial. It's always been two boats at one time, one against the other. And you used to set them up with sails and you used to push them out, and they used to pick up the wind. And they used to tack and everything like that. The boat was shaped like a racing skiff. We used to put the jib up, and the spinnaker.' *James* had a sailing boat too. His was called Effie.

Adults and kids would play cricket on Sundays in the back lanes, and more than 30 cricket clubs played in Centennial Park. One year there was a special event, The Ginger Meggs Derby. 'We all decided to put a cart in. Anyhow they said, "Who's going to drive it?" And so I offered. And anyway we got it over there and it had big pram wheels on it, and all good axles and all good stuff. It was a very hot day and it was picking up all the tar on the road, and we couldn't get enough speed on it. And it was won by a sponsored thing. I think Wrigleys won it. You raced in divisions from the gates at the top.' (*Bill*) The kids really preferred the thrills of the Paddington hills. 'I had my own billy cart which I built myself. It was just a box and it used to have what they call a centreboard. It had a fixed axle on the back. And we used to steer it by a bit of rope. I'll tell you one adventure. That's why they put the axe to my billy cart. I was coming down William Street, and these are the days when motor cars weren't too prevalent. And I'd turned into Underwood Street, and there was a car coming up Underwood Street, and I nearly went under the wheels. An Aunty of mine seen it, and she told my Mum about it. And she said, "Go and get the axe", and she chopped up the billy cart. And she said, "That's the last billy cart you'll ever get and you'll never get a bike." Which I never ever got.' (*Bill*)

James wasn't allowed to do 'silly things' with his. 'A colleague of mine who used to have a billy cart, got run over by a tram in Glenmore Road, and had both his legs cut off, so I think that frightened most of us.' *Albert* used his to get to the beach. 'We used to go down to Rushcutters Bay Park in the baths there, and we used to take the billy carts. And we used to come down Cascade Street down the bottom there. It was pretty safe. We had no idea of what the speed was, but you could put your foot on the front wheels to slow them up, and it used to wear your sandshoes out. The Rushcutters Bay Baths, they were a penny, but most kids walked further to Seven Bob Beach where it was free, and spend the penny on lollies. I used to swim from there round to Double Bay.' (*Albert*) Bill learnt to swim at the Rushie Baths even though D*olly* had seen water rats swimming there. 'A fellow called Alan Riggor taught me to swim. How they used to teach us, they used to have a big boardwalk all around the pool, and they used to have ladders that you climbed down. And he used to tie a rope around your waist, and he used to walk along the side. And once he thought you were good enough to swim, he'd throw the rope in, and you had swim up the thing. It was a 50 metre pool, 50 yards. But we never had any trouble.'

Fanny Durack was the daughter of a Paddington publican. She was a sensation in the swimming scene which had previously not permitted women to compete, because it was considered unladylike and improper.[10] She set a world record for 100 meters in March 1922, and won a gold medal for Australia at the Stockholm Olympic Games in 1912.

The kids were nomads. *Dolly* and a friend hopped on the back of an ice cart and every time it stopped they'd jump off. It was a very popular game called scaling. One day they went so far, they ended up getting lost. They were allowed out until nine at night but they kept in their own territory. *Bert* spoke of other people in Paddington as foreigners and regarded the tip as his turf. He had a barrow with two pram wheels on it with long shafts. He would 'go fossicking on the tip for empty beer bottles, oyster bottles, clear skins. Quart bottles used to bring a tray, [3p.] beer bottles were a deena [1/–] a dozen, lead, copper. zinc, all precious metals, we got 'em all. We used to get ten bob, [10/–] and that would help Mother with the rent.' (*Bert*).

The kids collected cigarette cards to swap, cricketers for the boys, and for the girls, satin, with beautiful butterflies. Everyone played marbles, three holes, big ring and little ring. And there always seemed to be a dog. 'I used to have me billy cart and me dog Spot, and he followed me everywhere.'(*Jo*) *Albert* liked to play football at Trumper Park, the 'shirts' and the 'no shirts', and they played with an old sock padded out. 'You had to climb the paling fence, and you weren't allowed to go on the cricket pitch, and poor old Paddy Ryan, he'd come out chasing you.'

Then there was the Five Ways pictures. 'It was very steep, and the old chap, if he was on the door, he'd turn his back and let you in for nothing. He used to have singing contests and all, and we'd go in there with a packet of jaffas and roll 'em down, and the old bloke used to come chasing you.' (*Albert*) *Frances* preferred the Oxford picture show, just down from the Paddington school, where there were lolly shops. When she went, it was 6p downstairs, 9p upstairs.

Childhood could end very abruptly. Most Paddington children left school at fourteen and then it was time to get a job.

My first suit *James*

Chapter Six
Gettin' a Job

When *James* turned fourteen he was told to start work the following Monday as a copy boy for the Sydney Morning Herald, where his father worked. 'They bought me a suit. I thought it was marvellous, a coat and a pair of trousers. A matching suit. We had to sit on a seat, it was called 'The Seat', and every morning two of the members of the Fairfax family used to make it their business to come into the building, via The Seat. And when they got near The Seat they docked their hats, and said, "Good morning boys," and we all stood up like three little angels and bent over and said, "Good morning Mr. Fairfax", but it was the thing that was done.

Miss Mary Fairfax, who was the matriarch of the Fairfax family, started the Sydney Morning Herald School for copy boys and junior and senior apprentices in 1921. And Monday to Friday we went to school. Copy boys went for one hour, junior messenger boys or junior apprentices for one and a half hours, and senior apprentices for two hours. Five days a week. No matter what we were doing, we had to knock off work and go to school. We had English and Mathematics and when you got over into the senior class you got two hours a day. One of the hours during the day was General Knowledge, and Appreciation of Opera and things like that. But Mathematics and Spelling, English and Grammar, was the number one thing. Every six months there was a prize day, the top boys got prizes. You'd get an open order to go to Fairfax and Roberts, which was a big jeweller's shop and get a comb and brush set, or a travelling set. You know, I think it was maybe five pounds, which was a lot of money in those days as a prize, donated by Miss Mary Fairfax.

My job was mainly going around with reporters and bringing copy back from the various courts and sporting facilities and things like that. On race day, after each race, we'd have to bring the copy to the nearest post office, because they weren't allowed to transmit anything from the racecourses. They were trying to stamp out SP bookmaking. There were three trips a day to the Observatory to get the weather report. We started work, I think it was 8 am, and from 8 o'clock till 9 o'clock we were cleaners. We had to go out to all the Fairfax Director's offices, put the current newspaper on their files in their office, and then with a feather duster, dust their offices. Then at 9 o'clock we had our various duties to perform. We had to keep going back to the office, because if you was doing a weather bureau job, you'd have a couple of hours to fill in, so you'd do petty little messages, and get a ham sandwich for someone. I used to have to go into their darkrooms. And that was another job that copy boys did for sporting events, cricket matches and things like that. After the photographers took a certain number of pictures, if he wanted to stop on, he gave the copy boys the negatives, or plates in those days, of what he had taken, to take back to the office.'

Maisie left school when she was fourteen. 'A fellow was going up past me in a horse and cart and he seen me standing there. He said, "Are you looking for a job love?" I said, "Yes, I've been everywhere." He said, "Well they're putting on a few out at the match factory." And they said, "Oh you can't go and do that", but I did. I was out at Zetland and I got 15/– a week. You had to put in these things as fast as you could, and that's where I got my finger jammed. It got caught in the machine. What you had to do, you had this stack of cartons alongside of you, so then you know those little books of matches. Anyway it went click, click, click, it went ten, and when it got to ten you had to put your fingers in. I was going really good for about a month, and I got it in, and you had to get some glue and stick that, make another before the next ten came on. And this day it went around before I got it. It went click you see, and I had to get seven stitches in my finger, I don't even know which finger it was now. Anyway, Dad wouldn't let me go back there. It's funny how things happen. They were going looking for Mr. Miller to get my finger out of the machine and it was jammed in. This poor old French lady was saying, "You are pale, don't faint, don't faint." I don't think I've ever fainted in my life. You're either a fainter or you're not a fainter. Anyway she told Gracie to get some brandy. She got me some brandy and I nearly choked. It was pure brandy. Anyway they took me to the hospital and I got the seven stitches and then I had to go back. And they said, "You can't work in that place." So I didn't get a job then till I was seventeen.'

Albert got a job with a firm of Office Requisites. 'I used to ride a push-bike with a box on the front, delivering the papers all around the city. It wasn't a bad job, but my poor old Mum didn't know for years that I had it, she knew I was working in the city but she didn't know what'. He was then a messenger boy for Baden's shoe factory in Waverly, then was put off, and there was no

Hardware Shop, Oxford Street

The Butcher
Glenmore Road
1950's

more work until he went to work for his brother. 'I used to do deliveries all round the eastern suburbs and western suburbs, in a 1927 Dodge Tourer, what they called a reverse Dodge, it had reverse gear. It had a canopy, which you could fold back, and two seats, and if there was roll of lino, I'd put it on the running board, and a big case on the back and a luggage rack. I used to get pulled up by a fella called 'Lenin', a big copper, he used to be on the corner of Market and York, and he was christened 'Flags Lenin', because he always used to pinch the taxi drivers for driving with their flag up on an empty cab, and he used to pull me up all the time with an obscured number plate.'

Bridie O'Shaunessey left school when she was fourteen. 'A lady across the road was a very good dressmaker and she employed several, so I went over there. I got 10/– over at Mrs. Gilmour's. We used to make all sorts of things. She had about four big power machines, and was a very clever dressmaker. But sometimes she used to suffer badly from migraines. And she used to like playing cards, and if she'd had a night playing cards she used to have a migraine the next day. She'd say, "I can't show you, I can't tell you, just do what you want to." *Mary's* first job was as a milliner in York Street, sewing bands on the model hats. 'Not the ready–to–wears, the models. Wasn't there long. I hated it because I hated sewing'.

Jo did twenty-five years on the City Council as a labourer. 'On wet days we'd play cards or get drunk. Well some of 'em would get drunk. When I got older and was a ganger I used to follow the shade around if possible. You couldn't always do it, you'd have the engineer watching you. When I started, we were picking up wooden blocks in Eddy Avenue and we put concrete down later and they used to send them down to Wattle Street and bag 'em up for the old age pensioners, for their stoves. I got as far as acting inspector, that was a good job'.

Bill wanted to be a carpenter or a motor mechanic, but just before he left school, 'a fellow came up to Paddington School and he said, "I'm offering a position for an apprentice plumber." Now my mother got wind of this and she went up straight away and applied for me. I says to her, "I don't want to be a plumber, I want to be a carpenter." And she said, "Well I've got the perfect job for you and you're going to be a plumber."

After work he and a lot of other young men went to footy training, and played at the weekend in Centennial Park. *Jim* played for the Paddington Colts. 'We used to play the 'Loo and Woollahra. It was Rafferty's Rules then. You had to be tough to take some of the knocks. The 'Loo was a bad team. They were very dirty players. You'd go to pick up a ball and if you didn't watch yourself, up would go the fist.'

James was always playing out of his age group and didn't play for the Paddington Colts. 'I was a marked man when we played against them. I trained hard. I had an ambition to play football, rugby league for Australia, which never happened unfortunately, but I was selected to play in the combined High

Maisie and friends late 1930's, all in home sewn dresses

School team. When I was going to school there were couple of famous Paddington boys that were playing football for Australia. One, Ernie Norman, was one of our heroes. His father and uncle were the local garbage men so everyone knew the Normans. He was called The Pocket Hercules, and toured England in 1937. *James* also swam with the Bondi Amateur Swimming Club, and was coached, 'by a famous bloke called Claude Seabrook', who lived in Paddington. *Bill* played with the Paddington Colts early but shifted to Bondi United, because most of his mates were there. He also found the colts the toughest team to play against. They had some supporters. 'All our girlfriends'.

In the evenings, Paddington danced. When *Maisie* was young she went to the Palais Royal, at the Showground. 'Then the Trocadero opened up, down near the Regent, because the Palais Royal closed down. That was good at the Palais Royal. That's where there used to be a lot of do's I think. They used to have tables and chairs around the side, and you'd dance in the middle. It was all the good dancers that used to go. It was 2/– to get in. Then I ended up teaching ballroom dancing, up in Oxford Street, Danny Lowes. Three of us, we used to get 4/6 a night, teaching. That was good money in those days. We had some good times there. That's when I got the pneumonia. I was no sooner out of the hospital when I was back up there, and they said, "Oh no you'll kill yourself."

Dolly's Mum 'out on the tiles'

Mary, one of 'The Paddington Girls', liked the Trocadero too. 'I'd go with Cath Lyons who lived the first house as you come round from the corner shop in Glenmore Road, opposite the hotel. Cathy lived there and she was a wonderful ballroom dancer. Oh marvellous! Anyhow she used to win cups and goodness knows what. I used to go down there with her, and she used to dance, you know. And if I got picked up for a dance, fair enough. But they always wanted the ones that were the exhibition dancers. You went up the steps and went into the foyer and there was this great big round seat, and in the middle was always this beautiful arrangement of flowers. And from there you went inside, and the dance floor was there, and there were tables and chairs all round. The big band was, like as you came into the dance floor, the tables and chairs would go right round there, and then there'd be the big band there, which used to turn around. Alice and I, this girlfriend and I, at this time she didn't have a boyfriend, and her and I, we used to dance together. She was very good. She could lead and I wasn't too good on this jitterbugging, but she used to teach me.'

Jeannie and *Jim* went to the Maxine Hall in Oxford Street up near the Centennial Hotel. 'I used to make long frocks out of silk for 9p a yard, they were only plain with a little frill around the bottom and a little frill around the sleeves. That was a good little hall with little platform things built all around. There was a drum and a piano, it was only a little turn out, but we used to enjoy it. Then we used to go to the Paddington Town Hall. They had mirrors all round the wall and you could see yourself dance. It was lovely. The men used to have to wear a dinner suit and you had to go dressed fancy, it wasn't just an ordinary suit. I only had one long, black, evening gown, and silver shoes. I used to always get me hair set, go to the hairdressers and get it set.'

Bill taught dancing at Bill Chown's on the corner of Newland Street and Oxford Street. 'We were good dancers. My wife was an Australian Champion. She was an Irish dancer. We went to a hell of a lot of dances and we'd go three nights a week. I used to have special shoes, laced pumps, and they used to be waxed every time I took them out. I taught for about two or three years, I suppose. But I used to get 7/6 a night for it you see, which was good in those days.'

Albert didn't bother learning. 'Oh no. I'd get up and dance. I was in the Army one time and I picked up some piece, and she said, "Can you dance?" and I said, "Well I don't think I'd pick you up if I couldn't", that was as it went. My wife had taught me to dance at the Paddington Town Hall. You walked up into the main hall, the back hall was a smaller hall than the main hall. The back hall was the jazz dance. Down the bottom end towards the Barracks there was the toilets, and then a passageway that led from there into the main hall and there was a milk bar there. There was Old Time and New Vogue. We done a bit of everything. Mr. and Mrs. Prendergast used to run the cloak room up at the Paddington Town Hall for years and years. It was a pretty rough old place at different times, the Paddo Town Hall. There was plenty of fights up there if you wanted them. Most of the time it was alright. I can't fight, I'm a coward.

If I wasn't out dancing, I'd probably be down the billiard room at Five Ways. Or there was the Vaudeville before it was the Oxford Picture Show. It was the Vaudeville every Thursday night with Jo Gorman and Stella Lamond. They did all their acts, singing and dancing acts, Scotty and Stella Lamond tap dancing, and all that type of thing. The Vaudeville days up there was a beauty. Same as the Tiv and they used to come up there, and then all of a sudden it disappeared and then the picture show was pulled down.'

Bert wasn't too keen on dancing. 'I wasn't a soft shoe man. I qualified, but if there were balls on…You know they were 50/50, 50 per cent dance, 50 percent fights. But we had good parties. What you had was a lot of people who played musical instruments, a lot of people who could sing. You might get pianists, you might get mandolinists and violinists, all sorts of people would turn up at a party and you'd get invited because you had a specific ability with a musical instrument. I played the banjo.'

He enjoyed staying home. 'We bred canaries for years, canaries and greyhounds we were involved in, two complete opposites. Lots of good greyhound trainers in Paddington. You'd go to Centennial Park of a morning, and sometimes you'd take 'em to Double Bay and swim them. You were allowed to do those things then, it was a free country in those days. We used to exhibit canaries. There was an old fella called McMahon up in Hargrave Street, a great old bloke, an old ship's engineer retired, and he had a big aviary in Hargrave Street. He used to breed Norwich canaries and I used to breed Yorkshires and the fella up the street bred Border Fancies and it was a great camaraderie. I showed them and reasonably successfully.'

Dolly went out dancing at Petersham Town Hall. 'We used to wear frocks and skirts about that wide and you had frills and sleeves. You'd carry them on your arm and put them on with press-studs when you got there so they wouldn't be crushed in the tram. We'd be out almost every night of the week.'

Kath knew of a couple, Jo and his girlfriend, who was a barmaid. 'They lived in Mary Place and she had a girlfriend who lived over the way. The house they lived in was so small, she used to keep her clothes in a wardrobe across the street and she ran across the road in her nightie to get dressed.'

By 1933, more than 60 per cent of Paddington houses were shared by two or more families. The population was 26,500, and was to remain unchanged for another twenty years. The basic wage was 3 pounds 6/6, and women's wages were about half. Seventy six per cent of the breadwinners in Paddington received less than the basic wage.[1]

But the doors were always open in Paddington. For *James*, whose Dad was in permanent work, the most important things in the front room were the piano and the bass fiddle. In *Mary's*, the front room had a leather chaise lounge, which was underneath the window. 'There were army photos on the wall of my father and his brother and of his mother. And my grandfather was a Justice of the Peace, there was a thing up on the wall with his certificate. That was the front room, you see, lino on the floor, and a lovely big old sideboard and there was a miniature Harbour Bridge. That was fantastic The hall was calcimine both sides. And right along the centre down, was this horrible yellow, like paper, yet it was sort of a shiny sort of a thing, with scrolling around it. It was the most awful stuff. Everything was calcimined. Out here the walls were sort of a dark green, a sort of a bluey green colour'.

There were corrugated iron fences between the back yards, and everyone had fuel stoves, sometimes augmented by a gas ring . They were always hot and *Bridie O'Shaunessey* got into trouble for putting her feet on the stove and burning the soles of her shoes. 'One thing about the houses is that they were always warm in winter and cool in summer. They were designed very well for that reason. They'd always get a breeze right through. And the fireplaces were in all the rooms upstairs. Dad used to light the fireplaces up in the bedrooms, so it was warm of a night time. And because there was always two to a bed it was warm in winter! Our parents had a huge bed, and they also had another bed in there because there was always a child coming in there. Half the time there might have been someone a bit sick and they used to sleep in there. And then everybody bunked up in rooms. There would be three in a double bed. It was fun when we used to have our girlfriends stay. We'd top and tail… That front door was never closed. We never locked the door. Even into our teens, if a girlfriend was late and couldn't get into her own house, she'd just come over here and crawl into bed. And my Aunty, when she'd come home and she'd be out of sugar or tea, and she used to come and leave a note 'took some sugar.' We always scrubbed the front porch. The women used to congregate and talk to one another outside. Always the same time. The back lane and your front veranda and everybody used to hose the street down.' *James* remembered women in Wheedon Avenue who scrubbed the footpath, 'that's how prim and proper they were'. 'Everybody polished and waxed their floors. There was no running down the hall, and you didn't scream out, you kept quiet.' (*Mary*)

Dolly's brothers slept on the front veranda, that was filled in with lattice and a canvas blind. They were paying 14/6 rent a week, but 'my mother used to always paint or paper herself.' They didn't have a bathroom. 'She'd boil the copper up every day for my father when he came home, and on Mondays when she washed, we'd have a bath and slippery slide in the suds, other times it was clean water out of the copper.' The *O'Shaunessey* kids used to be bathed in the copper by their Dad. 'You know the two tubs, well he'd put us in there and it was like an assembly line.'

Nobody had a phone and the corner shop would take a message in an emergency.

For some, this way of life was deemed unacceptable, and Paddington was declared a slum. Demolition was advocated. This devaluing label, slum, was a middle class expression, a class bred term, a judgement of the values of another class. Maurie O'Sullivan had become a Member of the Legislative Assembly, and in 1936 he spoke about Paddington. 'I resent people referring to areas in Paddington, Surry Hills and Newtown as slums. There are no slums in Paddington, as far as I know, there are congested areas. If you look at the dictionary you find that slums are 'dirty streets, dirty houses and dirty back streets!' People who live in congested areas are just as clean as those living at Potts Point. Go into their homes and have a look. Go into the most congested areas beside Victoria Barracks and you will find that homes are like palaces; the women take a delight in seeing how clean they can keep them; they are scrubbing, polishing, and cleaning from morning till night. Certainly the places are small, and some have no space to build verandas, but they are scrupulously clean. Let them be called congested areas, but not slums. Health returns show that Paddington is one of the healthiest parts of Sydney. It is certainly one of its highest points.'[2]

The debate continued. 'Experts accept the view that bad housing conditions must be largely associated with mortality and health figures. In Paddington, 75 per cent of the buildings are more than 75 years old, many of them in a dilapidated, or semi-repaired state. Bad health and poor development of the children here are due in no small measure to the lack of fresh air and sunshine. Families are huddling in damp hollows, unlighted and unventilated'[3]

Mr. Prendergast, the Paddington Health inspector and part time cloakroom attendant at balls at the Paddington Town Hall, replied. 'There are no damp hollows in Paddington and few houses are unlit and unventilated. Paddington is situated on hilly ground, well drained, with many parks surrounding it, Moore Park, Centennial Park, Rushcutter's Bay and Trumper Park. There is only one 'flat', on which mostly factories have been erected. Admittedly Paddington is an old settled area, and as stated, a great many of the houses are possibly 75 years old. This however does not make them unfit for habitation. Neither can it be said that the people look any different from those in other neighbourhoods. As to sickness, the Paddington School boys were instrumental in winning the Five League football competitions in 1941, the only school ever to do so, and a local girl, one of a family of eight, born in a street narrower than average, won the 'War Savings Certificates' Essay competition against all comers of her age in the Commonwealth, also twice winning prizes in the Police Essay Competition. These facts offset the statement made of 'bad health and poor development!'[4]

Bill played football for Paddington School. 'I captained what they call a Five Seven side'. I think they entered seven teams in it that year and they won all seven competitions. It was a record. We used to have a very good sportsmaster there at Paddington School, and he was very much into football and cricket and things like that'. In adult Rugby League, perhaps the greatest scoring combination League had

Mrs Prendergast

ever seen, was Les Cubitt, The Kangaroo Captain, and Gordon Wright, both Paddington Central Old Boys. 'James Carruthers held the world Bantam weight title between 1950–56, and Judith King won the junior high jump at the New South Wales School Carnival in 1945. At twelve she was third in the open high jump and went on to represent Australia at the 1954 Empire Games. 'Is there another school in the metropolitan area capable of boasting such a proud record?'[5]

Eighty-seven per cent of Paddington houses were still rented, and the rent was about half the income of an average Paddington family. The real issue of importance was overcrowding, which was itself a function of a more deep-seated problem: the general level of poverty among Paddington's majority of working-class residents. 'Some people had to be poor, and unfortunately, Paddington's working-class population were among the poorest in early twentieth century Sydney.'[6]

It was the Second World War that would relieve Australia of the effects of the Great Depression. Economically, the War created new manufacturing industries, prosperity increased, and full employment was achieved, as the War effort provided jobs for all. Sydney became a major naval base for the Allied Fleet and operated as an international city, with a floating population of soldiers and sailors. The Army had taken over the Showgrounds, and more than 700,000 troops passed through the camp. Less than a mile and a half away, there was a raid by the Japanese on Sydney Harbour. The HMAS Kuttabull was sunk off Potts Point on the western side of Rushcutters Bay at 11.30 pm on 31 May 1942.[7] Nineteen men were killed by the torpedoes from Japanese midget submarines, and 10 wounded. Windows were taped. Teachers enlisted, and there were air raid shelters in Hyde Park. Slum clearance was not only shelved but forgotten.

Dolly remembered Sunday bomb scares. 'Frieda had a baby, Kerry, she was only very small. I'd run from Comber Street round to Green's Road and bring her back, and we'd sit under the stairs. That's where they told you to sit and we had earplugs and something to put in our mouth and then finally in the end we didn't bother getting out of bed. My friend, she lived at Tamarama, and her place, she had a bomb come through her brick wall. At *Frances'* house, in Sutherland Street, all of her windows had to be blackened out, so her Mum painted them with Black-it, 'because we had the big Cosi warmer and she used to do the hearths. We had an old chip heater which you know you'd have to chop the timber for, and what have you, and I knew I blew it up a few times. But when I'd hop into the bath, because I always bathed first, then my brother, because we never wasted any of the hot water, I used to try and scratch the black off the window because I never liked to feel I was confined. I remember the search lights, I remember the sirens and I remember at a very young age, the sirens going off. My father was a warden, he didn't go to the war, because he'd taken his thumb off, so he would put on his hat and his gas mask, which was my favorite toy, and race out with his warden's stickers into the night, with the search lights, and it was very close, because my mother put a teething ring in my mouth and pushed me underneath the dresser in the dining room and I was told to stay there. Or else we'd have to sit under the dining room table. I used to wear the gas mask and frighten my brother. My uncle was in the Air Force. He was overseas in New Guinea, and my girlfriend's father was in the Army.'

James was called up. 'After we finished our basic training at Georges Heights, which is over at Mosman, we were allocated to different 3.7 anti-aircraft gun sites around Sydney, of which there was several. And I was fortunate or unfortunate enough to have the one at Long Bay, because it was quite close to Sydney's number one power house, the Bunnerong Power Station. It was very strange, because being in an artillery unit you were on 24 hour duty all day and night. And being so close to home and not being able to get home was the cruel part of it. There was always the possibility, the threat, like the submarine attack. They had gun emplacements underneath the Botanic Gardens where the Railway, Circular Quay railway loop now is. I got transferred later on to Rose Bay. It was a hard life, right in the middle of Royal Sydney Golf Club. They had a gun and battery there. There were about 80 people involved in a site. Japanese submarines did shell Sydney and one of the unexploded shells did land in Rose Bay. It didn't do any damage, but it frightened half the population of Sydney, and all the rich people that lived in Bellevue Hill and that, soon packed up and moved out and went to live at Bowral and you know, that part of the world. Then I was sent to New Guinea. But again in artillery and anti-aircraft gun sites in New Guinea. Mainly in Morseby, around Port Moresby.

The girls take a break on the roof of Lustre Hosiery. *Dolly* second from right, front row.

It could have been a lot worse. There were a lot of soldiers so much worse off, but we were reasonable, because we were so close to the mainland, we got regular supplies of the necessaries. It wasn't too bad.'

Maisie was packing lollies at Steadman's for the soldiers, in Zetland. 'You had to ask if you wanted to go to the toilet. "Miss Stenson can I go to the toilet?" "Well hurry back *Maisie*". I lasted there three weeks. And this doctor told me I wasn't fit. "You can't work here", he said 'Then someone said, "If you want an outdoor job, put in for the buses. That's an outdoor job." So *Maisie* puts in for the buses, so I didn't tell them I'd had pneumonia or rheumatic fever, a clean bill of health I gave myself. So I worked on the buses for three years. You carried six on the back platform. The Watson's Bay bus was the only bus that ran right through from Central to Watsons Bay. My mother cried, and my father was saying, "You can't do that, you can't do that". He said, "It'll kill you, your heart, running up and down all those stairs". Some of the passengers were quite nice. Some used to bring me chocolates. Someone said once, "That girl, that conductress, they're always bringing her chocolates and things." There was one, I used to hop off at Rose Bay and give him the paper and then hop back on the bus. You'd only be a second you know. In the peak hour, it'd be a non sit down one, a 5p fare out to Rose Bay, to stop the people who were only going short distances. Anyway, a lot used to get on that were getting off at the Cross you see, and because they'd know it would be impossible to get through the Cross without slowing down, and they'd be hopping off right and left.'

The Paddington Girls – *Mary* second from right, at the Trocadero

Dolly started work down at Lustre Hosiery. 'I was pretty frightened, you didn't know what to do and where to go. I had just gone down and asked if they had any vacancies. I was in what they call the finishing room and I was on the underwear floor, and they make the underwear and you had to cut off the cottons and things like that. You didn't get any morning or afternoon tea, and every Christmas they'd say, "Off till further notice", so therefore sometimes you'd be off for six weeks and you got no holiday pay at all. Overtime you had to work, whether you wanted to or not. They always had an Eight Hour Day procession and there'd be all kinds of floats and that. Lustre Hosiery, they used to have a float, with the girls in nightdresses and all decorated up with the materials and that, and they used to throw chocolates off and we used to go up and watch it up at Taylor Square because it came up Oxford Street and went down Flinders Street over to the Park.

We had a lot of fun. We all used to go out together, after work, down to Bondi for a swim or dancing. We used to go to the Trocadero, and Luna Park. They had the Giggle Palace with all the different mirrors and they had a floating pontoon where they'd have dances and we'd go down there and dance. The people from the American Red Cross or the Australian Red Cross, if there was a boat, and they wanted so many girls, well you went. We'd get dressed up in evening clothes. We'd go dancing and we'd go out for picnics. A friend and I, we went out with the same fellas, they were stationed here. I didn't like the English. If they bought

The bus conductress off duty

you home and they'd want to say goodnight, you'd be doing up your buttons and they'd be undoing 'em as fast as you were doin' them up. I didn't like them at all. Well, the Americans, you might be at the Trocadero and you'd be dancing with them and they'd say, "How about getting a room?" and you'd say, "I'm not a girl like that" or something similar and they'd just say, "OK" and that was it. There were no hassles, no problems at all. They'd always ask, yes, but as I say, we went with the same fellas every time they came in, they'd be in and out of Sydney. We'd meet them in town at Petty's Hotel. We used to go to Centennial Park and just sit in the sun, you know just normal things.

Sometimes they had dances at the Glaciarium but if you were just going around and learning, you were trying to keep yourself up off the ice. The same with the roller-skating down at the Palladium in Yurrong Street, where the trams used to go round. Well you'd hire the skating boots, and when we come to a space that had no rails to hang on, we'd stand up on our toes and walk across that bit. Then there were George Lane's picnics, launch picnics. We had camp pie and salad, and then we had crushed pineapple and cream. We had the same things every week, and my brother and his two friends, they would pay our fare, which was 2/–, and myself and my two girlfriends, we'd supply the lunch. We went to Rodd, we went to Putney, we went to Press's Pleasure Grounds, there was no alcohol. There were dances on Rodd Island. I mean they were all good. You'd go to the Trocadero and you'd end up at Romano's or Chequers after. That is after working overtime until 8.40, and then back by 7.30 in the morning. We used to go out to the loos to have a cigarette. The forelady would come out to see, so we'd jump up on the loo so she wouldn't know who was where. We used to go out before morning tea, and we'd go out before lunch, and then we'd go out again in the afternoon. We weren't, you know, we had to work and we did, but we had a lot of fun. When she was coming when we were at the machines, one would whistle, "She'll be coming round the Mountain", so we'd know.'

Albert was sent to Darwin and when he came back he was a wharfie. 'We had all our strikes in the world, we went on strike for the dancing girls. There was a heap of girls down at Woolloomooloo at the time, and the coppers came and pinched 'em so we lobbed down there, and went on strike and it went right across the waterfront. We had a lot of strikes, but it was mostly to try to improve out own conditions, sort of thing. The wharves was all alright, there was nothing light on the waterfront. I finished up a foreman, there was a few idiots amongst them, but the majority knew their work. You worked round the shift. You'd go to work on the waterfront and get a job at 6 o'clock in the morning. Before permanence come in, you had to go down to different centres. I was in the overseas centre. If you're, just casual, your numbers were on a board and they'd just call the numbers out, you'd go to a winder and they'd give you work.. You was on call 24 hours a day. In those days it was good money. One night I was on a double header, I had to work all day and then half the night,

A day at the races

and at dinner time the phone rang, and a chap said, "You". "What's up," I said. "Your wife thinks you've won the lottery", and I said, "That's very nice." So we went over and rang up the lottery office and that's it. I said, "Good. I'll see you later" and that was it, I haven't worked since.'

Dolly was in Martin Place the day the war finished. 'They let us all go home and we all went down to Martin Place and in that crowd everyone was shouting and screaming and going on stupid, most of the girls had boyfriends away, or husbands.' *Maisie* was working that day and they weren't allowed to go through the Cross. 'We had to terminate at Rushcutters Bay. The people were performing because we didn't have a Rushcutters Bay sign to put up. So I didn't have any fun on that day. No fun at all'.

By the time the War was over there had been 37,000 Australians killed in action.

After the War, the fight began against rent increases, due to a housing shortage. Mr. Osborne, Member for Paddington, argued in the Legislative Assembly for the Fair Rents Bill. 'It cannot be in the interest of the state or of the city that two or three families should be herded together in one house. The system of living in tenement houses does not commend itself to the average Australian. Every family should have a home of their own. They should be able to live under their own roof without interference by any section of the community'[8] *Bert* told a different story. 'Another politician, J. J. Dettman, in 1946, he was Minister for Housing, Labor minister, Chifley's Government. "Would you consider Mr. Dettman, giving Housing Commission tenants a low deposit and low repayment to relieve some of the housing crisis? You could spend the money building more houses." He said, "What? Make bloody capitalists of them?" *Bert* and his wife were living in a house which 'had little balcony flats. We were in the centre one. There was one below, one in the middle, me cousin had the bottom, we had the middle and me aunt had the top. A kitchen on the veranda, shared bathroom. And paint in the bath, so that you had a white arse when the paint came off. Bloody terrible.'

Mr. Osborne continued his campaign. 'In my electorate I know of dozens of houses which six months ago were only occupied by one family, but are inhabited now by two or more families. People are being driven into renting rooms, because they are not able to afford the exorbitant rents charged by landlords. Although I believe the best way out of the difficulty is to erect more houses at the earliest moment, still it is in the power of the Government to introduce a Fair Rents Bill to limit rents.'[9] The Act was passed.

Some disagreed. Wally O Connell of 41 Hopetoun St Paddington wrote to The Fair Rents Tribunal.[10]

I see by the reports of the newspapers where the Government is considering the reintroduction of the Fair Rents Court and they are watching very carefully any increases in rent.

The ball *Dolly* on the right

There is a terrace of houses in Hopetoun Street Paddington, 12 in number. The rent 25/– before the Interest Reduction Act (the last Fair Rents Act); that pulled them down to 19/6d. Some months ago the rent was increased to 21/–, that is an increase of 1/6d per week. There are four persons going out to work out of the two houses, three out of another, and two tradesmen out of another, and so on, and the agitator is up at the corner of Oxford Street every Friday night asking them to sign a petition for the Fair Rents Court. Every time the rent goes down so does the value of the property. In many cases there is very little equity left. It was no crime to bring the rents down. (i.e. during the depression). People will not buy property old or new, for a court to tell how much they should get for it. If Mr. Martin and his Government would equalise the sacrifice between the mortgagor and the mortgagee he would be doing more service to the community than listening to the half baked propaganda of half baked Communists. There would not be half so many evictions from Glebe or the other slummy suburbs if they paid their rent instead of putting it on the dogs. There is one of these gentlemen about Parliament who's got a lot to say about the Fair Rents Court and that is Mr. McKell, M.L.A. for Redfern. This Gentleman did not put his spare cash into houses and become a good Socialist and a model landlord. He went and put it into a farm down the South coast. The Fair Rents Court would not apply to that.[11]

The Paddington Girls just went right on partying. 'On a Saturday afternoon we sometimes went to Romano's or Prince's. Prince's was beautiful. You went downstairs, and in the bottom, and it was all beautifully laid out with tables and lamps. You wore your gloves and your handbag and your best gear. Whimsy hats and stuff like that. Whimsy hats are a veil, a bit of a veil or maybe a satin bow or something with a little whimsy around it. The whimsy was the veil, the net sort of thing. I used to wear these little waisted in things, with very full skirts. You'd sit at a table and the boys would come over and they'd ask you, "Would you like to dance?" They used to have sandwiches and scones and all that sort of thing, real afternoon tea sort of thing, really nice. Tables were always beautifully laid out and flowers and things like that.'

Back at home, families that had hung on in Paddington were getting older. In 1948, the NSW Labor government passed the Landlord and Tenant (Amendment Act). Rents were strictly controlled, and protected tenancies were created by the Act, which virtually created a perpetual lease in favour of certain lessees. Though many tenants were secure in the occupancy of their accommodation, their landlords, faced with a rent permanently pegged at a low level, and the impossibility of eviction for any reason, simply let the property fall into ruin.

Once again there was an attempt to clear the area because of its slum status, and there were moves to amalgamate Paddington with the City Council to facilitate this proposition.

Chapter Seven
The Transit Camp

In 1945, 90 per cent of Australia's population had been born here. A further 8 per cent were British, and 2 per cent were either European or Chinese. Aborigines were not counted in the census and were afforded no citizen rights. Immigration to Australia was controlled by the White Australia Policy, which was endorsed by both major political parties, and had been integral to the platform and philosophy of all major parties since Federation. It had been extended throughout the decades to virtually exclude all but British citizens. Migration had been limited by measures such as a dictation test, which could be in any language of the British Isles, such as Welsh, Gaelic and Cornish. It was specifically designed to exclude anyone that the government thought unworthy, and was only given to those it wanted to exclude. The test was not abolished until 1958.[1]

When the Second World War ended, it was apparent that Australia needed a rapid increase in population, 'factory fodder', to stimulate the economy. It demanded a growth in population far exceeding natural increase. The War had also raised awareness of threats of invasion from Asia. Australia was a large landmass with a small population.

The War in Europe had a created a situation where people wanted to flee nations whose infrastructures and economies had been smashed. However, these people were not the target of the Australian government, which wanted to maintain a British Australia. Arthur Calwell, the Labor Minister for Immigration, travelled to the United Kingdom to promote migration to Australia for British citizens. These people were offered an assisted passage and paid ten pounds to emigrate. 'This country offers opportunities for a new life to all those who are not afraid to work. Australia welcomes her British kinsmen and women

Maria's house Murello, Italy

wholeheartedly. There are no prejudices, no social barriers. There will be new jobs for skilled workers in the industries of her cities and towns, and for workers on farms, in the forests and mines, and on the sheep-lands.'[2]

But there were still shortfalls in the number of migrants needed, so offers were made first to Northern Europeans, and later to Southern Europeans, but not to Asians. Ironically, Arthur Calwell quoted an old Chinese proverb, 'If you are planning for one year, plant grain: if you are planning for ten years, plant trees: if you are planning for a hundred years, plant men. Australia is planning for more than a hundred years.'[3]

Australia's migration policy changed the social fabric of Australia. It would change the view from that of Australia as a province of the British Empire, to a global one.

Maria was a young woman living in Murello, Italy, when she experienced the horrors of war. 'We were in the middle, there were the Germans there, the Fascists there, and the Partisans there, and we were right in the centre. They made a mistake bombing. Instead of them getting Fiat in Turin, we got it in our back yard. We were all in the square because it happened to be the feast day, but it was at the back of our farm, the three bombs that came down. Three were killed and six or seven damaged. We could hear the bombing every night in Turin. My three brothers had to go to war. John was local, and Louis was sent home when my father was sick, and George was a prisoner of war in Tripoli. They all came home. We kept on working.' *Maria* came to Australia in 1948.

Nicolina came from Malta, where she and her family had suffered bombing raids. In one of these raids, her father was killed. Most of the family were in a shelter, while others had stayed in the house. 'After the bombs, they come and open the shelter because of the stones closed the doors of the shelter, we was from 4 o'clock in the morning till 8 o'clock in the morning. My mum and my two sisters were in the house, they were there because the other two sisters, they didn't want to come down to the shelter, and my father, who was shouting, "Come to the shelter", so by the time he was talking to Mum it was too late. So we come out, but we couldn't hear anything, so we couldn't understand my father die, and I remember I was crying because we hadn't got a house. We lived in the garage, my father had a garage for the horses and the buggies, and my mother didn't even take us to the cemetery, because she thinks we don't understand, and then I had to leave school, to go to work for one pound a week, and I used to give it to Mum, and then when my brother, he decided to come here, he said, "I'll take my sister with me", so we come here for two years to help Mum.'

Maria was singularly unimpressed with her first sight of Sydney. 'I thought the mast of the ship was going to touch the Bridge. It didn't look anything'. She was unimpressed by her accommodation in Dillon Street, Paddington. 'It was nothing, it was just a room. I didn't have much to do because all my clothes

Nic before migrating   *Nic* six months later

were new, and I couldn't speak English.' Her husband, *Enzo*, described the
boarding house. 'They were quite big places, there were five bedrooms. The
balconies were balcony kitchens, they would put the stoves in there, and then
the bedroom. You had the stove there and that was it, you didn't have any water
and you had to get it from the bathroom, and then you used to take it down
and put it in the toilet, and it was share toilet and share bath, but everybody
was really good and every one was really nice, really considerate of everyone
else. I used very little of the kitchen because I used to eat at the hotel.'[*Enzo*
worked as a waiter] When *Maria* had a baby, she was the only woman there,
apart from the landlady. 'All the boys were coming in and asking me if I want
anything. "Can I carry the bucket down for you? Can I do this for you? Do you
want to use the laundry?" It was multinational down there. One was Polish, one
was Czech, one was Australian, one was German. They were working in
factories, delivering mail.'

Nic also came from Italy. His first impression of Australia was the opposite
to *Maria's*. He fell in love with Sydney at first sight. 'When you come in through
the Heads the most fascinating thing is a picture I still have in my eyes, that's
why I never leave Sydney. When I saw the Harbour Bridge I thought, "I hope
we stay here in Sydney. I hope we never go to live further away", and I didn't

realize that my Dad had purchased the house just around the corner in Paddington. I've been in Paddington ever since. After the Harbour Bridge — to me, Sydney forever.'

Paddington was an affordable place to live in, and close to places of work, a major advantage for new arrivals. There was the potential to rent rooms first, and save a deposit to buy a house. *Mario* moved to Paddington from Italy, in the 1960's. He found a room, boarding above a shop owned by *Christina, Paula,* and *Nico.* 'It was a triangle shop on a corner, and the old shelves they full of pasta, tomato paste, that was imported from Italy. It was completely Italian except for soft drinks, and they used to make sandwiches in the back room. They had their own machine to slice salami, ham, cheese, and *Christina* was outside serving people, and it was very busy. They had been there for ages. It was like a Southern Italian village shop, not very neat, things were there, just chucked up in any corner, everywhere. *Paula,* even today she is hopeless in English, because she has been there with her brother and sister and speaks Italian all the time. She had no chance, but *Christina* was better because she was in the front of the shop.'

Dr. Lerner emigrated to Australia from in England in the 1950's, and he described Paddington as a 'transit camp for migrants'. He observed their effect on Paddington, as they formed a large part of his practice. He learnt Italian so he could understand his patients. Today there are only a handful left. 'Most of them had little English, they were the first generation, they were insecure people. Most of them, the overwhelming number of them, had never been educated past ten or eleven, educated by the nuns, and then they'd worked in the fields or in some heavy craft industry …This [their lack of English] was a general problem, and was a cause of stress to them. The overwhelming number of them came from southern Italy from a village society, or else small towns, where there was compactness and togetherness and everyone knew his neighbours and everyone chatted over the garden wall, and that had gone in Sydney. Your neighbour was Australian and you couldn't chat, and the women had even less English than the men, because they never got out. The men, to a certain extent, learnt English at work, and the women when they were shopping.'

Migrants were unable to make a gradual adaptation to their new life. It was a matter of sink or swim. They had to contend with the impatience of locals who had never met Europeans before. *Con,* from Greece, was forced to learn English by himself. 'I been to Glenmore Road School a few nights, and then I tried to listen the news from the radio, and television and the papers. I have the paper trying to figure out what the news says, Sydney Morning Herald it was, and it was the Grand Final of the football, and I think it was St. George and Balmain, and another young fella come next to me and he sat talking me about football. I couldn't understand, and he got angry, why I didn't understand what

First time in shorts, first time in a car, first trip to the beach, *Maria*

he was talkin' about. In Greece, the foreigner learning Greek, they laugh and they enjoy it, because you trying to learn. They didn't say, "Oh! a mistake", or something, they didn't say, "Why you didn't learn before you come?" They didn't say that to you did they?'

The first quest for a migrant was to find a job, and most learnt the language there. Others went to classes, or started serving in shops. 'The Italian community was there, but because I didn't speak English, I didn't want to mix with them. I said I have to mix with English speaking people and when I had spare time, I used to go to school for immigrant people.' (*Mario*) *Nicolina* was helped by a countrywoman. 'There was a Maltese girl, she was a floor lady in the Silk Knit. They used to make underclothes. She say, "I'll get you a job with me". I said, "Look, I never touch a machine in my life". She said, "Don't worry about it. I teach you". I said, "Look, if somebody talk to me I don't know what they talking about." She said, "Don't worry you will learn". So anyway they put me on the overlocker machine. "Oh *Gina*," I said, "How am I going to do that?" She said, "You do what the other one do." My goodness, in two days I learned this bloody machine. The factory was in Surry Hills, underwear, so we used to work with bonus, the more we sew the more we get, in those days we only get seven pounds a week, and my goodness, the forelady come and she said, "Jesus Christ, *Nicolina*, you do it really great, did you done that before?" I shook my head and *Gina* said, "Yes she did", and I looked at *Gina* and she said, "You should see her face," because I never tell a lie, and so I used to get good money, twenty pounds.'

For children, the lack of English could be traumatic. *Gino's* family emigrated to Australia from Malta when he was eight. He lived in Boundary Street, and spent his childhood and teenage years in Paddington. 'I remember going to St. Joseph's up at Edgecliff, we used to cut through Trumper Park. Now, I could speak one or two words of English, that was about all I could do, so you go to school, and you got nothing and you want to borrow a bloke's ruler, I can remember this. "Can I have your ruler?" and the bloke says, "No, you can't have the ruler". So through misunderstanding, you could get into a fight. He thinks you want to pinch his ruler and you want to say, "Why can't I borrow your ruler?" but you don't know the word for 'borrow', and you don't know the difference between 'take' and 'borrow', but he doesn't know what you mean. So those are the sorts of memories you have, but then you eventually mould in, but we were lucky, one good thing we did, we never got involved in a clique, and as a result we soon learnt the language, to assimilate. We never got into a herd like a lot of 'em did. I've never been very big on Maltese heritage. Our parents spoke bits and pieces, probably more Maltese originally, but we always answered in English. I think it just happened. You're here now, this is it.'

Australian government policy was one of assimilation. Migrants were not encouraged to retain their own culture. To be Australian was to be a British Australian. *Nicolina* was freed from the constraints of a strict Maltese upbringing and the workplace provided her with friends and new social possibilities. 'I used to mix with Australians all the time, because *Pearl* used to say to me. "*Nicolina*, if you mix with the Maltese all the time you never learn", and then I met a black girl, and she used to sit on the table with us at morning tea, and she was lovely. There was about five of us, a New Zealand girl, the black girl, *Pearl,* and two other Australians. They all looked after me. We used to go to the pictures, we used to go to the dance at the Trocadero. Oh, lovely, beautiful. *Pearl*, said, "Come here," she said, "I'm going to introduce you with Australians," I said, "*Pearl*, I can't speak that good." She said, "Come on", so he comes and he said, "I know a few words in Maltese," and I said, "I know a few words in English", so we used to dance together. When the dance finish, *Pearl*, she used to put me into a taxi straight home.'

Mario had little time to socialise. He was very busy establishing himself in the city. 'I tell you after I start working at the Wentworth Hotel, I think there is an opportunity for young people in Australia, I look at myself in the mirror and I say, "*Mario*, use your brain, work hard, and one day you will have what you want." So I work hard and I had three jobs in the same hotel and I was sleeping four hours a night for four years.' *Nic* was working with a European barber. 'For the first nine months, every night I went to the Oxford Theatre, the most beautiful theatre. It was a big theatre with a big entrance, with a milk bar on one side, and a milk bar on the other, and there used to be the front where all the kids used to go, and the back stalls and the upstairs. It was the dress circle, and for an extra 6p I always used to go upstairs. Since I came to Australia I never been short of money. I had nothing else to do until I started to meet other friends and we used to go dancing.'

Gino's pattern of family migration was typical of many families. First his father came a few weeks before the rest of the family, so he could find work to set the family up. About a month later *Gino*, with his mother and the rest of the family, arrived. They stayed with an aunt in Glenmore Road, then when they had established themselves, they played host to relations who later moved next door. *Nic's* father also migrated before the rest of his family. He came out one year before his wife and children, and worked to save a deposit for a terrace house in Paddington. This was unusual, for Paddington was still a place that was dominated by renters. Few of the working class families that had lived in Paddington for years, actually owned their homes.

The suburb had the reputation of being a slum, and the issue of slum clearance was raised again. In 1948, the bankrupt Paddington Council was absorbed into the City of Sydney, and in 1952 a Planning Scheme was launched, which proposed the extensive remodelling of Paddington. Alderman Reginald Murphy, wanted to see 500 acres of slums, the semi-detached and terrace houses, which surrounded the inner city, eradicated. Policies such as these were proposed by people who did not live within the suburb, and did not understand the culture of the inhabitants.[4]

Nic loved Paddington and he was surprised by other people's attitudes towards it. 'There was quite a big Italian community, a lot of Italians used to live in Paddington, because in those days Paddington used to be the poor man's suburb, which I couldn't believe it. I'll tell you a story. 1963–4, I used to always like dancing and I was in this dancing place, Petersham Town Hall, and I was dancing with this nice looking girl, and to make sure, I used to ask first, "Where you live?" just in case you offer to give them a lift home, and then you have to drive to Penrith, and I said, "Where you live?" and she said, "I live in Guilford." "Oh how nice," I said. And she said, "Where you live?" and I said, "I live in Paddington", always been very proud of living in Paddington. And she said, "Oh yuck, you don't look, you don't dress like you come from Paddington."

Wedding Day

"Well", I said, 'Paddington is a beautiful place." My father was the first one to paint the house, 88 Underwood Street. He painted the outside, he painted the inside, even pulled the chimney, which today would be a crime to do that, all the things that a newcomer done. He pulled out the chimney. He said, "Make more room here", then he painted inside. A beautiful little terrace.'

Max's description of Windsor Street where he grew up gives an impression of the impact of new migrants' renovations. 'Nearly every house as I can recall was brown. The house on the opposite corner was then acquired by Italians, and that's been some very interesting colours. I remember at one stage there was an Italian gentleman there, and he even painted the house pink with white mortar, and purple window sills.' The acquisition of individual houses by the Greeks, Italians, and Maltese broke up the pattern of ownership from one where one owner might own a row of terraces, to one where there were now multiple owners. Migrants either did basic maintenance, or renovated, and this increased the value of the property.

For the second time, slum clearance faded from the political agenda. As values increased, the cost of Government acquisition became prohibitive, and the focus was moved to the Rocks area. Paddy Pearl used Council rate books to count migrant householders between 1950 to 1960. He found they owned 679 of about 4000 dwellings. The largest groups were Greeks (341), Italians (304), Yugoslavs (42), Spanish/Portugese (39), Polish (13), German (12), as well as French, Russian, Dutch and Hungarians. This did not include renters.[5] To some of the older residents, this trend seemed like an invasion which threatened their way of life. *Bert* did not mince words. 'How would you feel about it when someone puts the guts of a goat out in the gutter to putrefy, when the old ladies in Paddo used to sweep from the fence to the gutter and the bloke would come through with a big square barrar with two tins on it, and he'd pick it up, and Paddington was bloody spotless, and the wogs come in and the first thing that happened, you've got goats' heads, sheep's guts, chicken feathers, dead bodies, everywhere you went? The place started to stink, and people started to shift.' At the same time, one of the largest factories in the area, Hardy's Rubber, closed down. It had employed many hundreds of Paddington residents. *Bert* was disgusted. 'Most of the people who lived in Paddington worked in these factories. Yeah, most of them did. You could be born in Paddo, live in Paddo, work in Paddo, die in Paddo, and never have to move out of bloody Paddo. It was efficient. They destroyed all that.'

The Paddington branch of the Labor Party had its first meeting on March 14 1956, in what had been a solid Labor area since the beginning of the century. Many residents were union members. The Paddington branch passed a resolution in August 1956 and asked for its submission to the central executive.

> 'That the Paddington Branch of the A.L.P. is of the opinion that the present intake of migrants is placing a too great a strain on the economic resources of Australia and is contributing substantially to the inflationary situation. This is endangering the living standards of the Australian people.
>
> We therefore declare that immediate action should be taken to restrict the number of migrants permitted to enter Australia to the near relatives of people already settled in this country.
>
> We further declare that the restricted intake be continued until such time as the housing lag is overtaken, and employment is assured to all workers.
>
> Finally, that a copy of this resolution be forwarded to the NSW State executive and the same be forwarded to the state executive of the A.L.P.'[5]

Migrants voted conservatively on their arrival. However, their vote began to swing from conservative parties to Labor, and is clearly expressed in the following letter of warning to the Prime Minister published in Fiamma, in 1961, when employment opportunities were decreasing.

> 'Free Translation, La Fiamma 13. 6. 1961
> 'Open Letter to His Excellency, Mr Menzies
> Your Excellency, We are unemployed.
>
> Your Excellency, We have seen and heard you on television last Thursday. The whole of Australia, after all, had remained at home that

Mary's daughter Prospect Street

evening to listen to you. Italians who did not have television met at clubs, restaurants and in the homes of more fortunate friends. At 7.30 there appeared on TV your face, the most photogenic face in Australia, the prosperous face of an honest man, sure of himself, which claims both faith and admiration.

We believe that the electoral successes of the Australian Liberal Party are fundamentally tied to your face, Your Excellency. Irrespective as to how many mistakes might be made by your party and your government, when you decide to descend amongst the people and to speak to the country, there is no critical situation that can be healed, except from your words, by your face of father and protector.

You see, the Honourable Mr. Calwell might have all the reasons in the world to occupy your place at the next elections. But he does not have the face going with the role, nor your overpowering fascination.

Cartoonists have a field day when they draw Calwell; but when they draw you they approach nervous breakdown.

This preamble partly explains why Italians last Thursday at 7.30 gathered in religious silence — to the very end — to listen to your splendid English. As usual they remain seduced, conquered, fascinated by your face, by your assurance and your optimism. And they went to sleep happy and full of hope like little pupils.

But the following day, on waking up, the Italian — and especially the newly arrived ones, asked themselves: By Jove, it might be alright for the country to have an Unlimited Future but where do we take the money in order to spend it 'in a normal way'? From where do we get the money to spend it, if we don't know how to earn it?'

Your Excellency, one can come to a compromise with one's stomach and one's debts for an evening, but on the next day the problem becomes more serious than before. Your Excellency, the Italians like you, but they cannot spend the money in any way because they are unemployed. Those that bought a home have to sell it, because they have lost their work and their overtime; our women who helped us during the first years round up our incomes, have been sacked; the families that depend on our remittances are desperate because we are no longer able to help them.

Of 90,000 unemployed, 75,000 are new Australians and 20,000 Italians.

It is not enough to tell these people that Australia has an Unlimited Future, that the 'squeeze' was necessary to stop the 'boom,' and the inflation. These people do not have the savings to await the future, nor influential or generous friends, They have nothing and nobody in the world except their hands, the will and the right to work.

Maisie's children Christmas Day

These people must work otherwise they don't eat!

These are the thoughts which crowded the minds of Italians on the morning after your speech, Your Excellency. We are certain you have good tidings also for the 20,00 Italians who have been sacked.

Perhaps you did not have sufficient time for new Australians on Thursday night. It doesn't matter. We will wait because your face, your experience, your common sense, always inspire us with faith.

With devoted observance,

La Fiamma

Despite the ill feeling of some Paddington residents, *Nic* did not face any discrimination. 'Never. Perhaps it was before, but not in my time. I used to go to the Police Boys' Club, we used to do a bit of boxing, a bit of weight lifting, but I never had any problem. Mind you, it's always me, that I make the effort to say good morning first, to say hello. Only once I got very annoyed. I really gave this bloke, well, he insulted me, he called me a wog, he said, "You stupid wogs that can't fight for peanuts", so I couldn't help myself, I gave him a … but that's only once you know.'

More strangers appeared at this time. John Thompson with his wife, Pat, who later was the author of several books about Paddington, and their sons, Peter and Jack, moved to Goodhope Street in 1956. They were the first representatives of a middle class group who began to migrate from the north shore to Paddington. They saw the potential in inner urban living. John Thompson wanted to live closer to his work in radio for the ABC. They witnessed the effects of the Southern Europeans on Paddington and the reaction of the long-term residents. 'The Europeans moved in, probably several families, and worked terrifically hard and got a lot of cash together and they would walk into a house in Paddington and say, "We want this house," and put the money on the table and eventually people started to yield to this, you know, walk away with the money, and so on the one hand there was an exodus of the old Paddington residents, many of whom were on controlled rent and were pushed out, and others who voluntarily left. There were these big bustling families, crawling with kids. A man came into the corner shop and stood at the back of the shop and waited his turn and got to the counter and said to *Les* in a foreign voice, "Do you have any salami?" And *Les* went a little bit redder and said, "Oh no mate, we don't sell that sort of stuff here." He was really saying, "Get out of this shop, you wog. You don't belong here and we don't want you in here ever again". Well, within a few years *Les* had been forced to sell his shop and it had been taken over by an Italian. On the other hand, I had my parents absolutely rejoicing in this change. Suddenly Paddington was becoming a much more varied and interesting place.'(Peter)

In time there was a guarded peace. The kids, whose parents had called the newcomers 'wogs', were marrying Italians, Greeks and Maltese.

Saturday morning

Church groups sought to keep the youth of Paddington in order, and maintain moral standards. They provided meeting places where young people of the same denomination could meet under supervised conditions. These groups were attended by the same people who went to the milk bars, and listened to Rock and Roll. The Catholic Youth Organisation was one of them. It was where *Janice* met *Gino*. This was what the Catholic Youth Organisation was designed for, to maintain the religion by encouraging Catholics to marry Catholics. Religion was a common ground for Maltese, Italian, and the old Irish community. 'It was held underneath the church at the hall at Sacred Heart, Darlinghurst, and it was a group, a priest used to run it, he was trying to get rid of the bad influences and was trying to give us something to do. Like playin' cards for money, and darts for money, and they also had Housie there in the Hall, Wednesday and Friday nights. When I was down there sellin' tickets *Bob* came in. "Oh, howya goin' sis?", you know, and I was a new face, and they said, "That's *Bob's* sister". And that's how we started. *Gino* said, "Hey you", he said. And I said, "Are you speaking to me?" "Do you want to go to a cabaret on Friday night?" And I was actually goin' with a guy at that stage but I said, "Oh yeah", and that's how we started going out.'(*Janice*)

Children from all backgrounds quickly became friends. *Gino's* childhood was not dissimilar to that of *Max,* who grew up in Windsor Street. Both of these boys earned money by selling papers and both boxed. As children, they played the same games, such as hidings and billy-cart races. Peter Thompson too, played the same games, and recounts, 'I was very much a builder and maker of things, and I built Jack a billycart and myself a billycart. We went and got ball bearings from the garage, and we made these billycarts and I endlessly modified mine by putting brakes on it. How my parents or anybody else in the street put up with it, I've never been able to comprehend, how they used to put up with the noise the kids used to make around the streets. We used to make so much noise racing up and down the footpaths, and in the street itself as well.'

Janice had moved to Paddington with her parents, *Jeannie* and *Jim,* when she was thirteen. At first she was unhappy with the move, as she had been well established in Glebe and was top of her class. When she arrived in Paddington, she kept up her relationship with Forest Lodge and Glebe, but soon got up to mischief in her new neighbourhood. 'We used to play cockelawra. You'd knock on people's doors and then you'd race off and then you'd hide. Or you'd go up and tie black cotton across their door, then knock on the door and then they'd come out, and it would be draped around them and they'd think it was a spider web. Or you'd do it across the street so they'd catch it across their legs. We used to pinch the old street cleaner's cart and race it across to the hospital. He was a grumpy old man and he used to come around with a barrow to clean the streets, and he'd go off for lunch somewhere and we'd pinch his cart and hide it in the bushes… We used to give the Salvation Army hell. They used to come

A boy and his dog

Janice

and sing under the light at the corner of Prospect Street and Spring Street. They'd come down there and play their things and we'd sit down and sing all the Catholic songs at the tops of our voices, because we were all Catholics. When I was with *Laurie* and them, we used to go down Oxford Street and stand on the corner, and the trams used to chug up the hill and we'd stand there throwin' eggs or tomatoes into the tram. And we'd go down to Hyde Park for the Christmas Carols and we'd chuck rotten eggs into the crowd. Oh, we were dreadful. We were buggers of kids. We used to have a ball. I don't think it was a dangerous place. It was considered slums. It was poor. We thought we were quite tough living in Paddington. It had a reputation for being tough, but you never actually saw it in Paddington itself. *Bob* had a couple of friends, there was one that was murdered, when *Bob* was about 17 and *Lenny*, *Bob* said the police got 'im and belted 'im up and he died. And then this other *Ted* up the road, he was the biggest thief, he'd pinch the eyes out of your head. Oh you wouldn't let him in your house. He'd walk out with anything if it wasn't nailed down. We all used to nick things in those days. We all used to go down the corner and pinch the iceblocks.'

Gino and *Max* grew up at different ends of Paddington, one born in Australia, the other in Malta, but they shared similar tastes in clothes. *Gino* thought he was really hip. 'I bought myself a green pair of pants and a green shirt. I don't know why I picked green. I had jet black hair pushed back, used to have it cut by a bloke called Archie round in Glenmore Road, where now there's a little restaurant. He was fashionable and we thought he knew how we all liked our hair cut. It turned out later that he was giving us all the same hair cut anyway, but we thought we were special. Shoes, we're getting serious now, we're fifteen and we're gettin' very serious. So you have to save your money and you have to buy a good pair of shoes called Mellers. They were in King Street, only one store in Sydney, and you polished them till you saw your face in 'em, and because it took so long you only did the toe, I mean you'd polish the whole shoe but you concentrated on the toe. Some were pointy, but not the real pointy ones, and we used to go and get those shoes, and spend a lot of time with a handkerchief and a tin of polish, and you used to light the polish to make it soft, and you'd put your finger in the water and you'd just go round and round like that and you'd really see your face in them and you'd get dressed up. And then later on as you got a bit older, we used to go to Andy Ellis somewhere down Pitt Street, and that's where you got your suits or 'your bag o' fruit' as he used to call 'em, your trousers with your twelve or thirteen inch bottoms and big knees and pleats going everywhere. They were very tight stove pipes. You could put your foot in but you couldn't get it out. And you'd get jumpers that were Robert Mitchum blue and Sinatra red.'

Max's favourite clothes were 'Elvis Presley purple socks, Sinatra red socks. I had black pants, they were that tight you had to sew up the last inch after you

The Boys

put them on. Peg pants were all the go. I had these black pants with pink metallic flecks. I bought these second hand, off a chap called *Chris* who was at school. I loved them, I bought them off him for so much money. I had a flat top. And this was called a Kramer hair cut in those days because of the tennis player. Not many people had them, but Tony Curtis was the style, and everybody wanted to have hair like Tony Curtis, you know the grease, Californian Poppy. Then just after that, I changed completely on my style of clothes and went to Ivy League. That was a change. Also at that time Crash Craddock jumpers came in. I never had one of those and I was glad I didn't, because they only lasted for about three months. They sort of came and went quickly. But Ivy League came. They were the button-down shirts. Searsucker sort of material, the grey pants. More the clean cut kid look'.

The girls were wearing pedal pushers, rope petticoats, hair in a ponytail, heaps and heaps of petticoats that would stand up by themselves, beach dresses with little straps, or else 'something really tight that you could hardly move in, and black shoes. We played netball for CYO. We went with our hair in rollers all over Sydney. Then we'd get all spruced up and go to the movies and then for a hamburger and a milkshake. Then you'd have a 'pasho' in the street for about three hours. Mum would say to me, "Do you have to come home with the milkman every night?"(*Janice*)

Police Boys' Clubs were meeting places for teenagers. Local kids trained to box. *Max* started boxing at Paddington Police Boys' Club when he was about thirteen. He went with a friend, whose brother was an Australian Champion Boxer, David Floyd, 'and he lived in Sutherland Lane and across the road from them was Jimmy Carruthers. And I was with Laurie Floyd, we used to go to school together. I used to watch them box, and then I started to have some lessons and then I started boxing. I had a few amateur fights, and I had a trainer. When I was about fourteen or fifteen I fought for the NSW title and I had to fight heavyweight, and I got beat on points. And I fought in the Golden Gloves, and got knocked out in the finals. And I fought a coal miner from Bulli at the Stadium'.

Crowds at the boxing had started to diminish as other forms of entertainment began to compete with it. Certainly the Paddington locals provided Stadiums Limited with little revenue. 'There was a canal running through there that used to run under the Stadium, a storm water channel, and you could sneak through there and get up through the seats without paying. All the young Paddo blokes used to do it.' (*Ted*) There may have been an even faster decline if it had not been for the influence of Italian migrants. They brought with them traditions in boxing as a sport, and Stadiums Limited capitalised on this new audience by importing Italian fighters. Two of the more prominent boxers were Carlo Manchini and Luigi Coluzzi. Carlo Manchini came to prominence as a middleweight and achieved the national title. Crowds who attended the Sydney Stadium were often rowdy, and in some cases brawls broke out between Anglo and Italian Australians. In 1954, after Luigi Coluzzi had been awarded a win on points over 'Bronco' Johnson, fights erupted in and outside the stadium and five Italians were arrested.[6]

The Stadium was also used by entrepreneurs promoting Jazz and Rock and Roll. Two of the most prominent of the men who brought out overseas and local talent to the stadium were Lee Gordon and Kym Bonython. Some of the acts that performed at the venue were Johnny Ray, Chuck Berry, Frank Sinatra, Buddy Holly and the Beatles.

Rugby League was the other big sport. There were many small teams, some of them established for many years. They were based on very specific areas within suburbs. These teams emphasised loyalties even within areas of suburbs. The Paddington Colts were under the jurisdiction of the Eastern Suburbs Rugby League Club. 'We had plenty of parties too. They'd sort of come from the football teams that you were in. I used to play football with a mob called the Wharfies. In those days there was the Paddo Colts, Bondi United. The Wharfies trained down Rushie Bay, and a lot of us played for the same team and some of those people, their parents were also interested, and they would put on a do or have a barbie.'(*Gino*)

Teenagers in Paddington took on the American culture they saw in films. There were many rebels without a cause. 'I was a quiet kid, didn't look for trouble, but I wouldn't walk away from it. There used to be a lot of gang wars, this and that. But I wasn't warring in a gang. I remember there was this big fight between the Swallow Inn Milk Bar which was in Oxford Street, and the Odeon which was down at Darlinghurst there. Milk bars would be the place. But the Paddington people weren't like Coogee. There used to be milk bars there where you'd be fighting to go in, and there'd be leather jacket people you know that would be around that area, and they'd look for trouble. Most of them couldn't fight but would cause trouble. The Paddington boys could always fight. They were good fighters.'(*Max*)

'You used to go up to the two milk bars and then you might go to the movies and then you went back home. So you probably covered about two hundred yards, there and back. Up from the picture show and the Albury Hotel there was the two Milk Bars. One of them is still like a café place and I notice they've got chairs with all the movie stars names on them. The other one was directly across the road. They were owned by the same people, Mr. and Mrs. Green. They owned the two of 'em. You walked in and on your left hand side was this counter that went the length of the shop, and in that you had a few lollies, you had your milkshake machine and your cigarettes stacked up the back there with a few boxes of chocolates, not much because they didn't sell. Then you had a juke box over here, and you had pinball over here, and that was it. That was all there was to it. There wasn't room to sit, everybody was crammed in, everyone was bumper to bumper, shoulder to shoulder. Now on any weeknight, you would have thirty people, you'd go there of a Saturday night and the bar wasn't much bigger than this room and you'd have thirty or forty people there. You could buy one cigarette for a penny, that's when I started smokin' when I was fourteen, Capstan cigarettes, Ardath, Craven A's. If you had a bit of money you could buy two for 3p. Sometimes you'd get someone to give you a bit of paper and a bit of tobacco and you'd roll your own. You'd have three or four cars parked outside the milk bar. Now a lot of them came from that area, a lot of them came from Paddington like the Five Ways. Some of them came from the Moore Park area, some of them came from Woolloomooloo, but they were all what you'd call part of the gathering, 'cause they were there every other night but then occasionally, and that was when the fights used to start, you'd get people from Marrickville, from Newtown, and they'd come in three or four carloads and there would be twenty of those and that's when the problem erupted. They stood out, and they were there for one reason, and one reason only, to pick a fight. They did that by sort of pickin' on the girls, either abuse them or say, 'Come on, jump in the car', and maybe even just grab 'em or something like that, because they knew that would start something. One person would go up and push, and then another one would come from behind, and it was all in, and then the coppers would come and we'd spread like birds everywhere, and they'd chase you, and if they caught you, they'd give you a kick in the backside and tell you not to get caught again.

In those days a lot of American sailors used to visit Sydney, so they'd go up there, and they were on R and R, see, and they'd take you back on the ship and they'd show you around because you were with them, and you'd come back with three or four packets of Camel cigarettes or Lucky Strike, it'd be good. One time a ship came in from England and there was a lot of Teddy boys on it. Now about six or seven of them just happened to wander into the milkbar and they saw a few girls there and obviously they had been at sea, and they tried to pick them up. A fight erupted and there's only six of them, and thirty or forty of us, so obviously they come off second best. Then they came back with a mob of about fifty with iron bars and God knows what, and there's windows goin' and fights goin' on everywhere, and it stretched from the West's picture show way past the Paddington Town Hall. You could see fights, two or three here, half a dozen there, one on one over there, cops everywhere. I'd have been eighteen, I suppose, so we're talking about '57 or '58. Bumper Farrel and his gang would chase you up, he was a detective, one of the most famous.' (*Gino*)

David joined the Police Force in the early 1960's and has memories of Bumper Farrel. 'One day we were all mucking around, we had water pistols. The detectives' office was upstairs, and right at the back of the building. You'd go up the stairs and then you went along the corridor, and then you walked along a steel walkway above the cells, it was like a steel platform. And *Graham* was annoying everybody, the meal room was up there. I said to him, "Mate you're so big with that bloody water pistol, I bet you're not going to squirt the next bloke who walks through that door." As it turned out, *Graham* said, "I'll do it", and it was Bumper! And he squirted him with the water pistol, and Bumper had not even a change in expression on his face. He just grabbed him by the scruff of the neck, dragged him down the corridor and stuck his head down the toilet and flushed it and said, "That's my water pistol, son". See he worked in the Vice area of the Cross and he knew probably all the prostitutes, and also he knew a lot of the knockabouts. He never took a step backwards, and he already had a reputation, even before he came to Paddington, how to handle himself in the street. To be quite honest, I never really saw Bumper in a real fight. He belted a few of us. If he took a dislike to a particular person, you could be just having a beer, and if he didn't like you, all of a sudden he'd let go of one. He knew everybody, everywhere he went. He knew a lot of people in the street, and he wouldn't tolerate any nonsense. Any of these young hooligans hanging around on a street corner if he told them to go home and they didn't, he'd be out of the car, and he'd give them a good kick up the backside, and a clip under the ear. But I never ever saw Bumper display any excessive violence to anybody.'(*David*)

The local police would patrol the bars. 'Hoodlums? Well you wouldn't put everyone in that class. There were the ones just hanging around, causing trouble. That was the attitude. There wasn't many girls with them. They were always doing something, whether it was belting up some other young kid in the street, or one of the biggest things in those days was the old gas meter. You used to put a 1/– in it for your gas. They used to break the gas meters open and rob them. They never did anything really bad, they just generally made a nuisance of themselves and annoyed people. If kids were selling papers on a street corner, they'd go and throw them all over the place. And you got to know them. I 'spose you'd have to say they were nearly a gang. They all hung around together in a group. But there never seemed to be the territorial problem. They always kept away from one another. You never seemed to have out and out gang warfare. They had their differences, or one bloke would start going out with a girl that belonged to someone from another group. I mean there was always the Paddo gang as such. A lot of it was linked to the Paddo football club, the Bondi gang or the Bondi United football club. When I say gangs, they might have played a particular sport and they all got together, so they'd call them the Paddo Gang.' (*David*)

Max worked for an SP bookmaker. So did *Gino*. 'They'd hire a room for a Saturday afternoon and they'd have four or five phones, and you'd have a clientele and you'd have maybe fifty clients, and you'd just write their bets down, credit bets, most of those. But the more attractive one was in that lane in Barcom Avenue and the back of the houses from Victoria Street, and there

Jim in the backyard

was a lane in between. Now the houses in Victoria Street, there was one or two of 'em there, who had a little shed in the back and that was where the SP operated from. Now you'd go in there, and you'd have your 1/– each way or whatever, and the bloke would scribble it down on a piece of paper, but also the coppers raided it just to keep it honest, every once a month or something. They wanted people to get pinched, and they didn't want their clients to get pinched because that wasn't good for business. So they knew when the coppers were comin', so they'd tell all their clients to buzz off, not to come for another half an hour and then get four or five stoolies like me, and pay 'em two quid plus the bail, to get pinched. You'd get taken up to Darlinghurst police, and they'd take your name and everything, and there'd be a bloke waitin' there to bail you out, and that was all there was to it. So for about two minutes work, you got two quid. In the meantime while you were up there gettin' pinched, the bookie was back takin' his bets, see. On Friday nights you had the trots, and Saturday afternoon you had the races, Saturday night you had the dogs. That lane was a hive of activity. It was like Martin Place. Two-up, there were a few places in what they call Taylor Street, up behind Taylor Square, but you had to have money there, you wouldn't go there unless you had at least ten pounds. No good goin' there with a couple of pounds.'(*Gino*)

John and Pat Thompson, Goodhope Street

And from the copper's point of view? 'The local SP, he wouldn't get locked up himself, he'd arrange for someone else to get his set day, so he didn't get a record. And one day the place was packed, there would've been fifty people in there putting bets on. And it was a narrow little door in this fibro shed, and this bloke I was with, the boss, said, "Whatever you do, don't get near the door". And we were trying to attract the bloke's attention behind the counter. We were outside looking through louvre windows and we were sort of waving to him, and finally he looked up and he yelled, "Coppers!" Well, they came out that door that was only about two and a half foot wide, three at a time, little old ladies with their shopping baskets. I even saw a woman, I estimate was in her sixties, with her shopping basket, she went straight over a six foot fence!' (*David*)

The pubs in the 1950's and 60's were still the main meeting places for men. '*Jim* and I and *Bob* would go down the corner pub, now it wasn't like it is now, it was all standing up, there was no seats, and there was a little room where women could go in. They used to sit down there and shell their peas, they couldn't go in the pub, they could only go in the little room, but we'd go down there and we'd order schooners and *Jim* would have the first one down before we picked ours up, and in half an hour we've had a shout, we've had three and he's had two or three extra and we'd walk up an hour or so later, with one or two beers in our hand and then we'd knock over a couple more bottles for dinner.'(*Gino*) *Ted*, a wharfie, among other things, moved into Paddington in the 1950's. His pub was The Rose and Crown. 'Great little hotel. You'd walk in there on a Friday night and you'd think you was walking into Davey Jones. There'd be suits and shirts and everything hangin' around the walls, some of them fallen off a back of a truck and selling. It was great. Plenty of cheap gear around in them days. My word it was. We'd just sit there and have a mag and that. You'd buy somethin' though. Somethin' would have come from the wharves or something, like that. There was always somethin' there. Always an SP Bookie. He was always sittin' in the bar. Every weekend.'

David started as a constable in the early sixties. 'Paddington basically hasn't changed. All the terrace houses were there, your little lanes, every pub was a busy pub. I can remember in Oxford Street there was the United Services Hotel. You wouldn't go near the place as a young constable, cause some of the worst criminals in the world used to drink there. It's now Kitty O'Sheas, but it used to be called the United Services. Paddington had that many hotels, there weren't many clubs. The pubs were pretty rough. Some of them were good, some weren't. The Lord Dudley's never changed — they drank on the footpath in 1962! We used to go down to the Windsor Castle and the fights we used to have in there to get someone out — we used to have to fight half the bar. You had to fight all his mates unless he was a troublemaker that no one wanted in the place. 'Cause in those days, I'd say 90 per cent of the time, if there was trouble in the hotels, they'd ring the police to come and get them out. And similarly, we used to have to go around doing the pubs at 10 o'clock when they closed. You had to have your wits about you. One of the worst was the old Centennial. The Centennial was a blood bath. It was nothing on a Friday night to lock up thirty people coming out of that hotel. We used to park the truck in the back lane and fill it up. It used to attract a lot of the bikies in those days, and it was a pretty rough pub. And the old Diamond Shoe Nightclub was next door. You know it's still there, and I've never ever been in there. I never got to go in. Probably whoever owned it in those days didn't want ordinary police in there. We were never allowed in.'

There were few middle class residents in the 1950's. John and Pat Thompson's renovations were a curiosity for the locals who speculated that the house was going to be a maternity hospital when they saw a hot water tank being lowered into the roof. Their move into a working class suburb was not readily accepted by their friends. 'People used to ask us, "Weren't you the first people to live in Paddington?" to which I had a stock reply, "Yes indeed, we came in with our black guides and our camels and we hacked away with our machetes."[7]

The changes to come happened quickly. Paddington's period of being a working class suburb was about to end, as bohemians, hippies, and the 'novo rich' (*Bert*) invaded the wilderness to the east.

Chapter Eight
Towards a Bohemian Utopia

In the 1960's, a middle class 'Bohemian' invasion of Paddington began. The arrival of this group coincided with the flight of the European migrants, in pursuit of the great Australian dream of a freestanding house in the suburbs, and at this time the suburb was at its most diverse. Southern European migrants, blue collar workers and a liberal-minded bohemian middle class co-existed. It was a period of class conflict, interaction and resolution, and was fought on various fronts, from Parents and Friends Associations at state schools, to attempts by some to standardise the colour of houses. The middle class had the desire to improve Paddington for the greater good. In an epic case of self deception they were unaware of the extent of the impact they had on long term residents.

Buyers in the 1960's had often travelled overseas. Some had found a base in London, and it was their first experience of inner urban living. It was fresh and exciting and was a total contrast to suburban Australia.

Rob and *Barb* came home from Europe full of ideas. They worked in advertising and also opened a unique antique shop in Woollahra. They bought a home in Paddington 'because the style of living in Paddington, the type of houses, was reminiscent of areas of London we'd enjoyed and had lived in, and areas of London, which at that time, had been fully restored and had become extremely pricey and very valuable. So we could see, here was an opportunity for beautiful housing which could be wonderful. But we were daunted nevertheless, by the condition of them. The house that we found was in Windsor Street, which had all these wonderful little architectural details, like little urns outside, wonderful lace and the whole bit. But it was a terrible wreck. We bought it for the detail, not for the house.'

Off to school — 1960's

Ken and Jenny decided to open a shop. 'We eventually found a little run down grocer's shop. It was festooned with advertising signs, rusty Coca-Cola, Peter's Icecream, Watsonia Hams and Bacon's. I took my daughters to see the shop and I said it was going to be our new home. I said, "We're going to change it into an antique shop", and my daughter burst into tears because she thought she was moving into an icecream shop.' (Ken)

Tom lived in Paddington in the late 1950's when he was working as an architectural draftsman. To pursue his career as an architect, he travelled overseas with his wife and worked in London and Montreal before returning to Sydney. Their experiences overseas helped them see Paddington in a new light. 'I wasn't as aware of it when I first lived in Paddington. What I liked about Paddington was that it was a unified precinct of beautiful buildings that architecturally had great merit if they were cleaned up, and I liked the topography, the things going up and down hills. When I went to Europe I was an absolute child, and got off the boat in Naples with a rucksack and bought a Lambretta and drove off with my wife on the back. I was absolutely stunned by the urban qualities of Italy. I just love the plazas and the big spaces and the urban life. We kept on thinking, "Why don't we have anything like this in Australia?" but it reminded me of Paddington.'

Apart from their appreciation of the Victorian architecture, the situation of Paddington made the suburb attractive to those working in the city. The houses were affordable for the first-time home owner, and they had plenty of room for a family. A cosmopolitan atmosphere had developed through post-war migration. It was an atmosphere suburban escapees could enjoy.

Claire moved to Paddington in 1965 from the north shore. She and her husband were librarians. 'I just liked the idea of Paddington. The houses seemed to have a bit of character. In those days it was just a tiny bit unconventional, which is probably not a good reason for doing anything, but I'm afraid I was always a bit like that. A few people told us that we shouldn't. "Where will you put the vehicle?" As soon as we bought, we realised it was the right thing to do. Because in those days Paddington was very multi-cultural; there were very interesting people living here.'

Multi-culturalism was not developed as a concept by policy makers until 1973. Al Grassby, Minister for Immigration in the Whitlam Government, was inspired to use the term, which had been coined by the Trudeau Government in Canada.[1] Not all of Australia's middle class were as enlightened as *Claire*. But the diversity of cultures in Paddington was embraced by some middle-class residents, especially if it was interesting or exotic. The middle classes migration to the suburb was, in fact, one of the incentives for Europeans to move out to the suburbs, or back to Europe, because prices began to rise.

Henry and *Louise* moved into Glenview Street in the mid 1970's. 'This was a Portuguese neighbourhood, strongly Portuguese, and they were known as the 'Ports' at the time. They would meet in the street because there were so many people living in these houses, every room there was a family, and there was a guy with a piano accordion and he used to sit outside on a chair and they were very friendly, lovely people. In the seventies the Portugese were cashing in and going back to Portugal, they all did it in this whole row, about half a dozen of them. We were in our thirties, they were probably in their forties and we enjoyed their company and got on well with them, but over a period of years they all left.'

Claire became friends with her Southern European neighbours, who lived in a house up the road, with 'Portugal' in stained glass over the door. 'Two of my daughter's best friends when she started going to Glenmore Road School were Greek girls, and they lived just down the street. That was lovely, it probably started me on my great passion for things Greek. I'd go down and have a glass of ouzo. It was really nice. I loved them.'

'Paddington was full of fabulous shops in those days, run by Greeks and Italians. There was a Portuguese deli, and it was because of this fantastic mix, and prices were still reasonable, you didn't have to go far afield, and because they were continentals, they would stay open till six, half past six, to eight o'clock. There was a famous fruit shop and there was a little old man in there, in his eighties and he would still feel up the ladies, this little tiny shrivelled nut, he was funny, he used to love the young ones coming in.'(*Jenny*)

Suburbs like Lanecove, Gordon and Pymble, on the north shore, from which these new middle class residents were fleeing, prided themselves on their exclusivity. The migrating group, dissatisfied with the conservatism of middle class suburbia, sought new experiences. They were prepared to fight for principles ranging from urban heritage to free-love. They were left wing. They were going to change the world. 'We were incredibly middle class really. In the beginning we thought we were rather Bohemian but of course we weren't. We were middle class to our boot straps. Although I suppose we had posters, psychedelic posters, and I had a thing on the refrigerator, 'You are a child of the Universe.' It's embarrassing to think of. We were more Marimekko than Caftans and we had a few hand made rugs that we brought back from our overseas trip in 1974. That sort of thing. It was more design than hippie.' (*Louise*)

Paddington was staunchly old Labor. The new group were left wing idealists, and typical of the groups that Whitlam hoped to motivate with his 'It's Time' campaign in 1972. But although they voted the same way, some working class occupants resented the influx of this new group into their suburb. Their values seemed to be different and it was difficult to distinguish hippies from bohemians. 'I never had a great deal of time for the hippies. They just weren't my type of people. They never seemed to go to work. And they were bludgers. They always relied on somebody to give them a kick along, which I don't reckon's right. You try to look after your family as well as you possibly can and don't employ any ill feelings about anybody else. And that's my philosophy in life. They weren't my type of people because I couldn't do anything for them, and they couldn't do anything for me. And I don't think they did anything for Paddington.'(*Bill*)

Middle class and working class residents pursued their different interests, the older residents passively resisting change sought by a more politically active middle class. The older group thought of Paddington as a convenient suburb close to the city. The new group who were migrating in from leafy green garden suburbs needed their trees. Two older residents, *Jim* and *Jeannie* believed trees were for the bush, not the streets. Many of the plantings died mysteriously.

Suburbia gave *Elizabeth* the creeps. 'You're on view to everybody, but once you slammed the door of your terrace house, people had to guess what was going on.'

Bill, an older resident, felt Paddington had become 'a little bit trendy. You know with the Paddington Society. I heard that they were going to have the right to tell you what colour you could paint your house. To me that's a lot of rubbish, because nobody can tell you what you've got to do. They can ask you to do something but they can't tell you, because they're not paying the rates and they're not paying any taxes for you. And I said to myself, "I'll paint the darn thing black and white if I feel like it. I don't care what they think about it." See they never even considered that people might not agree.'

Richard spent his childhood in Underwood Street. His father was an architect. 'There were some neighbours in Caledonia Street. I'll tell you what their mother was like. I saw her going to the shop, fag hanging out of her mouth, curlers in her hair, a scarf, and she was, like, in her dressing gown. So she was like that and her kids were all pretty tough. And we used to think they stole our bikes one year…or someone stole our bikes. So we used to have a bit of a thing with them.'

The divide between the aspirations of the newcomers and those of the longtime residents varied to such an extent, that sometimes the perceived differences were impossible to overcome. *Barb* was a designer. 'We tried to get along with them, we tried to be chatty and friendly, and they were always very aloof, because they felt we were…it was always like a class thing. Like you're a different class. They were not exactly very friendly.' For *Louise* it was different. 'Next door to us there was a funny old couple, and across the road was a funny old couple, and it was a mixture of the young people renting and the old denizens of Paddington. We all got on like a house on fire. Because the Four in Hand used to be their local pub, the guys, *Henry* included, used to go up with the old locals in their pyjamas for a final game of darts after dinner before bed.'

Paddington pubs were still the focus of working-class recreation, where some new arrivals felt like an isolated group. However other changes were occurring. Working hours were decreasing, six o'clock closing ended in 1961, and pubs were able to stay open until 10 or even midnight. The sly grog shop disappeared, and women were no longer excluded from public bars. Alcohol was easily available and the home became a prime site for entertaining. Eighteen year olds could buy alcohol and be on licensed premises when age restrictions were reduced from twenty one. *John* came up from Melbourne University to be an artist. 'I used to drink at the Windsor Castle. Not at all the glamorous pub that it is now. It was a pub that was essentially a working man's pub with a very small bar on Elizabeth Street, a little cubby hole about fifteen feet square and that was where the arty crowd would drink. Not many people would venture into the public bar, because that was where you'd get a fair bit of chiacking from the workers. They thought we were long haired pooftahs, you know. We were sort of strange people. I don't remember any fights. There was never any sort of outward aggression in that way.'

There were fights in other Paddington Bars. 'Even to this day, Paddington pubs still attract a criminal element. A lot of them are shoplifters, and some of the old safe breakers. A lot of the real good crims in Sydney always went to the eastern suburbs pubs. The Sheaf at Double Bay, The United Services was always well known for them. The Rose and Crown was one, I remember one big crim, he used to drink at the Nelson. If you ever wanted to find him, that was his pub. He drank there with his mates, he was known, and anybody that didn't like him didn't go in that pub. A lot of the other pubs were the same. We [policemen] always drank in the saloon bar of the Light Brigade Hotel when we finished work. There was none of the trendy pubs or all these gay pubs. They were pretty rough pubs in those days. You had to know your way around, and if you went in, you didn't tread on anyone's toes. Ninety per cent of them were full of locals. You didn't get many people coming in from outside like you do today. Paddington pubs have changed so much.' (*David*)

Although the middle classes shared some of these leisure venues with their forebears, they also had their own. Restaurants were almost an exclusive province of the middle-class, as were art galleries. Enzo bought a wine bar just opposite the Paddington Town Hall. He transformed this bar from a working class bar to one that catered for the new middle class. 'The old people used to go there and drink sherry and I thought, "Oh no, I have to change that if I have the opportunity". So I went there and I spoke to the boss who was there and I said, "Did you ever think to sell that place or rent it." It was very dark, filthy. It was for poor people on the pension. A little glass of sherry for 10 cents. He said, "If I'm going, I want to sell everything, lock stock and barrel", and I said I'd be interested. "Give me one week and I'll be back." So after one week I said, "You give me the figures and I'll tell you what I have." So he said, "The building only I want 16,000 dollars." I said, "OK". And here I was, I owned the building. Before I opened the wine bar I had so many Australian friends, and they were very helpful to me. "Why don't we do it with the Italian flags and columns all the way through into the back yard and put grape vines there just like Roman style?" So I was working very hard, painting, putting all those flags, and the bar.'

Enzo's Wine Bar attracted a diverse crowd. He still served the older residents in the afternoon, but the cosmopolitan environment of his wine bar attracted members of Sydney's gay and theatrical community. 'The first business we had there, there were some people from 'Les Girls'. Carlotta was number one and she was one of the best, so I said, "I don't like to allow transvestites in the bar but you are the only one because you look so feminine." She was the only one, but they bring their friends. It was a very social place, you know, about 4 o'clock, people finish work, they drop in before they go home, for a glass of wine or Campari or Cinzano. There were couples too, and old people come with mistress there, because they didn't want to be seen in other places. They were safe there to have an affair. It was an extremely exciting place to go. It was very cosmopolitan. We changed everything, even for gay people to have somewhere to meet, clean…Then the Vietnam war, and all those boys, a shipful used to come. It was like after the war, liberation, they come by ship, they were happy and had a good time, they spent so much money, they were loaded. I

Wine bottling

Fancy dress party

felt sorry for some young people really, because they have to go back and fight, which was awful. They were so happy, no fights, not in my place.'

However, most entertaining was done at home. Parties varied in size from those that took over a street, to the intimate dinner party. 'I can remember we used to cook things like, well we haven't had gazpatcho for a long time We would have six or eight guests or something like that. But that was really one of our main forms of entertainment, because we could bring the children and put them to sleep. I remember we had a wonderful wine bottling party in the garden next door, and people organised wine from probably Tyrells or something, and we spent the whole day doing that.' (*Claire*)

'Every one had parties, party after party. We all owned those Chinese dinner plates and if you went out to dinner, they'd say, "Bring plates." Well, we'd take ten plates and as you left you'd take ten plates. They wouldn't be yours but we all had our Chinese plates. We all had cooking pots, we pooled things and very casual, but wonderful meals. We were all good cooks. We all loved each other's cooking.' (*Elizabeth*) But dinner parties could be a chore for the wife of the household. The 1960's were not a time when domestic duties were shared. *Pat* was never really happy with the scene, because she found it very hard to flip from being a responsible mother getting the school uniforms ready, to going to a party where everyone was smoking dope and trying to get off with each other. 'I started to get quite moralistic about it, but I did get sucked into it, especially when my husband started dating people. I got very hurt, so there was a contradiction there. I always liked things to happen in a more informal, spontaneous way, while he would set up dinner parties, and he was very keen on dinner parties, and often they'd be visitors from overseas. I remember a Japanese professor coming, and a Russian professor, and he liked to ask people like that, and his Ph.D students and various colleagues. It would always be a three course meal, an entrée and a meat dish, and lots of vegies and a sweet. Something elaborate, I'd follow cookbooks. I tell you it really got me down in the end, because you'd have to feed your children, get them bathed and ready for bed, and then you'd have to turn around and get yourself washed and smartened up, and then turn on a three course meal, do all the serving, be entertaining, and then about midnight or so, turn round and wash all the dishes.'

The sixties and seventies were times of sexual and social experimentation. Paddington was supposedly a centre of middle class scandal and vice. The extent of these activities is open to debate. Much of the suburb's reputation was a media beat up, or a result of the envy of the more Puritan suburbs. The opening of the television show Number 96, was promoted as The Night Australia Loses its Virginity. It was the premiere of a soap opera about the lives of the inhabitants of a block of flats in the Sydney suburb of Paddington, but the block in the opening credits was actually in Moncur Street, Woollahra. Two million viewers tuned in five nights a week to Channel 10 to see the first bared breasts, the first gay hero, the first gay kiss on a prime time television program."[2]

Robert Burns, in his article, 'Pushing Paddington,' *Nation*, December 1967, wrote, 'Feature writers for glossies discourse of those infinitely tiny backgardens planted with bamboo clumps and Japanese rock pools, or of the 'with it' young, who shuttle continuously from automat laundry to the footpath outside the Windsor Castle Hotel, dressed in striped pants and black navvy's singlets regardless of sex. These writers cater for a public, who would no more think of abandoning the level lawns, patios and feature windows of better suburbia for Paddo, than would Mrs. Norm (Edna) Everage herself. Yet those who live thus, within hearing of the Sunday morning Victas, still need to feel there is a place, distant, but not too distant, over the Bridge, rather than over the rainbow, where permissiveness is the only rule, sex is the only routine, social manners are as exotic as the bonzai-ed backgardens, and It Is On in ways not to be exactly specified, all night and right through the working week.'

The mythology of decadent Paddington made it to the mainstream press. 'Somebody's friend who was a journalist for the Woman's Day said, "Can I come and interview you about husband swapping?" And I said, "Oh sure, yes." And they did this interview for Woman's Day and at the time I was minding a child from up the road, and I had my two, and my theory was that we were too busy swapping children to be swapping husbands. But it was just so typical of what the press were trying to make out of Paddington, as some sort of slightly salacious place.' (*Claire.*)

A feeling of liberation spread through the community. *Lois* 'used to do things like go around with no shoes on. There was a real demonstration of freedom. I used to walk around with no bra, especially with no shoes. That was my favourite thing, to go across Oxford Street, I am the minister's wife and I am wearing no shoes, and you've no idea the pleasure that gave me.'

However there were some truth to the rumour. *John*, a bachelor at the time, remembered. 'Paddington parties were very simple. They weren't complicated or elaborate. People would tend to bring a few bottles of beer and there would be records and people would stand around and talk and dance. I don't think they were as noisy, because people didn't have big expensive stereos. They would often be very crowded because we all lived in quite small houses. There used to be a lot of cooking. We'd go quite early, at 7 or 8 and people would bring food and we'd cook. We learnt to do a lot of interesting things with chicken livers, because they were amazingly cheap and we used to make these huge dishes of sort of spicy chicken livers and rice and bread There was a lot of sex, an awful lot of sex. It was very free and easy. It was amazing. I think now how many people I went to bed with in a matter of two or three years. It just staggers me now. There were no holds barred. Very few drugs, a bit of dope, that was about all. I mean, some people were using marihuana, but not very many, and I really don't believe that it was in wide use. I think there was a bit of cocaine, but it was mostly dope, and lots and lots of drinking.'

The gay community created new business in the suburb. 'Up on the corner of Oxford and Underwood Streets was the Bar Apollo, which was a funny old place. You went in off the street, but it was very blank, there was absolutely nothing advertised, and inside, it was all furnished with flock wallpaper and fake oil paintings, and chandeliers, so it was a very old-fashioned place, with someone playing the piano, and there was the lovely Elena who was the maitre d'it. She used to walk around in caftans and serve the boys hors d'oeuvres. There was a large gay community and that was to increase in my time there.'(*Tony*)

'There were a lot of young people living in Paddington, a lot of share houses, a lot of parties, and they used their gardens and balconies. 'There was always something happening. So I think it was more bohemian, and I think it was more, in some ways to me it was more gay than it is today, because it was the first place, it was where a lot of gay people lived. It had started to get that reputation of being a bit more promiscuous that way, and then of course there was Enzo's wine bar at the top of Oxford Street.' (*Norman*)

Jane was the daughter of an academic. She observed her parents' parties as a child, and a teenager. 'I remember two parties in particular, two very big ones with about two hundred people at them, at my parents' friends. I would have been primary school age. I remember two men and I think they were quite well-known people having a big sort of explosive argument, that was the way at parties in those days. They drank too much, but the argument wouldn't be, "You slept with my wife" or something, it would be about some intellectual thing, disagreement about some philosophical matter or what ever.'

Henry and *Louise* were inveterate party givers and goers. 'It was a noisy neighbourhood. Only because of us. I suspect it had probably been a quiet neighbourhood. You'd decide to have a party, and you'd ring a few people up, and they'd ring a few more people up. We used to have great big casks of Fiorelli's wine, sometimes there was food, sometimes I'd make an effort and buy a whole ham and breads. We all spread out onto the street of course, and all the locals were invited and anyone who happened to be passing, would drop in and have a drink too.'

Elizabeth's son, *Adrian*, had a studio in the backgarden, and used to put on very loud music. Someone rang up, and complained that they couldn't study for their HSC. 'He said, "If they're leaving it till the last week its not worth studying", and in fact he should be given a grant from the Woollahra Council for putting this wonderful music into the streets and homes of Paddington, and in no way did he think he should desist.'

The noise did affect the lifestyle of the original residents. 'Well, some people moved out, like one neighbour, because she said she just couldn't stand the noise across the street. They were just having parties all the time. And there'd be about four or five, and they'd come in late at night and they'd be bang, bang, banging. We were never loud like that. Actually we were taught to consider our neighbours. I don't think people today regard their neighbours. And they drink a lot too. They start at about 9 o'clock and it gets to about 12 o'clock and they turn the stereo on, and they've had drink and they get rowdy and all try to talk over one another.' (*O'Shaunessey sisters*)

Jannie Southern described the parties in the Paddington Journal, December 1968.

'Parties, yearly duty, find a date, who to ask, what it costs, wine or spirits, choice of menus, hot or cold, where to have it, kitchen help, preparation, busy time, can't trust anyone, irritation, engaged telephones, no parking, hard floors, trestle table, paper cloths, curried egg, squares of cheese, best dresses, white shirt sleeves, giggle and squeak, same old faces, red or white, roar of talk, background music, fixed smiles, mindless laughter, prepaid hospitality, clever chat, secret boredom. Gossip exchange, fork food, unmanageable salads, no chairs, spotted clothes, ungauged strangers, name forgetting, cigarette butts, paper napkins, open windows, traffic noise, sticky heat, sausage rolls, oyster patties, wilted parsley, crumby platters.

Intoxication, indiscretion, ersatz fun, good sports, silly goats, late leavers, funless bores, tight shoes, wilting make up, sweating faces, scruffy floors. Which to go to, which to leave, baby sitters, fractious children, drunken driving, Christmas road toll, upset stomachs, mornings after.'

Artists had moved into the area. Paddington was a cheap place to live at the beginning of the 1960s. 'People like Margaret Olley and Donald Friend, who lived just opposite Trumper Park in a sweet little house down there. Geoff Smart lived briefly at that time in Paddington and Colin Lancely and Peter Kingston. Most of them couldn't afford to have a studio, they painted in a room set aside. They would paint in the living room or in a back bedroom, but there were very few, I mean Colin Lancely was one of the few, and I think he did have a studio. His works even then were large and complicated composite pieces, using timber fragments and he had extraordinary, three dimensional sort of constructions.'(*John*) By the end of the 1960's, many of the artists had been pushed out by increased rents. Art galleries were opening, pioneered by Rudy Komon, who migrated from Prague in 1950. He found an old wine bar on the corner of Paddington Street and Jersey Road and opened his gallery in November 1959. Exhibitions varied from Tom Roberts to John Molvig,[3] and in 1965 the building was redesigned by Neville Gruzman. Barry Stern opened another in Glenmore Road.

Jackie Barbe was a French chef, who emigrated to Australia in the 1960's. He bought the Hungry Horse Restaurant, below the Gallery of the same name, from Madeleine Thurston. 'It was the opening of the galleries that brought the people, and the two things, food and art combined together, I think, that made the artistic scene in Paddington. We made it very Parisian. We had the awning coming down and white tablecloths. I got a French flag outside. After a while, we really swung to the French menu and we had snails, we had onion soup. Then I served lambs brains, tripe, sweetbread. We started to have soufflés as entrée, and we were the only restaurant in Sydney to do that, and soufflé as a dessert, hot soufflé, which was quite a revolution in Sydney. Ruth, my partner, was like an icon, with her bike and her plait, going shopping. A guy bought me half a bucket of black mussels one day, and after three or four weeks it was three or four buckets a night and people were raving about them.'

The Hungry Horse Gallery and Restaurant was one of Paddington's great successes in the 1960's. Betty O'Neill, who was managing a small gallery called Chattertons near David Jones, was approached by 'Robert Haines who was the director of the Queensland Art Gallery, and he said to me that there was a Major Rubin up in Queensland, who was a philanthropist, plenty of money, great collection and he was interested in opening up a gallery in Paddington, and would I be interested? I was. Major Rubin was a difficult man to work for. The gallery was launched with an exhibition of his impressive collection of Impressionist paintings. He commanded that the paintings weren't to be hung, and people lined up to look through the paintings, which were stacked against the walls.'

Later, Betty established a stable of artists. She produced a calendar with the images of these twelve artists and a photo of them on the balcony of the restaurant. One artist was shown each month. The first show was the work of Bob Hughes. 'Slowly then, the atmosphere of the building itself, the artists, Paddington, there was a tremendous sort of spirit of, a feeling we were creating something. We were proud to be people who were getting on with their lives, and we were a part of something that was growing. And there was an appreciation of Paddington itself. People would come, they would come to the gallery, they would have lunch in the restaurant, they would stroll around and look at the buildings, and go over to the Windsor Castle and have drinks. First of all I painted the gallery, then I bought in some matting. And there was an old shed at the back of the gallery, and this friend of mine opened up a framing shop up there. And we used to have a string from his shed to the back of the kitchen window and we used to send messages back and forth. I used to hand-write every envelope and every invitation, and they were very personal. And we'd have a preview the night before an exhibition, and also there would be time for the critics to come. There was Wallace Dawson and James Gleeson, really good critics and nice people, and it was terribly important to have them on side. Woo them. Because you always wanted the Galleries to buy, you know, the National Gallery, it was very important to be represented. There would be lots of white wine and red wine. The crowds going up and down the stairway. You couldn't move through the rooms. There was a tremendous noise, nobody looking at the paintings! But it didn't matter, they always came back. And these

Betty O'Neill with her stable of artists from right to left Bill Rose, John Olsen, Robert Klippel, John Coburn Stan Rapotec, Colin Lanceley, Betty, Emmanuel Raft, Robert Hughes, Leonard Hessing, Charles Riddington, Carl Plate.

would last about two or three hours, they were exhausting as far as I was concerned. And hanging paintings, every month they would change, and the walls got thicker and thicker because we never used wire, we only nailed into the walls. We were all making something of our lives. We were pushing ourselves beyond what we really came from. And I think that's very important. There's too much education today in a way. And it's too easy.'

Kym Bonython took over the Hungry Horse Gallery from Betty O'Neill, and later converted a factory site in Victoria Street into the largest private art gallery in the Southern Hemisphere. Betty O'Neill managed Bonython Gallery, which achieved fame for its beauty and scale. It was a very fashionable place. Kym described the opening in his book, Ladies, Legs and Lemonade. 'It was a most spectacular launching, although, like every launching, it caused a few waves. Victoria Street, like many Paddington streets in those days, was dirty as well as narrow, and its residents were not as sophisticated as they might be. They resented their street being crammed with Rolls Royces, Jaguars, and Bentleys, and the sudden influx of the 'upper crust' into their then humble suburb. Some of them discharged a barrage of raw eggs over adjoining roofs into the courtyard, and I had to settle a few claims for new shoes and dry-cleaning during the following days.'[4] Betty remembers, 'We only had one toilet. Well we had one for the men and one for the women, and it was really bad news. And people were knocking on the doors of the houses in the street and asking if they could use their toilet. It was just the most extravaganza, civilised opening. You could have been in New York, you could have been in London. And the paintings…it was a mixed show of the best.'

John remembered Brett Whiteley's exhibitions at the gallery. 'They were always brilliant. Brett was the golden boy in every sense, in appearance and in every other way. I mean he and Wendy were the two most amazingly beautiful people and his exhibitions were ravishing.'

Fashion boutiques were opening too, and Paddington was a popular location for fashion shoots. 'Honey Wilson had a shop opposite the London Tavern, and everyone was wearing Honey Wilson clothes and caftans, practically nothing on your body but these big floaty caftans and brightly coloured sandals. There was a great feeling of effervescence and Honey made a lot of batiks.'(*Elizabeth*)

These were times of excess and conspicuous consumption. One shop that was the epitome of the excesses was the Dandy Dog, opened by Cecil Sykes. 'I had a wonderful bath with His and Hers and it was an old fashioned bath and all the places for the girls to groom out the back, and then the front part was a little boutique. We had pyjamas, boots, umbrellas and coats for the dogs and when we opened in Double Bay, Cornelius made me a poodle mink coat and a fake diamond collar and we put it in a glass container on the fake grass that I had on the floor. Eventually it sold. Some dogs would get red nail varnish on and they had to have their bows. The colour of the bow must match the nail varnish. We had one dog, learnt to come to the Dandy Dog by itself, it would push the door open, the girls would wash him, groom him and I'd open the door and away he'd go and the owner would pay me, once a month. He lived in Paddington.'

Bill Blinco with his wife, Maggie opened Maggie Blinco's Showcase in Underwood Street. It was an antique and bric-a-brac shop. 'The opening day was absolutely fantastic. Fantastic. We had set it up beautifully and we'd painted it bright yellow, and it looked super. And it was filled with things to bedeck and bedazzle and shawls, and beautiful showcases and lovely glass and dolls and painting. It was Aladdin's Cave brought to life. We'd sent out a lot of invitations and I think they invited their friends, so the street, well it looked like the storming of the Bastille. Without any exaggeration, there must have been at least three hundred people outside. So when I peeped out through the brown paper and saw all these people gathered for the 10 o'clock opening, I became very frightened and very worried because I thought when we opened the doors we were going to be killed in the rush. They surged through the place and they

Enzo's Wine Bar,
Oxford Street

Backgarden
Underwood
Street

Children's birthday party

Young mothers in Duxford Street

Guriganya

Successful bidders

kept surging until they filled the front, the back, the upstairs, every inch of it, and the street was still full of people. And no one could move and no one could do anything, and no one could get a drink, no one could buy anything, which was even more important. So it was a case of overkill. We'd overdone it, but the day went on, and somehow it was a most exciting day.'(Bill)

In the 1960's, the Presbyterian Church amalgamated with the Methodist Church to become the Village Church. It was after this union that the idea for the Paddington Market developed. The concept was to have a trading table with goods to sell, from a group called Trading Partners, that were made by people in the Pacific Islands and Indonesia, and especially Asia. It began on a Saturday morning in front of the church, and developed into the Paddington Bazaar. It was only one of the functions that took place at the venue. There was a community clinic conducted by Mr. Neville Yeomans of St. Vincents Hospital, in the vestry behind the church. Massage, naturopathy, and acupuncture were later added to create the Village Healing Centre. The church hall was converted into the Village Theatre by Barry Donnelly. 'La Turista' by Sam Shepherd was performed in June, 1971. Two chickens were killed on stage each night, the RSPCA objected, and there were no more chickens killed on stage.[5]

Despite the objections of the Festival of Light, a gay congregation, the Metropolitan Community Church, held services in the church on Sunday nights, and a faction of the Greek Orthodox Church was there for eight years from 7 to 10 am on Sunday mornings.[6] The original aim of the Bazaar was to support the local community. Goods sold were not allowed to be in competition with local shops, and the emphasis was firmly in favour of hand made goods, produced in cottage industries, by the stall holders themselves.

Guriganya was a progressive school, which opened in Paddington in 1972, and like many others of its kind at the time, placed an absolute premium on freedom and self-expression. *Christine* was one of the founders. 'There were enough birds of a feather who felt they wanted to be part of their children's schooling, and as none of us were working, we were totally involved and devoted to our children, and enjoying it. We decided to start an after school centre at the Paddington School. It was a pilot project, and it seemed stupid for the school to close at three o'clock as there were a lot of latch key children. We had a big room, which we set up with craft activities, and we allowed children to take their shoes and shirts off, which freaked the Principal. We even brought in the cast of 'Hair' to give a concert. We were axed after one term. Then we set it up in the Village Church Hall and student teachers came to help. Some of the children were a bit unruly and I think we tested the patience of the minister.' Russell Davies recalled the scene in the church hall as one of 'absolutely delightful mayhem.' However it was not long before the noise of the young inhabitants began to disturb Mr. Neville Yeomans, and his mental health patients, to the point where Russell Davies had to take action. 'There they were in glorious Technicolour. I went in and it was clear that a heavy handed approach was not going to work with these hippies. So I said, "Hey man, we want peace and love and you are going to have to be quieter and more considerate of these people." They looked at me as if I was an alien. Then one of the long-haired hippie teachers stood up and said, "What the Rev. is trying to tell you is that if you don't stop fighting, this bloody great gargoyle is going to fly over the church and come down and piss all over you."[7]

Christine then invited the children to come to her big conjoined back gardens, which had been created when her husband bought three terrace houses. 'We had semi-open sheds, and the kids could climb trees and paint on the walls. One of my sons made his first coil pot and he was transfixed. It was an inspiring time, messy, chaotic, but great. It was part of the whole magical energy that flowed right through the Western world in the 60's and 70's. The flow of creative, innovative people aware of the absurdities of the bureaucracy.

Then we found a building and a large paddock between Oxford Street and Underwood Street, which had been a laundry, and set up the school, Guriganya. There were 90 children on the first day, with four teachers. We had Pre-school, Kindergarten, Primary and a few Secondary children, which was very ambitious, and everyone was inspired. However, the architects had neglected to inform the Council that we were starting a school, so until we conformed to the regulations, we had to move. The Kinder came to our place, and the rest went to a hall in Randwick. We finally got permission to come back to Paddington and the school ran for five years. There were some very good times. At the end of the first year we had this wonderful Indian Festival. Finally some parents decided it would be better for them to start their own school, so there was a split, the numbers went down, and we were burnt out. But there were some amazingly interesting times and real contact with the community. Looking back I think a school like that would be better in a rural community.' (*Christine*)

The Uniting Church in Paddington was going through a revolution and old barriers were broken down. 'One Christmas we all had a service in the front of the church and then we went inside and there was rum and Christmas cake and cocoa and two or three of the girls got all sorts of Christmas cake bits and they took 'em over to the pub over the road. It had not reimaged itself at all in those days, and they were passing round this Christmas cake, and one of the blokes said, "Where are you from?" and she said, "We're from the church over there", and he took another pull on his beer and he turned to his mate and he said, "The church has sure changed." We maintained all the old people and we didn't lose a single person through hurt feelings. That group hung on very loyally.' (*Tim*)

The cultural diversity of the suburb was useful when it came to forming soccer teams. 'The school sent a note that said, 'Bring your boys and we will train them for soccer'. We arrived there and there were all these little boys and no one to train them. So *Graham* and another man called John took it on. He

1c Paddington Primary School 1928, *James* second from left in the second back row

3d Paddington Primary School 1968, *Richard* fourth from right back row

had three little boys, so we formed these two teams which were the Eastern Eagles and the Queens Park Magpies, always bitter enemies, and there were little brothers coming up, and the next year it went to three teams, and then to sixteen teams. All ages and then we had two older age teams. It was the largest soccer club in the eastern suburbs. And we had every nationality in, everyone. We organised a trip up to Brisbane… First they came down from Brisbane, maybe ten teams and we played for this trophy which we won, and we billetted, and then we went up there and everyone wanted to come, and we hired two carriages to go up. It was the largest movement of junior sport ever in Australia. About twenty parents came with two hundred boys, two teams of under 6's, under 7's, and under 8's, under 9's. Most of them were from Paddington, and a Maltese club gave us some help.' (*Graham* and *Lorna*)

Local schools were now dominated by children from middle class families, although some continued at Guriganya. After school, traffic was a problem. Kids could no longer play in the street and they had to adapt to the local environment and use the spaces available to them. The children, whose parents had set up Guriganya, played games sometimes reminiscent of the children of earlier times. 'We used to play this game which we made up, where you weren't allowed to tread on the ground, because it was dangerous to tread on the ground. So you had to have pieces of wood and put them down, and then get the one from behind you and put it in front of you. That was fun. We used to climb the trees a lot and make cubbies a lot'. (*Richard*). They mixed with the children of artists and intellectuals who provided stimulating activities for this group of children. They made ceramics, built cubby houses and billy-carts, played sport, watched television and ate gelato once a week. They participated in parties and were expected to be clever and amusing, to be able to mix with adults on adult terms. They too, lived through The Age of Aquarius, were influenced by the social revolution of their parents, and were expected to adopt their liberal philosophy. They sometimes saw their parents behaving badly. 'I remember them round at our house one time, the adults sometimes would be a group having lunch together, and Mr. Whippy came along, and they asked us to go out — this makes my parents sound more irresponsible than they actually were — we were asked to go out and ask for a fix, because I think there had been this rumour going round that Mr. Whippy dispensed drugs, and we, the innocent children, went out, not for an ice cream but a fix, and the Mr. Whippy man told us to get lost, but they were just having a drunken joke.' (*Jane*)

For local teenagers, Paddington could be exciting or very traumatic. Drugs were a major legacy of the liberal sixties and seventies. A certain level of experimentation was condoned as a rite of passage.

'Parties, you'd get invited sometimes, written sometimes or a phone call and they would be at someone's house, with varying amounts of supervision from

Not the Brady Bunch

the parents, there would always be loud music playing. You would wear long dresses and there would be alcohol and cigarettes from when I was about fifteen, not in huge quantities, and dope was being smoked. Marijhuana was just terrible. You'd go into a room. You'd have red lights on. This was not necessarily a party, this was just hanging out at someone's house, maybe playing very loud music so it was impossible to talk, the lights would be very dim and they'd shut all the windows and doors, light incense, and smoke. And it was just the most, I mean everyone would just sit there, and say not a word, it was boring, just as boring as anything, and all these boys thought it was just the coolest thing on earth to do as well, and they'd talk endlessly about it. There came this sharp divide. You were cool or you were not.' (*Jane*)

Most of these activities went on without the parents knowledge. 'I'm not sure how much they got up to. You see when they got into their teen years, I was a bit of a dead loss myself because my marriage was breaking up and I took it very hard, and the kids ran a bit wild in those days. They were a bit scruffy looking.' (*Pat*)

An essay titled, 'A Teenager in Paddington', by Christabel Blackman was published in The Terrace Times, December 1972. It gives a different view of teenage life in Paddington. 'If it's raining we sit at home alone — or with a friend or two (or ten), listening to records, chatting to one another (or yelling). Teenagers don't look at television much...Because in Paddington we all live so close to each other, there is always a lot happening...There are so many different galleries, we could spend all Saturday just wandering from show to show... The average teenager goes to a party at least once a fortnight...We do have to spend a bit of time at home...sometimes we get round to baking a cake (which by chance might turn out edible), or making up our own plays or holding mock auctions and fetes of things we have made. Last year some of us made a film...We do a lot of walking in Paddington. To look for each other, to walk the dog, or maybe just to poke our inquisitive noses round corners because Paddington is a curious place. It's different to other places.'

Chapter Nine
Conservation and Conservatism

As middle class residents of Paddington explored new lifestyles and spiritual beliefs, they were also to form the first suburban led heritage movement in Australia. It was a movement that would not have been initiated by the working class residents of Paddington. The buildings that they lived in were so familiar to them, that they did not see their architectural uniqueness. They did not have the money or resources to influence public and government opinion. But the middle class group that founded the Paddington Society, was sure of its convictions and confident of its power. They had moved in from the garden suburbs of Sydney, and to them, terrace housing was unfamiliar, exciting, and beautiful. It was symbolic of their new found values, which were often opposed to the values of their parents. They renovated and gentrified the terraces, and without them far less of Paddington would have been preserved. However there was a price for the successes of the urban conservation movement, because the gains in the prestige of the suburb, caused the loss of the suburbs' working class identity, and also of most of its cultural diversity. These were features of Paddington that left wing, middle class residents enjoyed most in the seventies, but one that their invasion would eliminate. 'We were all very keen on being egalitarian. When I look back on it now it was terribly presumptuous of us. We didn't think we were gentrifying it at all. We thought we were back with the real people.' (*Louise*).

Those moving into Paddington were often faced with properties that were severely run down. Paddington was a renovator's dream!

'I would say that all of Windsor Street at that time was unrestored, like most of Paddington. It was pretty well as it had been since the 1930's, and earlier. And this house was that sort of tea colour, which was very popular. The veranda had been filled in, and the windows were all sliding out, and falling onto the ground. A woman was living in it, *Mrs Mc Carthy*, dear old soul. But she was living in a couple of back rooms, because it was just falling apart. Luckily all the cast iron was OK, it was all there, but the rest of it was desperate. As you walked in the door, the entrance hall was wonderful, a lovely big entrance hall with big archways. But the smell was terrible. It had rats living in it. It had everything. And you walked into the two main living rooms. There were big holes in the floor, everything was rotten. The reason was, the house suffered from damp in three directions. It had damp coming downwards from a broken roof. It had one exposed wall, so damp was penetrating the exposed side wall, and there was rising damp like you wouldn't believe, about five feet up from the floorboards. And the smell of rot and damp and everything was terrible. But the courage we had, we just couldn't wait to get into it. It had a lovely staircase, a cedar staircase going to the top. Wonderful panelling. It was 21 feet wide. And you walked out into the back kitchen area and little breakfast room, and again that was terrible. There was water and damp everywhere. One of the reasons was that the land the house was built on, sloped towards the house, and drains were non existent. So that when it rained, all the water lapped up underneath the house and into the walls. Upstairs wasn't quite as bad, the floors were OK, but you couldn't open a window. It was all rotten. There were four bedrooms, but we ended up with three, because we made one into a bathroom. We had to replace the roof, the rafters under the roof, the window frames, floors downstairs. And instead of putting wood back downstairs, we built piers down to the ground, and put a concrete slab all the way though. We then put terrazzo tiles down. So the whole floor looked like white polished marble. And we put under floor heating below that. So in the winter, we had a thermostat, so the heater automatically switched on and heated the whole house. But they were later days in the restoration. The early days were horrendous.

The front of the house was painted all white, which was very popular in those days. We bought all these wonderful black and white tiles and we put them on the veranda when you first walked in. The walls were painted a wonderful sort of dark green, a cool blueish green, and the ceiling was white. And we had all the antiques and things we'd found, and nice furniture from London that we'd bought over there. All the wood looked wonderful against the green. We had a chandelier that we'd bought in a small village outside Paris, which looked great. And I made these indoor shutters that I'd covered with fabric to go across the front windows, because I wasn't mad about curtains. We found a mass of Victorian tiles, each one was different. So we covered the whole corridor to the kitchen in these Victorian tiles. I think they're still there. And that looked spectacular at the time.' (*Rob* and *Barb*)

By the end of the sixties there had been a steep rise in Paddington prices. Robert Burns, writing in Nation 1967, wrote, 'Paddington houses are hard to shift because vendors insist upon asking boom prices for them… One reason why there are few urban adventurers is that for people with our tradition of layering new suburbs about the central area as each generation marries, it is such a hell of a Big Step To Take, to sink your mortgage money in mouldering inner urban glories. Another reason is that to obtain the bank loan, which will permit you to purchase this sort of present ruin and future glory, you need to offer the sort of extra, rock-solid, institutional guarantee which only members of elite groups, University staff members, for example, have access to. And members of University staffs are by and large a pretty suburban bunch. Add to this, that in asking boom prices and hoping to hook these big fish, Paddington vendors have tended to freeze off, increasingly, those natural buyers of near city terraces, our migrants from the Mediterranean countries, for whom a lira is a lira. Most of the home buyers moving in, equipped with bank capital, are intent in buying into the ideal rather than the actual. They are impatient to get on with the renovations and are apt to look at the house's potential rather than at its standing features."[1]

By the time of the 1976 census[2], Paddington had one of the highest concentrations of graduates in Sydney. Incomes were above average, with people earning more than $15,000. Paddington residents were paying above average mortgages.

Some individuals had organised local campaigns against proposed developments. John Thompson had fought a local mechanic in Goodhope Street, (a direct descendent of Robert Cooper of Juniper Hall), when he proposed an enlargement of his garage into a service station. *Margie* fought against the building of a football stadium and clubhouse in Trumper Park. Residents were concerned about the development of new flats. On the horizon they could see the massive tower blocks being built on Darling Point, and it was not a fate that most local residents wanted for their suburb. The rezoning of Paddington, after it had been placed under the control of the Sydney City Council, allowed for it to become a much more densely populated suburb. 'In 1948, a County Council planning report described the area as almost totally substandard, and requiring substantial clearance. Plans were afoot to replace the rows of terrace houses with stark high rise blocks of home units, and convert the romantic winding streets to barren highways.'[3]

Marea Gazzard met John Thompson in a Paddington supermarket. Marea had lived in Goodhope Street before she had travelled overseas with her husband Don. 'The old rooming house they had lived in had been demolished and replaced by a very ugly block of red brick flats which quite spoiled the appearance of Goodhope Street, otherwise rather handsome. So now, John and Marea, in friendly conversation, agreed that 'people like us' should get together and arrest the sinister trend to tear down nice old terrace houses and raise up horrible flats. "I'll send my husband Don to see you. He's an architect and

Victoria, Peter, Pat and Jack Thompson pour a libation to John Thompson at his memorial fountain

interested in town planning."[4] They set up a public meeting in the Town Hall, and Don was in the chair. 'From all accounts I made a hilarious job of it. "We're going to set up this Society and we're going to get the area properly looked after and so on", but the Labor party, the old Paddington Labor party turned up in force, and they all tried to take it over. Most of the newcomers were leftist like me, but they weren't card carrying members of the Labor party, and we thought it was obviously sensible that this not be allied with any one political party, if we were going to try and get politicians to do things for us. Anyhow, we elected a committee and I think there was someone from the Labor party on that committee, but he resigned two days later. The Labor party pretty quickly saw that they weren't going to get anywhere, and of course then they bitterly opposed everything the Paddington Society did for years. It was stupid really. It was all pretty trogladite, the Labor party in those days.' (Don)

The Paddington Society was a pioneering organization, travelling a path in Australia where no one had gone before. They adapted the Charter of the Chelsea Society, before they had really formed a philosophical base for a heritage movement, and a number of questions had to be addressed. Did restoration diminish diversity? How did architecture reflect and create culture? What was important to preserve in Paddington? Who were they preserving Paddington for? There was little time to consider these questions. There was a battle to be won.

Late in 1967 the State Planning Authority announced its plan for running expressways through Paddington, which would necessitate the demolition of 400 houses and create new barriers between different parts of the suburb. The whole of the 1840's Paddington Village was under threat of demolition. The Paddington Society printed 'Save Paddington' leaflets, and they raised $2000 for a fighting fund. Four hundred and fifty people attended a public protest meeting. They approached the Local Government Minister, P. H. Morton with a petition. An election was due and he was convinced to appoint a commissioner to enquire into the matter. Don Gazzard suggested Walter Bunning, (designer of the National Library). Bunning was appointed and listened to 55 witnesses and considered more than 2000 written objections. One day he suddenly adjourned the meeting, and went on a walk of the suburb with John Thompson. "This is an unusual course," said Bunning. "but, I don't give a fig about that, if the true purpose of the enquiry is served." He inspected houses and talked to residents and was trailed by reporters and television crews. A month after his eye-opening walk, Bunning delivered a report that was to become Paddington's Magna Carta. He found that the proposed roads were neither necessary or desirable, and he recommended that the existing character and identity of Paddington be preserved. Furthermore he asked the government to declare it a protected historical area. Later he recalled, 'As I walked through the streets of Paddington that day, I was impressed by the sensitive way people had responded to the original architecture, and by simple means recreated the old feeling of the area. It hit me forcibly then, that preserving the occasional old building of character is a vain exercise. It is the enclave, the precinct of houses, where the space in between is as important as the houses themselves, that we should preserve if we are to have cities with souls and traditions.'⁵ The Paddington Society were triumphant.

'Paddington had been zoned as an area of special significance and we thought, 'We've made it so that they can't knock it all down', and then the Department of Main Roads suddenly announced that they were going to widen Jersey Road, and in traffic engineering terms it seemed a nonsense, because what they were doing was sort of drawing a ring around Sydney and they thought, "Oh well we'll bung it through Jersey Road", but what it effectively did was knock the houses down on both sides so it would have made a dreadful gash through Paddington. So we jumped up and down, and Wally Abrahams was appointed as a special commissioner to hear that. We were much more organised. Bernard Smith wrote evidence and we all weighed in.' (Don) Not every one in Jersey Road supported the Paddington Society in its campaign. 'We went to collect money to pay for the court case, and I met lots of people who were renting and some said, "I'm not giving any money to you lot, you're the yuppies, you lot are putting us renters out." Some were genuinely antagonistic. One house was all pensioners all divided up with each paying 20 dollars, and when that got sold they were put out, it went to one family.' (Lorna).

But more than 3000 people were at the Rally in Jersey Road in 1969. 'They wanted people to look around the houses, it was just marvellous the way everybody pulled together. 'To widen Jersey Road is to destroy Paddington.' We had black crepe over all the balconies and everyone dressed in black and there were thousands there. The whole street was blocked — TV and all.' (Lorna).

'They decorated Jersey Road, they came along the night before and gave us big black wreaths and bunting and signs. They had an open day where people could come and look through the front windows. I had a robbery after that actually.'(Marion).

'It was like a picnic. You knew everyone there, it was a wonderful day. Small children, we all felt that right was on our side, us against the Philistine Council. The feeling was one of euphoria.' (Louise).

The RTA retreated and abandoned the scheme. Other forces were working against the RTA too. 'The Askin government was vocal in its support for roads, but its Country Party members effectively blocked many urban road building plans in favour of rural roads.'⁶

At the same time as the Paddington Society became active, NSW unions also started to voice their opinions and fight for environmental issues. Working class activism was different in its methods of protest. While the Paddington Society had to rely on theatrics to attract media attention and attract public support, the

Builders Labourers' Federation had the power to withhold their labour from any development it considered destructive. Jack Mundey and the Builder's Labourers Federation, were working to save other parts of Sydney by imposition of the Green Bans. 'Workers control to us wasn't an empty phrase used to form part of a romantic future. It meant using the industrial muscle we had, to help otherwise powerless citizens to retain their inner city residences, to prevent the erosion of park areas and to make people pause and ask who was really benefiting from the boom.'[7]

Working class activism went beyond issues relating to their work. It was not polite and members were prepared to take risks with their liberty. John Phillips who lives in Paddington, was a waterside worker and a friend of Jack Mundey. He became concerned with apartheid in South Africa. 'When the Springboks were out here in 1970, there were lots of demonstrations. One night when the Eastern Suburbs were training at the SCG we walked in with them, and when they were finished, me and Bobby got in there with a couple of hacksaws and got through the goal posts. And on the Saturday the blokes were going to go in and pull them down so they couldn't play the South Africa and Australia game. Well, we got pinched and had a coupla days at Long Bay, and a coupla days at Parramatta. We finished up with a bond, and we appealed and we won the appeal. It finished up they got the game on. There were just too many police there!'

A sub-committee of the Paddington Society began to write a plan for the development of the suburb in 1970. This committee was made up of Donald Gazzard as chairman, Keith Cottier, Brian Cassidy, Terry Dorrough, Elias Duek-Cohen, John Luscombe, Charles Moess, Stephen Oquist and George Clarke. George Clarke had just completed a similar plan for Battery Point in Tasmania. All, bar Charles Moess and Stephen Oquist, were architects. Donald Gazzard was the driving force of the committee, and his concern was for the height of buildings, with their comfortable human scale. The Paddington Plan, which had been the most influential piece of planning shaping the area in the last fifty years, was however, forced to consider the heritage value of the area in a wider sense than just height restrictions, to preserve it. The Preamble stated, 'It must be stressed that the basis for all our thinking on controls for this area, is that what exists is not a slum which must be replaced with modern sanitary housing as soon as possible, but that the existing pattern provides a pleasant, healthy, and sensible environment for inner city living. Therefore any new regulations must be based on what exists and not on some suburban image of the ideal.'[8]

Some members loved the old Victorian style and disliked modernity. Others wanted new development to reflect the time that a house was built, rather than counterfeit the past. Some members of the Paddington Society, though they professed a love of Victorian style, were entirely ignorant of its architectural components, 'as can be seen by the numerous colonial restorations of late

Victorian houses, which would make the architectural historian or purist shudder.'[9] All future modification and new building in the area needed to show a sympathetic relationship to the buildings in existence. There was, in fact, a wide divergence of opinion even within the Paddington Society.

The question of authenticity of individual houses and of the area as a whole, was perhaps the most contentious of the heritage areas to resolve. At the same time as the Paddington Plan was being written, similar values could be seen in other organisations such as the Historic Houses Trust, and The National Trust. However, their houses were restored to a state of grandeur that they did not possess in their original state. An example is Experiment Farm at Parramatta, a modest property, which was, when first restored by the National Trust, fitted out in a much grander style than the original occupants would have contemplated.[10] These buildings had had many owners, all of whom had left some mark of their occupation on the properties. Through restoration, much of the evidence of these houses' complex histories were lost.

Historic restoration of a house to a state of total authenticity, would make the house un-liveable by modern standards. Professor Freeland working at the University of New South Wales in the early 1970's, wrote, 'It is impossible to reconcile the two requirements successfully. While it is possible to make an old building attractive, and at the same time retain much of the character and atmosphere of an earlier age, the result should not be supposed to be a historic restoration — it is a renovation, and a romantic one at that. A fair amount of freedom should be given to individual taste, because the area is large enough to take the resultant diversity, as long as the scale and pattern of the building is consistent.'[11]

The Paddington Plan divided the area into four precincts. It valued the large body of Victorian Terraces as most significant. Other areas were more difficult to classify, and contained houses of a different character, or factory buildings. These areas either received a B, C or D classification. The Paddington Village received a B conservation listing because there was a diversity of style, and some factories. Shops received a C classification, while the small factories on the fringe, received a D classification.[12] The classification valued one aesthetic over another, the Victorian over the Georgian, over the modern, and early twentieth century factory buildings. Aesthetic significance was valued independently of the cultural significance of the buildings, in a historic or social sense.

The Paddington Plan placed little importance on the preservation and restoration of shop fronts in Oxford Street. There were proposals for the redevelopment of the street, putting in a number of arcades to Victoria Street, and the demolition of seventeen houses to build a car park and shopping complex. 'Oxford Street is far too long to be walked comfortably. It is south facing, cold and drafty in winter, and generally unattractive.'[13] The plan never eventuated, and the strip is now a popular promenade.

The Paddington Society added the comments of academics in their submission to Council. Bernard Smith, the Professor of the Power Department of Fine Arts, University of Sydney wrote, 'What we are witnessing, I believe, is the emergence of an increasingly urban society in the inner suburbs of Sydney, one which finds a sense of recreation and refreshment, not so much in the home garden and in nature, which the suburban resident looks to, but to the historic fabric of the city itself, as expressed in older buildings. For such people the raw newness of inner-city multi-unit development does not provide an acceptable alternative. The emergence of this type of urban sensibility is of first importance for Sydney, for it can succeed in connecting the present with the past, and provide a community with a sense of continuity and direction. In preserving Paddington, we shall be preserving a very important chapter in the history of the veranda and balcony, elements that are almost endemic to an Australian architecture, and provide it with a great deal of what ever continuity it may possess.'[14]

In The Paddington Plan, comparisons were made to other areas of the world, such as Chelsea, Paris's Left Bank, and Greenwich Village in New York. These rather romantic comparisons made by Walter Bunning, reflected the fact that many artists, writers and intellectuals lived in the area, and hopefully would result in a café society where a cross fertilisation of ideas could occur between members of this group. Robert Burns writing in the Nation in 1967, made the comment, 'Though schooner sinking on the pavement outside the Windsor Castle is really not very much like pushing back cognac in a Montparnasse street café, some of the iron fringed first floor balconies above the fruit and lolly shops, do look like places behind which a local Modigliani could slowly be falling to pieces, along with the unsold rainbow cake.'[15]

The other key element in the case to preserve Paddington, was the argument that it was the most intact Victorian suburb in the world, which was a claim made in the Paddington Plan. Whether this is actually the case, is open to contention. Savannah, USA, for instance has grander and more elaborate terrace house districts. However this claim was strong enough to elevate the status of the suburb from an ill thought-of slum which only rated one sentence in Morton Herman's book, Victorian Architecture in Australia, to a desirable suburb which was of the greatest architectural importance. Few terrace houses have been pulled down in Paddington to build flats since The Paddington Plan's publication. The fame of Paddington's architecture was, in part, the product of the self-fulfilling prophecy of its bohemian middle class residents.

It was a logical step for the Paddington Society to back a candidate for Council. However they underestimated the difficulty in gaining a seat. 'I think they obviously thought all these middle class people were somehow intruders or were at least going to change Paddington in ways that they couldn't foresee, and saw their political base being threatened. If all the old prole Australians were moving out and New Australians weren't very interested, these middle class people seemed like a threat. The Thompsons were very left wing and so was I, and we were all Labor voters. When we contested the elections, it was a shemozzle. We designed these snazzy election posters and thought we'd shit it in. Leo Schofield was running around making slogans and I scrutineered at one of the booths afterwards and we won on all the polling booths. Then they started to count all the postal votes, all the old ladies the Labor party manages to rustle up in situations like that, and they beat us easily. It was a great political lesson. We were very naive. We just thought it was enough to put posters around, and jump up and down, and every one would see the wisdom of what we were doing and go for it, but it wasn't like it at all.' (Don) In fact, they had underestimated the high concentrations of renters.

The Paddington Society, however, had become a significant part of the Paddington scene and social life. Their parties and fundraisers were popular and well attended. 'The yearly Christmas Party thrown by the Paddington Society was at Paddington Town Hall for 600 people. For $3 we all had as much as we could eat and drink, all served to us at tables, while we were entertained by an 1890's music-hall type revue from the Nimrod Theatre plus some outstanding local talent like Maggie Blinco, whose joyousness sweeps everyone up in it.'[16]

To preserve and protect The Paddington Town Hall, Lilian Horler was appointed the Executive Officer of the Paddington Town Hall Project. 'I was asked to set it up and then operate and run it — The brief was to restore the Town Hall and set up a venue for public broadcasting, TV studio and offices. The ballroom was beautiful and there were lots of Greek weddings and community groups having their annual party there.'

Juniper Hall was saved from demolition by a campaign fought by the Paddington Society and the National Trust. It is one of the last of the mansions that existed before the terrace development in Paddington, and is a significant site and building. By the late 1970's it was in a dilapidated condition, shops had been built in the front garden in the early 1900's, which hid the old building, and it had been converted into flats. The campaign to buy and restore Juniper Hall was launched when the owner applied to demolish the house. 'We had always looked at Juniper Hall and realized as we turned into Underwood Street, that there was this great mansion tucked away behind the shops, so it became a great fight. Max Kelly organized a rally and I think maybe, 250–300 came and we marched down Oxford Street and stopped the traffic, and we had lots of banners and I think we were calling out, "Justice, justice, justice for Juniper Hall." The National Trust managed to scrape the funds together to buy it. Eventually the shops were demolished and the house was revealed. That was very much a Paddington Society, National Trust based rally.' (Tony) The Trust had the intention of renting out the property for functions, but the rooms were not large enough. Part of the building became a National Trust shop and café, and the upper floors became the Museum of Childhood. Neither were commercially sustainable, and finally the house was leased to a Real Estate Agency.

At the same time there was a boom in the value of local real estate. Prices rose well over the inflation rate.[17] Credit to purchase a Paddington terrace house, that had been hard to obtain during the early 1970's, became more readily available, when resale value of properties proved to the bank that such loans were of low risk. Property was expected to maintain its value or increase over time, and neither the 1970's oil crises nor the 1980's stockmarket crash, had a significant impact on the value of Paddington property.

Alan became a real estate agent in the 1960's, which was a turbulent time. 'After 1968 we had that enormous increase in interest rates, which forced a lot of people into selling. Anyone who had mortgages, instead of paying 6 per cent or 8 per cent were paying 16 per cent to 18.5 per cent interest. We were flat out moving people from one house to another and what have you. People who were caught with high interest rates were having to sell rapidly, or they'd move into one room somewhere, and let the house out. I got an enormous amount of job satisfaction out of housing people…We worked well with the other agents. We were all helping each other, low key, laid back, it was quite a different atmosphere.'

More than 50 per cent of divorcees lived in the inner city suburbs. Paddington was typical of this trend, and by the 1980's the market had changed. 'We got a lot of people who were breaking up from the more salubrious eastern suburbs, the big families split and we'd get the wives or the husbands. Paddington was a sort of haven where you could get yourself a nice little house for a quarter of the price that you would pay in Vaucluse. Also it was the period when young people like *Jack*, young lawyers, were buying. It was a period of take-overs and mergers and banking became a big thing, which it never used to be. And people, bankers, were coming from overseas and paying huge rents here. The companies were paying the big rents. The English people came from London, Chelsea, and it was normal for them.' (*Alan*)

Henry and *Louise* bought in 1968. 'My generation not only had a great affection for Paddington but were terribly interested in what was happening here, and they were involved to a degree that I've never seen before or since. The Paddington Society group stopped the freeway and saved Juniper Hall so there was a sort of bonding of this community. Then people started moving into Paddington, not for what it was, or for what it offered, but for real estate reasons, like you can make a buck.'

The Sydney Morning Herald advertised a 3 bedroom terrace in Hargrave Street for sale at $23,000, and a similar house in Windsor Street for sale at $24,000, on April 1 1970. Prices escalated, and on April 7 1980, a similar 3

Leinster Street

bedroom house was advertised for $188,000. In 1988 a 3 bedroom in Cascade Street was selling for $455,000. The preferred method of sale of property in the area changed from properties being offered for sale, to their being auctioned, which was a sign of increased speculation on the local property market.[18]

When *Louise* moved in, her friends in Rose Bay and Vaucluse were a bit 'Goodness me. Paddington is the place you first move to before you move somewhere else sort of thing.'

By 1976 most of the population of Southern European migrants had moved out of the suburb. Greeks tended to move to Sydney's south-west, while the Italians moved to the west of the city. Although Paddington was surrounded by suburbs with high concentrations of people speaking English as a second language, there was only a small proportion of this group in the suburb in 1986.

Just as Paddington was a suburb of transience for migrants in the 1950's and 60's, so it was in the 80's for some on their way up the Sydney social ladder. They would seek to renovate, to make a profit, then resell. They were observed by those who had been there for a much longer time. 'The Paddington Society would alarm the National Trust and the Woollahra Council if they thought that anything untoward was happening, they'd buy a terrace and want to turn it into something else. They wanted to add huge dormer windows and completely alter the whole context of the house, so the National Trust employed myself and a couple of other students to do a survey of every house in Paddington. There was a form for each one, to fill out at what stage of originality it was, and what the key things were that had to be done to each house to put them back to their original condition.' (*Tony*)

Paddington had been split between two municipalites in 1968, the southern side of Oxford Street part of South Sydney Council, the northern side, Woollahra Council. Paddington had been incorporated into the very area it had rejected when it first drew up its boundaries in 1861. 'I think many of the councillors were skeptical, there was always this, Paddington doesn't fit. In the early 70's it was slightly bohemian, there were a lot of Greeks and Italians, a lot of gay people, a lot of Labor voting trendies in a sense, and the people associated with the Paddington Society might have come into that category, young professionals looking for a different kind of life style, and it never fitted with that established view of Darling Point, Point Piper and Bellevue Hill, which was still very much a bastion of conservatism. I don't think the Council ever gave it really high regard, it was never really considered an acceptable place, and it seemed to have its problems and was a bit outdated.' (*Norman*)

Buyers in the late 1970's and early 1980's, bought into a suburb where there were still remnants of its bohemian past. 'We had moved to Paddington, which wasn't the best suburb, but was respectable, and we were excited and sitting there with our drinks and watching the street go by. The Windsor Castle was a very popular pub, and this character appeared in the middle of the street and he was coloured, he had on a flowing white caftan, he had black dreadlocks and he had a great stockwhip of some sort and he was twirling it round his head and cracking it, and it was just so exotic, and we thought, this is Paddington, and that was our first night and we have never ever in twenty years seen anything like it again.'(*Jill*) Although some people were buying in the suburb with the intention to live there, a trend had started between 1971–76 when there was an 11 per cent decrease in owner occupied houses.

There was limited scope for new building in the suburb, but Don found a vacant lot in Hargrave Street, and built a modern house. 'In the Paddington Plan I said that I couldn't see when you came to build anything new you should try and imitate what was old. It had to be the same height, and it had to use the same materials, but it didn't have to be a mock Victorian sort of house. And some members of the Paddington Society agreed with that and some didn't. Council didn't necessarily agree with that either, but I took the view that it really is the street facades of the houses that are important and it doesn't really matter what happened behind. They were a real dog's breakfast, most of them, and you could quite happily let all sorts of things happen because it wasn't the prime architectural thing. I just wheeled in with the plans, and it got approved, and I built it. It's on three levels, you enter on the middle level, and because it's forty feet wide it's got a feeling of space that you don't get in a normal Paddington house. I mean, except for a kitchen and a toilet thing along one side, it was just

Paddington houses 1970's. The pattern of skillion roofs is one that is under threat because of current trends in renovating. Photograph Warren Turner

The Windsor Castle 1970's. Photograph Warren Turner

View above Caledonia Street 1970's. Photograph Warren Turner

Brown Street in the 1970's. Fewer and fewer of these filled in verandas exist in the suburb and the iron lace has been restored. Photograph Warren Turner

Corner of Hopetoun and William Street 1970's. Photograph Warren Turner

Corner Shadforth and Gipps Street 1970's. Photograph Warren Turner

one great big room with a stair going down and a stair going up. There was a living room, it was double height, there was an upstairs in a sort of L-shape, around a tall space in the middle of the house. It opened into a big terrace that faced north, that had a glass roof over it. Downstairs was the studio and the kids' bedrooms and sort of playroom and bathroom and stuff like that. There was a cliff below the road, and the house stood away from the cliff and you entered across a little bridge into the house. It was a great place to live.'

'If you look at Hillier's, Let's Buy a Terrace House, you cringe at the sort of things that people thought were basically acceptable in those days. Putting walls in front, chipping back the render to reveal the pecking of the brick work, taking the plaster off the interiors, putting through Spanish arches when you opened the place up, quarry tile floors were very big, everything whitewashed, walls had that sort of Mediterranean comes to Paddington look, making them more Europeanised. Maybe they thought that living in an inner city area was much more cosmopolitan and sophisticated. We've only got to think that it wasn't so many years before that people didn't have wine with their dinner at night and didn't eat in restaurants.' (*Norman*)

One of the most common renovations was to relocate the main family room to the rear of the house, and to open up the roof with attics. The applications were worded so that the roof was storage space. 'What is he storing there?' 'Children.' (*Henry*)

The Paddington Society kept fighting campaigns to preserve and improve the suburb. 'Our two great things in 1980, 1981 was getting the fences taken down around the Trumper Park Oval. They used to play Australian Rules there and it was effectively shut off from the Paddington community and they charged entry money. The whole thing had this horrible fence and you had canvas things around it so you couldn't peek, so I remember ringing up Margaret Throsby and got an interview, and the Mayor of the Woollahra Council was furious about the whole thing, but shortly thereafter they did Trumper Park and they did the oval.' (*Louise*)

In the early 1960's Paddington was still primarily a suburb of tenants. By the 1970's-1980's there were approximately 50 per cent rented properties. The transients were people aged between 20–29, many of whom were students. Accommodation in a boarding house was between $19–25, but there were only 25 per cent of places available in comparison with advertisements eight years previously. Share accommodation had replaced the boarding house, but it was a lot more expensive. In 1988, a 3 bedroom house cost $400 a week to rent. One bedroom flats were asking between $80 to $145 a week.[19]

The rise in rents forced many of the old tenants out. 'We had new neighbours and things were starting to change. Big piles of mattresses would appear in the street because every house had been a boarding house. Disgusting old mattresses and junk from the boarding house, and lots of pygmy stoves. Lots of tiny stoves would be chucked out. Houses were starting to be painted white.' (*Marion*). Enormous pressures were placed on some of the older tenants. '*Miss Jones* was a protected tenant. She was an elderly woman and quite deaf, and she was forced into one room of what had been her house by two airline stewards, who had bought the house. That was quite indicative of the change, I suppose. The old lady was taken over by these two boys but they were representative of the new Paddingtonians. She eventually moved out.' (*Tony*)

The 1986 Census shows that occupancy rates per dwelling had dropped to 2–3 persons per dwelling. Shopkeepers were suffering. 'We went through a crisis. There might have been nine or ten people living in a large house in Regent Street and then it sold to a married couple with no children, so you go from nine or ten locals to two, so that takes a period of time to adjust.' (*Michael*)

Alan built up strong relationships with the protected tenants in the properties that he managed. "We had *Mrs. Young* who was a delightful lady who lived down here, and there were rooming houses, terraces. They stayed for quite a while, the rooming houses. Then there was a very dapper little Englishman who had a little dachshund, and he used to be absolutely immaculate, they were all on Second World War rentals of $7 or $8 a week and we took them over. They were starting to really fall apart because there was no money to do anything. The tenants used to do their own repairs and one man who was an old boiler maker used to repair his floors with box wood. He used to break up the boxes and use the boards to replace the floors as they disintegrated. Eventually he died and there were two bankbooks in his house, one with $20,000 in it and the other with $75,000. The rubbish that came out filled five truckloads. We had the floors sanded and polished and these floorboards made a unique effect and the house then became a major attraction. The tenants in those days in a lot of the properties were mainly students. They were pretty good on the whole. They'd get a tin of paint and paint a room, and they'd do quite a good job, and the owners didn't want to spend the money or didn't have it. They were quite happy to take something cheap and paint it and do it up, but that doesn't apply now.'

The people who had moved in the 1970's and stayed, developed a community spirit beyond their own group. They were Paddington old hands who valued their contacts with older residents. 'Max was very much a sort of a neighborhood based person, and yes, if someone lived nearby they would be invited in for a cup of tea, but certainly there was a lot of talking at the front fence. If you were out watering the garden, or sweeping your share of the footpath, you would always end up chatting to someone who you knew, who was passing by, and you knew everyone who was living around. It was very friendly and everyone kept an eye on one another.'(*Tony*). Peter Madden, a chemist, developed long term, deep friendships with some of his customers.

'The elderly tend to go to what's been there the longest, and I probably have a higher percentage of the local elderly people than the next guy up the road as customers, and I treasure them because they've been with me a long time and they're part of my extended family. I really care about them and we try to look after them. There are ladies who come in here now in their 80's, who used to nurse my kids. Because we lived upstairs, I was involved with my wife and the children twenty-four hours a day. Judith would go shopping and she'd leave the baby in a bouncinettte in the corner of the dispensary, and if I was busy and the baby started to cry, I used to get whoever came in to the shop. I'd say, "Have you got five minutes?" and they'd nurse the baby. And they'd sit in a corner and say, "This is Mathew" and, "Look at him", and, "Isn't he beautiful?" I used to do the deliveries and I'd put the kids in a pram and with a black Labrador, away we'd go, and knock on the door and hand out the prescriptions.' (Peter)

Paddington in 1986, was still in the second highest bracket of renting areas, (25–54 per cent). *Jack* lived in a share house in Paddington Street in the 1980's. 'It had rental beige, Berber carpet. And what I called the oatmeal look. All the walls, floors, all blended into the same colour, it was painted beige, the ceilings had gone beige. Carpets were filthy, with cigarette butts stubbed into them. A pretty irresponsible bunch we would have been. It was never in good nick, nothing was in the fridge, kitchen was a brothel, rough and shabby. Bedrooms, usually just a mattress on the floor, and a clothes rack and a sheet over the French doors. Can't remember the back yard. Don't think I ever went in it.' He explained why this share house broke up after he graduated and was working.. 'You start to notice that the Paddington dig was a bit rough, well you start to need your privacy because you have to be too organised. I'd talked my way into the big time and I was up against people who came from the Blue Mountains who had a very sedate, calm, comfortable, family lifestyle, who would have been at home with their parents, and in your Paddington terraces, there were always people coming and going and sharing, one person would have three or four friends over, and that was my recollection of that house and all of the houses. Always people there. There was always a full ashtray, a bottle of wine opened, and a few beers and the TV going, and just general mayhem, which is not quite conducive to being a businessman, unless you're able to function with it all going on.'

Kristen also lived in a share house for several years. 'There were three of us in a terrace, right next door to a car repair place, so it was really noisy. But it was a really nice terrace for young people to move into. It was *Rex*, myself, and a girl I went to school with, who popped up out of the blue and was looking for a place at the same time. So we were all quite different. I was working in the box office of the Sydney Theatre Company, *Rex* was doing sets for film, and *Kate* was at Sydney University doing Archaeology and History. And *Kate* and I did the groceries together which was quite fun. We shared the food. *Rex* was fantastic on cleaning the back yard, and we had an outside table and did heaps of entertaining. Always having people for dinner, and it was quite a sophisticated way of living at such a young age. I think because we had a really nice place, people would come to us. In summer we'd sit outside and talk and listen to music. During the winter we did heaps of backgammon, a lot of scrabble, and a lot of monopoly and we still do. We just sit around with whole groups of people and play games. It was very quiet. Just us really, making noise. I didn't ever meet any neighbours. None ever complained.'

The 1980's, before the stock market crash, was a time of real affluence for some. 'A typical night out, well you would be talking about when I was in my early twenties, and it was the 80's and everyone was earning a lot of money for their age, ridiculous amounts of money for their age, and I was too, earning twice what my father was bringing home, I mean it wasn't uncommon for my peers to take home over $10,000 a week. Not that I ever did, but I was very comfortable. Designer clothes, Italian imports, none of this Australian stuff, $1500 suits. At twenty six I decided I wanted a car, and I bought that, at twenty seven I decided I wanted an apartment, and I bought that, all this is through my own bat, doing what I wanted, where I wanted. You'd go out and you know, it wasn't a habit, but you could go out to lunch every day if you wanted. It was just, your friends were in the same boat, and the people you associated with in the property industry. You'd go to Tech, and they'd be there and then you'd go out for drinks and they'd be there, you'd go out to a night club and when you'd finished, you'd go out till three, and you could always tell who went out the night before because no one would be answering their phones the next day. If you wanted to do some work with another agent, your peer in that agency might not be around until midday. People used to just go and sleep in their cars all day, and get over their hangovers. Oh, it was just terrible. If I could do what I did then, now, I would treat it with so much more respect. I didn't work hard at all. It was a big joke to me. I was terrible.' (*Nina*)

The stockmarket crash seriously effected the lives of many of the young in Paddington. 'Well my unfortunate career path was that I hit my straps as a boy, when the stockmarket crash had happened, and it was all down hill from there. In the late 80's Bond was collapsing, a whole lot of them had had it, and no one wanted to invest in anything, so trying to talk them into buying assets, three years out of Uni. was difficult. I didn't have a clue and I was at the most junior level, the firm is down to 30 and they say "Deutsche Bank are buying us, could you just knock your resume together by 2 o'clock tomorrow?" We're staying in a dingy hotel in Melbourne, trying to buy a paint company for $30,000,000, me and another young guy. I remember sleeping in my suit in this hotel, it was such a crummy hotel, freezing, so not so glamorous. "How do I get my resume together?"' (*Jack*)

The late 70's and 80's were traumatic for some families. There was an increase in divorce rates after the Labor Government of 1973 passed the Family Law Act. Families had been affected by changes in moral standards, by the women's liberation movement, and the aftermath of the permissiveness of the 1970's. It marked the end of the utopian dream of the bohemians.

'When you leave somewhere you go to something new. I left Paddington with a new husband to build a new place in the bush. Marriages all kind of broke up in a wave, and it was the end of an era, and the severance of marriage was part of the end of the era'. (*Elizabeth*)

'It was lovely at the start, it was beautiful, planning that home and moving in with all the children and all going to school, but I think my life fell apart when *Reg* went, it was like this dream I had, suddenly fell to pieces, and I had to try and find a new direction. I think in life you have to go through these really hard times, and something strong comes out of it. We call it the waves and nodes of life. My husband met someone in Paddington and moved off with her. I stayed in the house, I still had one son at home for a few years and I started renting rooms out to young people. By this time I'd been at University and done a social work degree and I got a job. My son liked playing drums and it was a bit embarrassing. The back room we padded out with egg cartons, that's supposed to break the noise, but there was a man in the back who periodically complained and said, "Face it, he's no Gene Krupa". I used to go to workshops all up around Paddington. There was a lot of that, a bit of hippie stuff. I found out about it when I went to University, and I thought, this is the way to go. Then I began to rent these rooms out. *Harold*, was doing an osteopathy course, *Hamish* was there for a while, he worked in the city, *George*, who was part of the Rajneesh, there was another girl used to do massaging.' (*Patricia*)

'I became part of the generation of kids with divorced parents, whereas the older children in the neighbourhood, my brother's group, who were eight years older, were part of a group, so they were the baby boomers children, so they were like 18, 19, before their parents divorced, but we were in the group ten years below that. They were all getting divorced because they were getting sick of having kids around and paying mortgages and they were getting into their forties and were discovering other things in life.'(*Eugene*)

Jane's social life as a teenager after her parents separated, revolved around Paddington. "Mandrax and acid which were big things and then a bit later speed and heroin started to come into the picture. I mean the Mandrax, people would take about six, and they're sleeping pills and then they might drink and then they'd just become wobbly. I remember taking them once and thinking, this is terrible, you get, if you had a bit to drink you got a euphoric sense, but if you took Mandrax you didn't have that, but you got really wobbly so you looked like you had all the bad side effects of alcohol without any of the benefits. I didn't think much of it but obviously other people did. A lot of this was centred around the Windsor Castle. The heroin was all very discreet. It was only later that I found out that it had been going on, it was right under my nose. People I spent a lot of time with, it turned out were using it, and one fellow died at eighteen, so I was perhaps seventeen at the time and there were some others who died and others who went to NA. It was only later that I began to realise just how much was going on at the time'. (*Jane*)

The working class kids and the migrants' children who had stayed in Paddington, behaved in much the same way as kids in the previous decades. They jumped the wall to get into the show. They defended their mates. They roamed the neighbourhood confident that this was their turf. 'We actually sort of claimed a couple of cars that we drove around, we don't know exactly what happened, but there was a couple of Vdubbs, Beetles that had been dumped in Furber Road. You know at fourteen, fifteen we'd kinda like jump in, clutch start them, never stupid enough to get onto the main road, but drive around Furber Road for half an hour at a time. That's where I learnt to drive.

Six of us went into the Paddington Town Hall and snuck in, and took our own tour. We were up in the clock tower having a good look around, best view in Sydney by the way, and the next thing you know we heard some noise and some guy coming up the stairs. So the four of us ran, a whole lot of empty rooms and passageways we were running through, it's huge in there and we had to dive through a window and fought our way through, pushing and shoving, every man for themselves. So we're thinking, "That's it, we're dead." It was just some guy in there, and he just grabbed us and said, "Who are you, what are you doing?, I'll call the police if you come back again", and that was it. And the three of us were sitting in there thinking we're going to get kicked out of school.'(*Phillip*)

By the end of the 1980's the bohemian middle class was leaving Paddington and being replaced by a far more conservative group with a lot more money. They retained some of the values of the departing bohos, but did not have the same attachment to the suburb and the sense of community feeling. The Paddington Society had preserved the aesthetic of Paddington, but they themselves were becoming a displaced group, encouraged to sell by offers of big money.

'We decided to build a house down the coast and move into an apartment in town. We felt that Paddington had changed a lot and Max always said that when he went there, everyone used to sweep their share of the footpath, but when we left, you were flat out sweeping your share of it, because it was often half parked on by a four wheel drive, everyone seemed to have red setters, and it was just very different. We were pleased to get out then, it seemed much of the niceness had gone, and in fact we found that here, in Potts Point, it was still down at heel here in a way, and very friendly. It was like a whole new lot had moved in with plenty of money to develop Paddington.' (*Tony*)

'The thing that eventually drove us out of Paddington were the people who came in from other suburbs at night. They would park up on the pavements right outside our windows, we would have gasoline fumes straight into our kitchen. If we objected to this, people would be rude, they pissed on our fences, on our back gates, and that wasn't Paddington people, it was people who came in.'(*Jenny*)

After they had moved out, the bohemian residents were left with a romantic vision of the past, and a resentment towards the new residents. 'Well, after moving to the inner west, when I used to come back to visit Mum, I really liked how bourgeois it was. Terrible isn't it. By that time it was. Around the streets were all these well-dressed people, I really liked looking at the clothes they wore, and into their front doors, and seeing how their houses were done, but I also remember that very quickly I tired of that. I'd look at the unfriendly behaviour and, I was twenty one or something, and feeling very much like my Paddington had been lost.'(*Jane*)

Chapter Ten
Money Changes Everything

Since the late 1980's, more of the nation's wealth has been concentrated in the hands of fewer and fewer people. Money has changed the character and social fabric of Paddington. Its desirability as a place to live, has led to such a high demand for real estate in the suburb, that house prices have contitnued to rise fast. And sometimes situations have arisen where greed has triumphed over social conscience.

The State government policy of urban consolidation often conflicts with heritage and tourism. Groups such as the Paddington Society, had firmly established the area's heritage significance in the 1970's, and Paddington is now a tourist attraction. Visitors are guided through the suburb in buses and on heritage walks. It is a fashionable area to live, close to the city and close to coastal and harbour beaches.

So it is not surprising that Paddington property is highly valued. Prices have more than tripled in the last fifteen years. A 1 bedroom cottage in Prospect Street, that was bought in 1984 for $70,000 is now valued at over $300,000 — and it is common for houses to fetch prices exceeding $1,000,000. The price rises create an illusion of increased stability through increased home ownership, but of 8459 dwellings, 3486 were rented, and only 3167 were owned by the residents or being paid off, in 1996. This implies a return to the absentee landlords of the past.

It is impossible for those who earn an average wage to buy in the suburb. New buyers are wealthy, and the average length of stay is only five to seven years. This is a destabilising factor in the community, for between 1991 and 1996, 48 per cent of the population moved.[1] Those who purchased their properties more than twenty years ago, are randomly distributed throughout the suburb. However every year less remain.

Paddington, once described as a transit camp for migrants, is becoming a transit camp for young business people, who are confident that if they buy a house, it is going to be worth considerably more when they sell a few years later, and they can then invest in a grander property. In 1996, 25 per cent of families with offspring had incomes over $100,000, but there were 25 per cent more households who had no children than those that did. The average age of residents is decreasing. By 1991, 50 per cent of the population were aged between 20–34 and there were many lone households. The highest proportion of people who lived in the suburb were managers or professionals, then those who worked in sales or personal services, and only 75 people were labourers or tradesmen. The social demographic of the suburb has been turned on its head.

Jack, a local real estate agent, has observed the latest trends. 'You've got bankers and brokers and yuppies from the city, and those who are successful in advertising. There are some empty nesters from the north shore, the doctor from Lindfield had heard it's a great investment, and he's met his groovy friends in Queen Street, and wants to be a part of the scene. You do get some tenants who start out renting in their twenties, and who get to their thirties and will buy the humbler houses. Some come in here to make some money, but as soon as they've got the kid and made enough, they're off again.'

For many who had lived in other parts of Sydney, the eastern suburbs were places which they had never considered living in. *Nina* had lived all her life on the north shore and the northern beaches. 'There was this barrier, I'd already crossed the Spit Bridge for heaven's sake, to cross two bridges was unthinkable. That place in the eastern suburbs, why would you want to go there?' *Susie* also grew up on the north side of the harbour, and during her childhood had not explored the south side. She grouped the entire area in one category. 'I always used to say that people who lived over this side of the bridge were in the western suburbs, were Westies.'

In 1994, *Lea,* who grew up in a far northern suburb, was engaged to be married, and with her fiancée, they searched for houses in the eastern suburbs. They found a house in the Paddington Village. 'From the north it felt like you were looking out into big wide open spaces, but here it is quite enclosed. Not claustrophobic necessarily, but enclosed and small, and cosy too. Everything is right there. I thought it was not posh so much, but wealthy people must have lived here. And you know the people, the women and men that walked down the street all looked like models, they were glamorous looking people in what I thought to be a glamorous place.'

Buying the house was a big step. 'We didn't look for a long time. And we had seen this house. It needed a bit of tidying up and cleaning and a few things done to it. I thought, "This could be a great house, we could make great things out of this house." It ended up getting passed in at auction for $460K, and the

John Phillips in his backyard

Kath caught the 1970's spirit

Paddington Town Hall, Photograph by Don Gazzard

Fondue Night

Often houses in Paddington are demolished to their façade and a new house is built at the back. This process almost totally destroys the heritage significance of the property, while it maintains streetscape.

This block of flats was situated on a block that once housed the boarding house where Don and Marea Gazzard first lived in Paddington. The building of this block of flats and the threat of similar development contributed to the formation of the Paddington Society.

Cafè on Glenmore

The last fish and chip shop in Paddington

Mid-week shopping fernzy

agent came over and started talking to us, and somehow or other we ended up with the house.'

Ed was a single man when he bought a terrace house in Paddington in the late 1980's. A bachelor unit was too small to live in. 'It was close to the city, it wasn't the lower north shore, it wasn't the inner west. The inner west was pretty downtrodden, the lower north shore probably was trendy, but that bloody Bridge made all the difference. Instead of being able to walk home, you had to get a taxi. And it was beautiful, and it was Victorian, and it was different, and it wasn't little boxes which was what I'd escaped from. I enjoyed the convenience, the culture, the people, the handiness of the pubs, I mean going out and having a good time is obviously a very important part of my life, and you can go out and it doesn't cost you an arm and a leg to get a taxi from A to B, because everything is very handy, and its more interesting socio-economically, because you have people that aren't too well off, living next to people who are the some of the richest people in Australia. We all live shoulder to shoulder and it seems to work. OK, there's a bit of crime, but it seems to work, whereas the north shore seems to be White Anglo Saxon Protestant, and there is no cultural diversity, and that just bores the hell out of me, and it's why I left middle class New Zealand. It would have driven me up the wall.'

Liz and *Pete* moved to Paddington in 1998. They formed a relationship after they had divorced their partners and their children had left home. They had previously lived on the north shore. *Pete* remembered when he first moved there. 'They were very sleepy suburbs full of widows, where nothing happened at all, and beautiful old houses weren't regarded as beautiful. It has been a phenomenon of the 70's 80's and 90's and they are beautiful suburbs, and the architecture is wonderful. I loved all of that and my kids loved it. I wasn't typical. I was a member of the Australian Labor Party, Mosman branch, for many years. I wanted to try the eastern suburbs and I knew it was going to be different.' (*Pete*) 'We sat on the bench at Five Ways and something sort of happened, looking out across the glimpses of harbour and I thought that was just lovely around that area, something quite uniquely special. I think I didn't really fit into Mosman, because it's pretty homogenous, pretty smallish and incredibly middle class. The eastern suburbs are more European, it's more cosmopolitan here.'(*Liz*)

John Normyle was a Councillor for the Paddington ward until 1999. He is a designer who specialises in renovation. 'I've done a lot of renovations for people who have bought houses for more than $900,000. This is interesting. I remember when a friend bought her house for $50,000 and friends said, "That's ridiculous. They'll never hit a hundred," and then, "You'll never get a quarter of a million, then half a million, you've got to be kidding, they're asking far too much, You'll never get a million." The style of renovations has changed. Warren Turner, the building inspector for Paddington for almost thirty years, has seen many changes in the demands of applicants to the Council for renovations. 'I've seen a big change by way of gentrification, certainly the people who choose to live in Paddington today are a much wealthier class of people, certainly a lot different to the people of the early 70's. It was very much working class then, and the type of work done was very minor alterations and additions. There were no major extensions — people really just wanted to upgrade the amenities. The bathroom, kitchens, and now and again you'd get somebody wanting to put a carport in the back lane. The people today want far too much. The thing that doesn't change is the small allotments. If you could see the map of the whole Municipality that goes all the way out to Watson's Bay, Paddington is like a small chequered blanket, the blocks are so terribly small. People have to accept that windows will always overlook the back yard, and probably one of the biggest sources of objections today, is somebody wanting to build a traditional balcony to the rear. We find that people are not as tolerant today as they used to be. I think they are much more guarded towards their investment now that they are paying so much. They want to go boundary to boundary, so rather than leave the breezeway, they want it utilised. They want the master bedroom with the balcony and they also want the ensuite, the walk in wardrobe, and that really is a big tendency. It's the upper levels and the breaking up of a common alignment that concerns us very much, and that the Development Control Plan addresses. That was something that was urgently needed.'

The Paddington Society initiated the writing of the Development Control Plan. Cedric Carle, a member of the Paddington Development Control Plan Committee explains. 'From day one, the Paddington Society started lobbying for conservation. It was an incredible struggle and it was only last year that it happened, and it happened because Paddington had always been the poor relation of the Woollahra Council. Lanes were filthy, and we were beating our heads against the wall to get some decent controls in Paddington. Bill Morrison and I put forward a document called, 'Towards a Development Control Plan for Paddington'. The Council gave us an audience, we had a historian, a conservation architect, and they adopted it, and they formed a working party of fourteen people. We spent a year on this document and it's now in place and it will stop these $1,500,000 things in their tracks. They don't really belong. If you want that sort of a house, you should go somewhere where you can build one, not try and pretend that a Victorian house is something like that. We tried to stop all the excesses but we weren't always successful. It's taken twenty years to get that document into place.'

There are no museum examples in Sydney of an intact Victorian terrace or one that shows evidence of changing occupation. 'You have Susannah Place in the Rocks, but they're not even typical veranda terraces and they generally don't have the service wing as a separate wing coming off the back. Five years ago,

I went to a house that had been occupied by Italians for a very long time, and it was absolutely fantastic, because all the wallpapers were patterned, and the furniture was very Italianate from the 60's and 70's, and the back garden was tiled and the chrome chairs were in the back yard with the vinyl seats and everything. Those are the things that we are also losing.' (*Norman*)

The Paddington Development Control Plan, gazetted in 1999, is now the major document that protects the architecture of Paddington. It seeks to combat the demolition of outbuildings such as old outdoor toilets, to prevent the building of carports in front of houses, and over-development at the back of buildings. The plan though, has already failed its first test in the courts. A recent application to build a garage in front of a house in Paddington was rejected by the Woollahra Council, as it contravened the guidelines in its legislation. The applicant took the matter to the Land and Environment Court. "Why is this person not entitled to a garage?" asked the Judge. The applicant won the case.[2] The Plan encourages the restoration of houses which have suffered unsympathetic renovation in the past. There are suggestions for home owners to renovate in ways that are specific in time to their house. Early, middle and late Victorian periods are specified. Windows, doors, balconies and fences are described. Allowable extensions, garages and dormer windows are proscribed.

There are a number of questions raised by the issue of renovations. Does this renovation effect the heritage value of the properties and community? Does renovation compromise local character? What are we defending, when we object to development? Who are we preserving the buildings for? One of the main reasons behind the desire to preserve buildings is so that the identity of past owners is not lost. People are forced to confront the transient nature of their occupation. The majority of the Paddington houses have been occupied for over one hundred years, and residents have had different aspirations and desires. They adapted the houses to their needs. In the 1930's, people filled in balconies and adapted back sheds to accommodate as many as possible, and reduce the cost of rent. Southern European migrants attempted to modernise and increase the area of the houses for the same purpose. These adaptations were frowned upon by the new middle classes residents in the 60's and 70's as intrusive. They wanted to restore the suburb to its former glory. The filled-in balconies were eliminated and the cast iron replaced. This group found extra space in the houses by building into the attics and introducing new additions to the rear. These were much larger alterations, than either the working class renters or the post Second World War migrants had performed, and the houses were accommodating fewer people. The population is now one third of what it was in 1933, despite the building of flats, townhouses and units.

Modern additions often wipe out all evidence of previous occupations, leaving only the merest fragment from which no archaeological and little historical significance can be read. In such cases, where the only concession made to the environment rests on the retention of streetscape, the heritage significance is decreased. They are not reversible changes like the filled in balconies of the Depression years. Changes are sometimes made out of desire, not need. They add glamour to their owner's lifestyle, but can reflect self-interest rather than community values.

Damage to the area's heritage values is caused by those who buy terraces expressly to renovate and to later sell. Such developers will give an architect a brief, who will be dropped in favour of another if they disagree with the proposal. Legislation requires an owner seeking to demolish all or part of a building in a conservation area, to employ a heritage consultant to prepare an impact assessment of the proposed works. However, if the assessment is not positive, a developer can persist until they find a consultant who is compliant. The consultant becomes an advocate of the property owner. If they do not promote the developers interests they will not be employed.

The Paddington Society sought to restore the suburb's aesthetics in the 1970's, but they also wanted to preserve its character and diverse social fabric. They felt part of it. Ada Louise Huxtable in her book, Unreal America — Architecture and Illusion, writes, 'The act of preservation turns what has been 'saved' into something else, at the same time that the improvements provide the economic base that 'saves it.' Paddington was 'saved' but has not become what the first members of the Paddington Society had envisioned or was ever there in the first place. Members saw a community of their peers, a 'café society', where ideas were exchanged, a Paris in Australia. But they made the area comfortable for a group of middle class people. They had acted with the best of intentions, but they created the property boom. A chain of events have marginalised them from the place that they love.

The proportion of people with degrees and those involved in the arts has declined. Only 19.5 per cent of people in the suburb in 1996 had a degree which is equivalent of a Bachelor Degree. Only 5 per cent had a higher degree. Forty two per cent of the people who live in the suburb now have no qualifications at all.

Don Gazzard, one of the most influential members of the Paddington Society, sees a loss of the identity of the area. 'I think the social character of Paddington has changed for the worse. I haven't lived here for four or five years but it had a very diverse character in those early days and there were lots of old 'prole' Australians. There was an old lady who lived across from us called Dolly, who, whenever there was anyone who came out to cut down trees, she would be there saying, "Cut it down. The roots all get in the pipes", and all the people like us would be saying, "No, no, you can't cut down trees." It was an absolute divide. They hated trees and we liked them. It was a very mixed social environment, and I loved it. I used to chart the degradation of Paddington by the number of phoney brass carriage lamps outside houses. I regret the loss of that social diversity, but it's very hard to maintain, because when something gets expensive and people can afford it, they tend to be the same sort of people. At the moment I'm spending part of my time in St. Kilda in Melbourne and it's like the old Paddington. There are Kooris and bag ladies and Melbourne's best restaurants and students and middle class people all mixed up together. Paddington used to be like that.'

Renters have always been dominant. Today, more than 50 per cent of houses are rented, but it is the cost that has changed, as advertisements in the Sydney Morning Herald, 27 January, 2000 show. '$1050 for an elegant four bedroom house on a tree lined street,' '$1500 Vogue entertaining!' ' Brand new Sun drenched corner terrace, 4 bedrooms 4 secure parking, near Trumper Park, $1100'. 'Stunning grand Victorian terrace located just moments from the Five Ways. Classical style throughout, tastefully compliments with ultra modern finishes and set over three levels. The property further boasts a beautiful rear courtyard, which is perfect for entertaining. $1500.'

The real estate agent comments. 'I'd say that the day of the beaten up house is not good enough any more in Paddington. The people who want to rent here are the executive types, who might buy here to speculate, and they want it to be nice and freshly painted with a timber veneer kitchen, and a sort of a look and they will pay endless money for it. I reckon there's a better market for the 'more' money than the 'low' money. You can do really well if you spend the dough. Houses worth a million dollars being rented out, lots of them. They weren't bought for a million, but they are now worth that. A person who is paying you $1000 a week is A, intelligent, B, well-heeled, and C, didn't get there by fun. If that blind doesn't work, they're going to ring you at 9 am and again at 4 pm, and say "The guy hasn't come yet. Why?" Then a fax will roll through. "If this is not attended to rent will stop."

Some of the owners have inherited or been around for a while. You get people who own four of them and stuff like that, and they were never Paddo-ites. Their daughter may have lived there for a while when she was eighteen. Sometimes they're from the country, gentry. That's the old guard of rental properties. Land tax is flushing them out, because land taxes mean if you're an investor, it is better to buy a unit, because the land value of the unit is very low. It is difficult for people with middle incomes or under, to live in the area. This has restricted the diversity of the area. There are no more young, struggling artists. Paddington is a valuable area so the gentry with four houses are slowly going to be squeezed out and will be bought by smart young bankers who appreciate how money works.' (*Jack*)

'Young, Hip, Urbanites. Gen X loves Apartment Living' are headlines in the Sunday Telegraph of 5 March 2000. 'A unique property market. The inner eastern suburbs covering Darlinghurst, Woolloomooloo, Potts Point, Elizabeth Bay, Paddington, Edgecliff and Surry Hills, has been created by Generation X,

Interior of house in Hargrave Street. designed by Don Gazzard. Photograph Don Gazzard

says a research report from PRD Realty. About half the inner–east population is aged between 20 and 39, compared with the Sydney average of about one third in that age bracket, and they are sophisticated in their approach to lifestyle, leisure and home choice. To them, the apartment has become a fashion item with the branding image based on the reputations of the architects and interior designers. As prices rise, young Sydney-siders are facing a rental crisis. Young renters in Paddington are paying at least $360 a week for an original 2 bedroom apartment. If they want something modern they have to pay $500.'

Many members of the shifting population live in share houses. There are many similarities between the old boarding houses of the 1930's and 1950's and share houses. In both cases, residents have to share facilities, the bathroom, lounge room and kitchen. In a share house there is less privacy than in a boarding house where individual rooms sometimes had cooking facilities on the balconies. All domestic aspects of the lives of sharers are on display, from what they are going to eat for dinner, to the identity of their latest lover. Not many share houses can survive the claustrophobic closeness that people are forced to live in. However, the biggest difference between the share house of today and the boarding house of the past, is the size of the rent, and the income of the residents.

'I was in a house the other day and it was rough and ready, which is now extremely rare. The ashtrays were full and it reminded me of my old share house. People dropping in, dropping out, three people going to bed and five waking up, and not feeling funny that they've got a partner in the bedroom. I remember that a lot, and there's someone else at breakfast, and you sort of shut up and you might see them again or you might not.' (*Jack*)

The suburb's fashionable image and convenience attracts young people to the suburb, sometimes despite surprisingly low wages. Most young people between the ages of 20–29 are employed in sales and personal services, which are at the lower end of the wage scale.

Cassie and Evan began renting a house in the Paddington Village in the early 1990's, after living in Glebe and Balmain. 'I still had to drive to get to the city. You felt you were so close to the city but you weren't quite there. I didn't expect the inner city area to be as friendly. I didn't realise that if you have to live closer to people, you can't be really separate, like you don't talk to anyone. You've got to be really friendly and this tiny neighbourhood of the village sort of engulfs you in love as soon as you step into it, so you feel like you want to know everyone and you want to be part of it. It's got that feel about it.'

Cassie and Evan set up a café on Glenmore Road. When the premises became vacant, they were excited by the idea of a local café. They did not want to see the shop being bought by people, who didn't understand the area. 'We were building our café. All the locals and our friends were popping in, and getting so excited, and that's when people started making it their own, and that's when our goodwill started, before we opened up, because it was people we knew. Between fifty to seventy people went through on the opening, and we had a sausage sizzle and coffee party out the back. It was like a pub in here, but Evan was serving coffee not beer, and everyone was crowded around the machine going, "I'll have a flat white, two long blacks." It was fabulous. All the local businesses love that we're here, because there's nowhere else close by where they can get fresh, fast coffee and a smile, first thing in the morning. A lot of artists come in to put their work up in the galleries in the neighbourhood.'(Cassie)

The café performs a service that the old corner shops used to do. Cassie and Evan keep an eye on the neighbourhood and on the elderly. '*Kath* lives in the house that abuts the back of our house, and if you ever have the pleasure of walking into her house, by invitation only, she doesn't take guests very often these days, it's like walking into a theatre. There's a little organ and she worked in a theatre in Melbourne and saw South Pacific how many thousand times. She's a very, very, colourful character and she loves the neighbourhood because she has friends. We see *Kath* every day, and she loves the fact that she comes out of her house and across the road and past the café to do what ever she does for her daily things. She is happy that we're actually able to hang for a while, we can help her out in any way.'(*Cassie* and *Evan*)

Restaurants cater for some locals but rely on most of their trade coming from outside the community. Darcy's Restaurant has been established for over twenty years. Attilio Marinangelo, the owner, explained that he has 'clients that have been here since we opened, we have newcomers to the area, we get people that are recommended by the hotels. Lots of overseas people who live in Australia or are recommended by people who lived overseas. A lot of people are moving into the area, there are lots of people who used to live on the north shore in huge house, with big families, and now the family is all married and so they move into Paddington, with a little garden and keep a dog and a cat, but they don't entertain as much.'

When Lucio Galleto took the lease on the Old Hungry Horse Restaurant he didn't know he was buying into part of the suburb's cultural heritage. 'The first one to talk to me about the Hungry Horse was Geoffry Dutton. He used to live in Paddington and he was a regular, he used to come two to three times a week, and he brought in a photograph of the balcony with all the artists.'

Henry mourns the loss of the use of restaurants for locals. 'Some are very high profile. There's a row of chauffeur-driven cars at lunchtime waiting to pick up. I think we all had this vision, like Paris, you'd walk out your front door and go to the next block and you'd eat at the local café where you would know the proprietor and it never happened. Ironically it's happened in Victoria Street, we eat there regularly, we can walk out our door, and turn right, and they've done that marvellous thing of widening the footpath and narrowing the traffic carriageway and that is what should happen in Paddington.'

There are more than thirty galleries. However, fewer artists live in the suburb than in the past. Trade for the galleries goes far beyond the bounds of the suburb. Dr. Gene Sherman runs two linked galleries, one in Hargrave Street and one in Goodhope Street. Like Betty O'Neill and Kym Bonython, she has a stable of artists, who each have a major show every two years. Openings are an important feature of the Sydney social calender. 'At least 300 or 400 people attend, and our mailing list contains three and a half thousand people, it's a huge mailing list and we struggle to bring it down, you can imagine what it costs, just the postage alone costs $1500 dollars every month. But I'm a very inclusive person. Some galleries have the policy, if you don't buy, you don't get an invitation, you're welcome to come in, but they're not giving you drinks if you're not a buyer. I'm not at all of that feeling.'(Gene)

Another group that is becoming less prominent in the suburb is the gay community. As the prices have risen, this group has tended to migrate to Surry Hills, Darlinghurst and New Town which are now centres of gay culture. But the Gay and Lesbian Mardi Gras originated in Paddington. The first parade, a protest march, started at the Paddington Town Hall, and proceeded to Taylor Square. There are fewer gay venues in Paddington than there were in the 1980's, and some bars have changed their style. The Unicorn Hotel, (now the Fringe Bar) once catered for a gay crowd and presented drag shows, as did the Paddington Green. The Albury Hotel is one of the last bastions of gay Paddington, and is on its boundary.

The local Independent member of State Parliament, Clover Moore, was represented in the Mardi Gras parade. 'I was very touched by that. A float was prepared over six months by a very good friend of mine who had since died, Tony Carden, and he got one of my suits from Peter and it was taken apart and twenty suits were made by Covers. Tony organised shipping in twenty wigs from the US and he got the make-up artist from South Pacific to do the make-up. They had a photo and they practised my walk, and it was just bizarre. We had a Christmas party and some one said to Tony, "Oh don't you love Clover's new hair do?" and he said, "No, I think it's a disaster, I've just imported twenty wigs." The night of the Mardi Gras I was down at Tony's about 6 o'clock and I met these twenty people who looked just like me and we all walked up to Elizabeth Street together. I remember this singleted old chap looking out his window and calling out, "Have a good night, girls." It was really good fun.'

Most of the local hotels have developed themes that cater for specific crowds. There are a number of Irish theme pubs for visiting Irish and British tourists, and to a much smaller extent the locals. 'It is sad about the pubs, when we moved in we all went to our local pub, now you feel like an alien in the places, they are full of poker machines. They've turned their backs on the community. For instance when our kids were at Glenmore Road, they used to have a dinner, an author's dinner for kids at the Royal Hotel at Five Ways, all these little kids. They'd meet an author and have dinner, and the publican set up a special table and menu.' (*Henry*)

James Couché has owned the Lord Dudley Hotel for many years. 'I think Paddington is a lot safer. There was a criminal element years ago, nowadays there are a lot of young yuppies as you call them. I was called a yuppie pub years ago, it was absolute rubbish. I like to call them young business people moving into the area. Yes, they're earning good money now and that's done a lot for the area. Paddington is rather like Camden, in London, like some little pockets of London, little villages within the city, and I think that's what Paddington has become.'

David returned to the Paddington Police station in the 1990's. 'House breaking has dropped off...they're going for your garage, for your power tools and your lawn mower, because nearly everybody you know has a video and a TV, so no one wants that sort of stuff. So they are looking at stealing entirely different things. And you can sell them anywhere. Paddington was always in trouble because of the way the homes are secured. Shoplifting is rife along Oxford Street. The demands of the locals are to keep the place quiet, get rid of all the tourists. They don't like tourists, but it is a tourist area. Very few locals drink at the hotels. You look around and you think there might be eight or nine locals in there. The thing that the locals hate is that they want to be able to park their cars, have no noise at night, and they don't like people coming into their area. Centennial Park is a problem for the local police because the area is difficult to patrol. The mixed use can start fights and they have trouble handling graffiti and vandalism.

Some people are struggling. Paddington is home to a number of street people. The Uniting Church feeds the poor in its church yard on weekdays. In nearby Darlinghurst, refuges accommodate many of Sydney's homeless, many of whom suffer from mental illnesses or alcoholism. Clover Moore remembers Diane. 'I had Diane living in the bus stop for many months. I talked to her. She used to say she had a husband and she had a house and it was being fixed up. She was directly opposite the office. When she first moved in with her trolley, she did her housework every morning, but there was conflict because it's quite a busy bus stop, and people would be wanting a bit of shelter and they'd all be standing out on the rain because Diane and her trolley and her blanket and all her worldly possessions were in it. And she refused to go anywhere, she refused help and it went on for months. The hotel behind her was getting very agitated because their breakfast area looked onto the street. One day, one of the shopkeepers came banging on my door, "The police have come for Diane," so I ran across and tried to talk to her, they were taking her to Caritas. She was in a world of her own. She just sat there all day. Sometimes another homeless friend would come and visit. It was sort of fascinating.'

It can also be hard for elderly members of the community to maintain their independence. 'All the little shops are going. Where you had lovely Tessareros, a fruit shop, and when the children were babies, and you'd cook one spinach leaf, a piece of potato, a tablespoon of barley and a bit of carrot or something, and you did that each day, well, you'd go down to Tessareros, you could buy one spinach leaf. They'd sell you one spinach leaf. Now if you wanted to do that you couldn't. And now you haven't got that local shop. And you had that nice ham and beef shop, you could go in and get three pieces of Devon or something. You used to get a half a pound of ham for 1/–. All those little things. Everybody knew all the local shops. I think they're the main things that you miss.' (*Maisie*)

Eugene lived in Paddington in defiance of the excesses of wealth. He found a very dilapidated place to squat in the Paddington Village. 'I came in through the window, like there was no window, climbed in and the whole house was full of trees and three feet deep with rubble. You couldn't work out what was in this rubble and there were building materials everywhere, and to the right there was a huge pile of gravel and you could just make out that there was a fireplace over to the right and lots of sand. All you could distinguish was the bedroom and the study, otherwise you couldn't work out the geography of the house.' He convinced the manager of the property that it was in his interest to let him stay in the house rent free, if he did it up. He made the place liveable and maintained it from further deterioration. But there was some resentment and suspicion from his neighbouring home owners. 'I chased one of them away with an axe one time, when I first moved in. They hated me because they wanted to buy the property and they knew I wasn't paying rent and they were paying exorbitant mortgages.'*Eugene* used the house as a base to launch a career in the arts. Before he became established in a successful career as a filmaker, producing documentaries, he was given a large load of marble off cuts for next to nothing, which he sculpted. 'It didn't take a huge amount of skill. You take an angle grinder, and a lot of patience, and a willingness to die of cancer from the dust.'

Another local artist is *Rosie,* a painter. She and her family live a bohemian lifestyle in an increasingly conservative Paddington. ' My house is partly an artist's house because my kids are all artists of one sort and another, so there are often interactive activities that bump into each other.' Their different attitudes to life in the suburb have caused conflicts, their celebrations of life just seeming noisy or messy to their neighbours. 'We've always been controversial in whatever neighbourhood we've lived in, because of the number of us, and because we've had so many noisy parties. We've not only had birthday parties for our own kids, but for other kids whose parents won't allow them to have a party, so they plead and beg and at one stage we had all the neighbours around us, wanting to throw us out of the street. They said they couldn't stand the noise any longer. 'I said, "Fortunately I don't think there are going to be any parties for a while because the last party has just happened and they're all starting to get married now." One of my sons was continuously dismantling Valiants in the street so there were all these car engines and car parts on the pavement. It irritated people. It wasn't tidy. Now there are only grandchildren and they're not too bad. We've had two weddings in the house and we closed off the street and had dancing for both weddings. I didn't tell the neighbours, I just got witches' hats and I closed off the streets and we had waiters and musicians and everyone was very happy to stand around watching the dancing till one in the morning. The neighbours were invited, but they didn't come.'

With the major streetscapes preserved, the Paddington Society and other groups have fought to place traffic controls in Paddington, to control development on major sites such as the Scottish Hospital and White City, and control air traffic noise.

There has been a massive increase in car ownership in the suburb. A significant number of households have three or more cars. In 1976, the average was less than 1 per household. John Normyle was involved in the campaign to reduce through traffic in the suburb. 'Glenmore Rd is carrying 20,000 cars a day, and we got a 40 k speed limit up. But people were still driving through here at 60 k, there's still a log jam of cars. The car kept coming up as the biggest negative force affecting the life and the quality of the area. We even got asthma counts and pollution counts. The neighbourhood contact had dropped to .001 per cent of people talking to one another over the fence. Clover Moore had a public meeting down in Boundary Street, there was unanimous support to take it further. Anyway, there was another group who wanted the motor car to go through. Freedom of choice. They ran full-page ads, and spent nearly $30,000 fighting it, to try and stop it. The traffic plan was approved by a slim majority in Council to go on trial, and the next day the Minister for Transport removed the delegations from every Council in NSW to be able to do such a thing. So it's now with the RTA.'

The development of the Royal Women's Hospital site is the largest development in Paddington this century. The Paddington Society were represented on the committee that liased with the developer, and they won a number of concessions. A park was included on Glenmore Road and the height of some of the buildings was reduced. However the owners have continued throughout the development to ask for changes. A building inspector on the site says, 'We are having a big fight at the moment, we all agreed on the master plan for natural sandstone for the main public domain area, and that is the real feature and now they're coming back saying they are doing a costing on the stone and they find that it's out of the question financially, commercially, and they now want to go to reconstituted stone. Once they sell the development, they'll be off, but the development is something that is going to be there for over 100 years so we want high class finishes and materials that will last for that period of time. Reconstituted stone, that's like comparing a Volkwagen with a Mercedes. I hear the sales are going very well.'

Paddington, despite all its problems and conflicts is still a suburb that inspires loyalties in present and past residents. All have different dreams for Paddington. *Mary, Maisie, Jeannie* and *Maria* wish that Paddington still had good local shops. John Normyle wishes for a release from through traffic. *Henry* wishes that his dreams for Paddington had been fulfilled. *Louise* would like people to have the sense that they live in a suburb with a wonderful messy past. So would *Rosie.* She would like 'to encourage the reintroduction of chickens and people chatting to each other in their pyjamas.'

End Notes

Chapter 1 The Wilderness to the East

1. Mulvaney, D.J., and White, J. Peter, *Australians to 1788*, p.343
2. Hunter, Captain John, Commander, HMS Sirius, *An Historical Journal 1787–1792* p.57
3. Tench, Watkin, *Tench's Narrative and Complete Account — Sydney's First Four Years* p.285
4. White, John, *Journal of a Voyage to New South Wales* p.134
5. Tench, Watkin. *Tench's Narrative* p.52
6. Hunter, Captain John, Commander, HMS Sirius, *An Historical Journal 1787–1792* p.93
7. Yarwood, A.T. *Growing up in Phillip's Sydney* p.31
8. Hunter, Captain John, Commander, HMS Sirius, *An Historical Journal* p.116
9. Tench, Watkin. *Tench's Narrative* p.159
10. *Ibid.* p.191
11. Hunter, Captain John, Commander, HMS Sirius, *An Historical Journal* p.143
12. Tench, Watkin, *Tench's Narrative* p.281
13. *Ibid* p.162
14. *Sydney Gazette* 27/1/1821
15. Ellis, M.H. *Lachlan Macquarie* p.493
16. Marriot, Edward West, *Thomas West of Barcom Glen* p.83
17. *Ibid* p.73
18. *Truth* 9/2/1913 (Bigges report No.1of 1822 — Major Druitt)
19. Marriot, Edward West, *Memoirs of Obed West* p.36
20. *Sydney Gazette* 21.2.1810

21. *Historical Records of Australia* p.732
22. Hainsworth, D.R ., *The Sydney Traders* p.125
23. *Sydney Gazette* 27/6/1812
24. *Sydney Gazette* 13/3/1813
25. *Sydney Gazette* 27/1/1821
26. Eldershaw, M. Barnard, *The Life and Times of Captain John Piper* p.129
27. Cunningham, Peter, *Two Years in NSW* p.71
28. Ellis. M.H. *Lachlan Macquarie* p.501
29. *Sydney Gazette* 27/1/1821
30. *Sydney Gazette* 22/5/ 1823
31. *Sydney Gazette* 2/6/1825
32. *Australian Dictionary of Biography* p.246
33. Simpson, Margaret, *Old Sydney- A Social History* p.150
34. *Sydney Gazette* 28.10/1824
35. *Sydney Gazette* 14.10.1824
36. Cunningham, Peter, *Two Years in NSW* p.71
37. Marriott, Edward West, *Thomas West of Barcom Glen* p.143
38. *Ibid* p.146.
39. Cunningham, Peter, *Two Years in NSW* p.143
40. *Australian Newspaper* 24/10/1831
41. *Sydney Gazette* 24/10/1831
42. Cunningham, Peter, *Two Years in NSW* p.53
43. *Ibid* p.20
44. *Sydney Morning Herald* 24/5/1882

Chapter 2 Paddington Hill.

1. Clark, D. *Baron Charles von Hugel, New Holland Journal. November 1833–34* p.178
2. Marriott, Edward West, *The Memoirs of Obed West* p.35
3. *NSW Post Office Directory and Calendar 1832*
4. Sharpe, Alan, *Colonial NSW 1853–94* Rushcutters Bay, Yesterday and Today p.74
5. *Ibid.* p.74
6. *Truth* 22/12/12 HSM. Geebungs are a type of flowering plant of similar species as the Banksia the Proteceae. A Geebung or Persoonia contained an edible nut. Five corners was a native plant which bore edible berries.
7. Ashton,P. Blackmore, K. *Centennial Park* p.21
8. *Truth* 22/12/12 HSM Fitzroy
9. *Sydney Morning Herald,* Old and New Sydney 1V 1882
10. Atkinson , A. & Aveling, M. *Australians* 1838 Vol. 2 p.256
11. Cope, I. Garrett, W. *The Royal, a History of the Royal Hospital for Women 1820–1997* p.16
12. Parkinson, Liz *The Underwoods, Lock Stock and Barrel* p.76–77
13. *Australians 1838* p.83
14. Birch, A. & McMillan, D. T*he Sydney Scene* "A Journal of a Voyage from London to Sydney" p.105

15. *Australians 1838* p.133
16. *NSW Post Office Directory and Calendar 1834*
17. Maclehose, J. *Picture of Sydney and Stranger's Guide in NSW for 1839* p.14
18. Mc Queen, H. *New Britannia* p.124
19. Pearl, C. *Sydney Revels* p.1
20. *The Sydney Scene* p.140
21. *Newspaper Cuttings FM 477111, Vol. 1* 'The Story of the Victoria Barracks", John F. Mann, 8/2/04 p.147
22. *Ibid.*
23. Gerald Dillon.*Navy, Army, Air and Munitions Journal Sept. 1982* , "Victoria Barracks Sydney reaches the Century." p.2
24. *Truth 22/12/12* HSM Fitzroy
25. Marriot, Thomas West, *Thomas West of Barcom Glen* p.178
26. *Ibid.* p.215–7
27. *Truth 3/10/09*
28. *Journal of the Australian War Memorial. Special Colonial Issue.* Deservedly Respected. Matthew Higgins
29. Cunningham, P. *Two Years in NSW* p.134
30. *Truth 3/19/09*
31. *Letters to 'Old Chum'* 7/11/09
32. *Navy, Army Air and Munitions Journal Sept 1982.* Gerald Dillon
33. Harries, Norm. *Monologue performed at the Barracks.*
34. *Letters to 'Old Chum'* 7/11/09
35. Matthew Higgins. *Journal of the Australian War Memorial. Special Colonial Issue.*
36. *Newspaper Cuttings vol.1 FM477111* John F. Mann 8/2/04
37. *Ibid.*
38. Fowler, F. *Southern Lights and Shadows* p.22
39. Baron Charles Von Hugel. *New Holland Journal* p.200
40. *The Sydney Scene* p.75.
41. Cunningham, P. *Two Years in NSW*
42. Pearl, C. *Sydney Revels* Charles Corbyn, court reporter for Bell's Life in Sydney. p 58
43. *Ibid.* p.80
44. Printed at the Sydney Monitor Office. *The Rights of Juries. Appeal of Mr. Robert Cooper, distiller, against the prohibition of colonial distillation.*
45. *The Sydney Scene* p.108
46. Parkinson, L. *The Underwoods, Lock, Stock and Barrel* p.73
47. *Australians 1838* p.243
48. *Truth 5/2/13*
49. Summers, A. *Damned Whores and God's Police* p.67

Chapter 3. Cast Iron Morality

1. Birch, A. & McMillan D. *The Sydney Scene* p.142.
2. Hardwick, J. MSS 448/113.
3. Ibid.

4. Pearl, Cyril *Sydney Revels,* p.8
5. Hardwick, J. MSS 448/113
6. Ibid.
7. Ibid.
8. Ibid.
9. Davidson, G. Mc Carthy & Mc Leary, A. *The Australians 1888* p.408
10. Hardwick, J. MSS488/113
11. Ibid.
12. Birch,A., McMillan, D. *The Sydney Scene* p.158
13. Hardwick, J. MSS 488/113
14. Kelly, M. *Paddock Full of Houses* p.34
15. Mc Naughton, *Australia, a Social and Political History* p.19
16. Committees of Enquiry, NSW State Archives
17. Rathbone, R. *A Very Present Help* p.51.
18. SMH *Letter to the Editor* 5/12/87
19. *Old Chum* 7/11/09 p.71
20. Ashton, P., Blackmore K. *Centennial Park* p.21
21. Kelly M. *Nineteenth Century Sydney* p.60
22. Sonder, R. *Paddington, its History, Trade and Industries* p.33
23. Marriot, T. *Thomas West of Barcom Glen* p.167
24. Sonder, R. *Paddington* p.12
25. SMH 21/8/1857
26. Sonder, R. *Paddington* p.42
27. Cannon, M.*Life in the Cities Vol 3.* p.22
28. Sonder R. *Paddington* p.49
29. Ashton, P., Blackmore, K. *Centennial Park* p.20
30. Sonder, R., *Paddington* p.50
31. Birch, A., Mc Millan D. *The Sydney Scene* p.67
32. Kelly, M. *Paddock Full of Houses* p.24
33. Sonder, R. P*addington* p.105
34. Kelly, M. *Paddock Full of Houses* p. 42
35. *Australian Dictionary of Biography 1850–1900* p. 301
36. Sonder, R. *Paddington* p.102
37. Portus G.V. *Happy Highways* p.50
38. Sonder, R. *Paddington* p.106
39. Larcombe, F.A. *The Stabilization of Local Government in NSW, 1858–1906* p.7
40. Kelly, M. *Paddock Full of Houses* p.74
41. *Ibid* p.85
42. Fitzgerald, S. *Rising Damp* p.40
43. *Ibid* p.25.
44. Kelly M. *Paddock Fullof Houses* p.83
45. Larcombe, F.A. *The Stabilization of Local Government in NSW 1858–1906* p. 193
46. Paddington Wesleyan Church. *Manuscript Journal* MLA 2435
47. Mc Queen, H. *New Brittannia* p.17
48. Yarwood, A.T. *From a Chair in the Sun* p.13
49. Fitzgerald, S. *Rising Damp* p.7

50. Max Kelly Private Papers, Box 10 Mitchell Library
51. Kelly, M. *Nineteenth Century Sydney* p.63
52. Sharpe, A. *Colonial NSW 1853–1894* p.240
53. Fitzgerald, S. *Rising Damp* p. 86. .
54. Sharpe, A. *Colonial NSW 1853–1894* p.240
55. Cannon, M. *Life in the Cities vol. 3* p. 157
56. Haggar, J. *Australian Colonial Medicine* p.51
57. Sharpe, A. *Colonial NSW 1853–94* p.110
58. Sonder, R. *Paddington* p.88
59. Prescription Books, 1887–90, Maddo the Chemist from Paddo
60. SMH 10/1/1882
61. SMH 25/1/1882
62. Cannon, M. *Life in the Cities Vol 3* p.319
63. Cannon, M. *Life in the Cities Vol 3* p. 36
64. Fahey, W. *When Mabel laid the Table* p.16
65. Portus G.V. *Happy Highways* p.50
66. *The Illustrated News*, 1870
67. Marketing Department, RAS.
68. Poole. P. *The Diaries of Ethel Turner* p. 30 August 1890
69. Portus G.V. *Happy Highways,* p50
70. Sharpe A. *Colonial NSW 1853–94* p.146
71. Ashton, P, Blackmore, K. *Centennial Park* p.62
72. *Ibid* p.77
73. *Ibid* p.101
74. SMH 12/2/1882
75. Birch A., Mc Millan, D. *Sydney Scene* p.219
76. SMH 12/2/1892
77. Sonder, R. *Paddington* p.72
78. Davidson, G., Mc Carthy & McLeary, A. *The Australians, 1888* p. 239
79. Flower, C.. *Duck and Cabbage Tree* p.118
80. Mc Intyre,S. C*oncise History of Australia.*p135
81. I*bid* p.135
82. Kelly, M. Papers Box 10
83. Sonder, R. *Paddington* p.63
84. *Ibid* p.59

Chapter 4 The Renters

1. Sonder, R. *Paddington, Its History, Trade and Industries* p.58.
2. Roe, J. *Twentieth Century Sydney* Studies in Urban and Social History p.193
3. Cope, I., Garrett, W. *The Royal* A History of the Royal Hospital for Women 1820–1997 p.26
4. Sonder, R. *Paddington* p.88
5. *Ibid.* p.54
6. Spearritt, P. *Sydney Since the Twenties* p.45

7. Larcombe, F. T*he Stabilization of Local Government in NSW.* Vol. 3. p,197
8. Sonder, R. *Paddington* p.64
9. Spearritt, P. *Sydney Since the Twenties* p. 153
10. Birch, A., Mc Millan, D. *The Sydney Scene* p 203
11. Factories and Shops Act 1912. Hansard
12. Kelly, M. Private Papers Box 10
13. RAS Marketing
14. Sonder, R. *Paddington* p13
15. *Ibid.* p.89
16. *Ibid.* p89
17. Roe, J. *Twentieth Century Sydney* p.185
18. *Ibid.* p.189
19. Corris, p. *Lords of the Ring* p. 103
20. Park, R. H*ome Before Dark* p.22
21. *Ibid.* p.52
22. *Ibid.* p.7
23. *Australian Dictionary of Biography* p.271
24. SMH 29/11/1913
25. Saalmans, J. *Growing up in Sydney before the Great War.* Assignment for the Uni.
    of NSW, School of Librarianship
26. *Ibid.*
27. Australian Hardware and Machinery Journal, vol 22 No. 8
28. Blaikie, G. *Wild Women of Sydney* P. 54
29. Ashton, P. Blakemore, K. *Centennial Park* p.119
30. *The Australians, Historical Atlas* p. 140
31. RAS Marketing
32. Larcombe, F. *The Stabilization of Local Government in NSW Vol.3* PAGE
33. Kelly, M. *Nineteenth Century Sydney* p.70
34. RAS Marketing
35. Larcombe, F. *Advancement of Local Government in NSW, Vol 3* p.438
36. *Ibid.*p 106
37. Labor Daily, 20th May 1927 p.120

Chapter 5. We Done it Hard

1. Mc Intyre, S. *A Concise History of Australia.* p.175
2. Birch, A. Mc Millan, D. *The Sydney Scene* p.292.
3. Cohen, E. *Paddington, Something Old, Something New* p.17
4. NSW Police Criminal Register, 20 December 1933
5. Blaikie, G. *Wild Women of Sydney* P. 28
6. *Ibid* p.42
7. *Ibid* p.41
8. *Ibid* P.177
9. PIX 123/11/1938
10. SMH 22/11/99

Chapter 6 Gettin' a Job

1. Labor Daily 2/9/33
2. NSW Parliamentary Debates 18/11/1936
3. The Sun Newspaper 8/10/41
4. Paddington Municipal Council *Miscellaneous Papers*
5. *Ibid.*
6. Spearritt, P. *Twentieth Century Sydney* p.31
7. *The Australians.Historical Atlas* p.233
8. Parliamentary Debates Mr. Osborne Hansard
9. *Ibid.*
10. Kelly, M. Private Papers Box 10

Chapter 7. The Transit camp

1. Cope, W . Kalantzis, M. *A Place in the Sun,* p.41
2. Ibid p.38
3. Ibid p.40
4. *Reader's Digest* p.44
5. Labor Party Archives, Mitchell Library
6. Corris, P. *Lord of the Rings* p.160.
7. Thompson P. *Accidental Chords* p.221

Chapter 8 Towards a Bohemian Utopia

1. Cope, W., Kalantzis, M. *A Place in the* Sun p.185–186
2. Good Weekend. SMH 2/10/1999
3. Edwards and Shaw, *The First Gallery in Paddington* p.11
4. Bonython, K. *Ladies, Legs and Lemonade* p.165
5. Mangold, M. *Paddington Bazaar* p.5
6. *Ibid* p.7
7. *Ibid* p.7

Chapter 9 Conservation and Conservatism

1. Robert Burns 'Pushing Paddington' *Nation* 1967 p.14
2. All the statistics in this chapter are from the 1976 and 1986 Census and from 'Sydney, a Social and Political Atlas', Poulsen and Spearitt 1976, and 'Sydney, a Social Atlas' 1986, John Wilson.
3. Cyril Pearl 'The Battle of Paddo' *Readers Digest* 1972 p.44
4. Patricia Thompson *Accidental Chords* p.236
5. Cyril Pearl 'The Battle of Paddo' *Readers Digest* 1972 p.44
6. Shirley Fitzgerald *Sydney 1842–1992* p.252

7.   Jack Mundey *Green Bans and Beyond* p.143
8.   *The Paddington Plan*, Paddington Society
9.   *Ibid* p.9
10. Ian Stephenson, *Lecture*, Power Department of Art History and Theory, 1997. This was the N.S.W's branch's, first acquisition and this was the main reason for the exaggeration of the style of the museums fit out, for they wanted to acquire a grander building and this was beyond their means at the time.
11. *The Paddington Plan*, Paddington Society p.20
12. *Ibid.*
13. *Ibid.*p.24
14. *Ibid.* p.36–37
15. Robert Burns "Pushing Paddington", *Nation* 1967 p.13
16. *Paddington Journal* Jan 1972
17. Sydney Morning Herald Real Estate 1970–1985
18. *Ibid.*
19. *Ibid.*

Chapter 10. Money Changes Everything

1.   Australian Bureau of Statistics 1996
2.   Heritage Net Workshop 25/2/2000
3.   Domain section "Sydney Morning Herald 27/1/2000
4.   Sunday Telegraph 5/3/2000
5.   Australian Bureau of Statistics 1991 census of Population and Housing

Acknowledgements

We are indebted to a number of good friends who have helped in various ways in the preparation of this book. These include, Ace Bourke, Bryony Cosgrove, Tony Fragar, Cherry Jacobsen, Annette Jameson, Russell McKean, Dominic Morice, Tara Morice, Tamsin O'Neill, Sue O'Neill and Gabrielle Storey.

Most importantly we would like to thank all those who shared their stories and photographs with us, John and Roma Agius, Cassandra Alley, Gavin and Robin Andrews, Nikki Andrews, Jackie Barbe, Sally Basset, Jim and Isobel Bishop, Rebecca Bishop, John and Julia Blacker, Barbara Blackman, Bill Blinco, Maggie Blinco, Andrew Blomfield, Anne and Peter Blomfield, Jan Bradbury, John Butterworth, Cedric and Penny Carle, Janet Chapman, John, Henrietta, Kate, and Jo Clark, Ken Clarke, Arthur Connelly, Natalina, and Don Costa (deceased), James Couché, Kate Couché, Steven Davies, Reg Delaney, Mick Dunn (deceased) and Sylvia Dunn, Kevin Dyson, Joyce Everett, Lina Farrugia, Don and Vicki Fish, Tony Fragar, Lucio Galletto, Marcus Gillezeau, Don Gazzard, Marea Gazzard, Kathy Golski, Jack Griffith, Norman Harries, Elsie Harrison, Lena Henson, Lillian Horler, Charles Hewitt, Patricia Huntley, Peter James and Joan Sinclair, Evan Jones, Robert Kay and Gina Toia, Su Lanker, Enzo Leone, Sean Linkson, Lorraine Lovett and Roger Shelley, Anne Lucas, Bill Lucas, David Lucas, Bonnie Mc Cormick, Howard McIntyre, Peter Madden, Attilio Marinangeli, Simon Martin, Ruth Mary, Johanna Minogue, Clover Moore, Independent Member for Bligh, Michael Nissen, John Normyle, Betty O'Neill, Pat O'Reilly, Margot O'Reilly (deceased) and Kathleen Northey, Dean Pantle, John Phillips, Maggie Prill, Sam Ricciardo, Peter Ricciardo, Drew and Marie Robertson, Dr. Marcus Sacks, Gaye Stockell and John Portus, Gail Shaw and Robert Hannan, Dr. Gene Sherman, Herb Smith, Jannie Southern, Cecil Sykes, Gabrielle Storey, Richard Storey, Susan Tooth, Peter Thompson, Warren Turner, Arthur and Vicki Tourgelis, Jim Waddell and Brigadier Woodbury.

The writing of this book was made far easier with the enthusiastic support of Rosemary Block and Jennifer Broomhead at the State Library, Faye Lawrence and Jane Britten at the Woollahra Library, Denise Syme and Fiona Johnson at the Paddington Library, Susan Ma, Tina Borserio, Jennifer Wilson and Susan Zipfinger of the SCEGGS Darlinghurst Library, the staff of the Mitchell Library, the NSW State Archives, Sydney City Council, the Victoria Barracks Museum, the Natural History Museum, London, the Salvation Army Museum at Bexley, Penny Carle, the former President of the Paddington Society, Bronwyn Myrtle, Reseach Centre, Australian War Memorial, The New South Wales branch of the ALP, Platinum Imaging, Oxford Street, Paddington and DAC Printing, Oxford Street, Paddington.

We are indebted to Dr. Shirley Fitzgerald for her advice as we embarked on this project.

We would like to thank the Woollahra Council for their financial support in the development stage of the project.

Bibliography

Abraham. Walter, "Address, AGM, Paddington Society", 1998.

Alexis. Effie & Janiszewski. Leonard, *Images of Home*, Sydney 1995.

Ashton. Paul, *The Accidental City*, Sydney 1993.

Ashton. Paul & Blackmore. Kate, *Centennial Park*, Sydney 1988.

Australian Dictionary of Biography, Volumes 1 & 2 Melbourne 1966.

Birch. Alan & McMillan. David, S, *The Sydney Scene 1788–1960*, Melbourne 1962.

Blackman. Barbara, *Glass after Glass*, Sydney, 1997.

Blaikie. George, *Wild Women of Sydney*, Sydney, 1970?

Bolton. Barbara, *Booth's Drum, The Salvation Army in Australia 1880–1980*, Sydney 1980.

Bonython. Kim, *Ladies Legs and Lemonade*, Melbourne 1979.

Bremer. Stuart, *Living in the City*, Sydney 1983.

Brimson. Samuel, *The Tramways of Australia*, Melbourne, 1983.

Brodsky. Isadore, *Sydney's Little World of Wooloomooloo*, Sydney 1966.

Cameron. Robert, Stewart, *Robert Cooper of Juniper Hall*, Woollahra, 1986.

Cannon. Michael, *Life in the Cities, Australia in the Victorian Age:3*, Melbourne 1975.

Clark. Manning, *A Short History of Australia*, Sydney 1963.

Clark. Manning, *Sources of Australian History*, Melbourne 1962.

Clune. Frank, *Saga of Sydney*, Sydney 1961.

Cohen. Eve, T, *Paddington, Something Old, Something New*, Woollahra (no date).

Conway, Ronald, *The Great Australian Stupor*, Melbourne 1985.

Cooke. Anne, *Going to the Show, Images and Memories of Sydney's Royal Easter Show*, Sydney 1966.

Cope, Ian, Garrett, William *The Royal — a History of the Royal Hospital for Women 1820–1997*, Sydney 1996.

Corris, Peter, *Lords of the Ring, a History of Australia's Prize Fighters*, Sydney 1980.

Cunningham. Peter, *Two Years in NSW*, 1827.

Cusack. Dymphna, *Caddie*, Sydney 1953.

Davis. C, Black. K, & MacLean. K, *Oral History, from Tape to Type*, Chicago, USA, 1977.

de Winton. William, *History, Walking Tour and Map of Paddington*, New Edition Bookshop.

Doors were always open. Recollections of Pyrmont and Ultimo, Sydney 1997.

Edwards and Shaw. *The First Gallery in Paddington*, Sydney 1981.

Edwards. P. D, & Joyce, R .B, *Trollope, Australia*, Queensland, 1967.

Eldershaw. M. Barnard, *Phillip of Australia*, An Account of the Settlement at Sydney Cove 1788–92 Sydney 1972.

Eldershaw. M. Barnard, *The Life and Times of Captain John Piper NSW*, Sydney 1973.

Ellis. M.H. *Lachlan Macquarie*, Sydney 1947.

Emanuel. Cedric, *Paddington Sketchbook*, Sydney 1975.

Fahey. Warren, *When Mabel Laid the Table*, Sydney 1992.

Fitzgerald. Shirley & Golder. Hilary, *Pyrmont and Ultimo*, Sydney 1994.

Fitzgerald. Shirley & Keating. Christopher, *Miller's Point*, Sydney 1991.

Fitzgerald. Shirley & *Sydney 1842–1992*, Sydney 1992.

Fitzgerald. Shirley & Wotherspoon. Gerry, *Minorities*, Sydney 1995.

Fitzgerald. Shirley, *Rising Damp, Sydney 1870–1890*, Melbourne 1987.

Flower. Cedric, *Duck and Cabbage Tree*, Sydney 1968.

Fowler. Frank, *Southern Lights and Shadows*, facsimilie edition (with introduction by R. G. Geering), Sydney 1975.

Fowles. Joseph, *Sydney in 1848*, A facsimile of the original text and engravings, Sydney 1962.

Fox, Len, *Old Sydney Windmills*, Sydney 1978.

Freeland. J, M, *The Australia Pub*, Melbourne 1966.

Garran. The Hon. Andrew, *Australia, the First Hundred Years*, Sydney 1974.

Gazzard, Sheldon, Architects, *Paddington Town Hall*, A Conservation Plan prepared for the Council of the City of Sydney 1991.

Geeves. Phillip, *Local History in Australia*, A Guide for Beginners, Sydney (undated).

Goodman. Robert, B & Johnson, George *The Australians*. 1996.

Greville. P.J, *A Short History of Victoria Barracks, Paddington* (no date).

Hagger. Jennifer, *Australian Colonial Medicine*, Sydney 1979.

Hall. G & Brash. N. *Above Sydney*, Sydney 1984.

Heritage Australia.

Hibbins. Fahey, Askew, *A Handbook for Enthusiasts. Local History*, 1985.

Hillier. Rob, *A Place called Paddington*, Sydney 1970.

Hirst. J.B, *Convict Society and its Enemies*, Sydney 1983.

History Today.

Holt. Patricia, *A City in the mind- Sydney Imagined by its Writers*, Sydney 1983.

Hoorn. Jeanette, *The Lycett Album Drawings of Aborigines and Australian Scenery*, Canberra 1990.

Hughes. Robert, *The Fatal Shore*, Sydney 1987.

Hunter. Captain John, Commander HMS Sirius, *An Historical Journal 1787–1792*, NSW 1968.

Ingleton. G.C. *True Patriots All*, Sydney 1952.

Jacobs. Jane *The Death and Life of Great American Cities*. New York 1992.

Kalantzis. Mary & Cope. Bill, *A Place in the Sun*, Melbourne 2000.

Karskius. G, *The Rocks*, Sydney 1997.

Kelly. Max, *A Certain Sydney 1900*, Sydney 1977.

Kelly. Max, *Faces of the Street William St Sydney 1916*, Sydney 1982.

Kelly. Max, *Nineteenth Century Sydney*, Sydney 1978.

Kelly. Max, *Sydney, City of Suburbs*, NSW 1987.

Kelly. Max, *Paddock Full of Houses*, Sydney 1978.

Kelly. Max, *Plague Sydney 1900*, Sydney 1981.

Kelly. Max & Crocker. Ruth, *Sydney Takes Shape*, Sydney 1977.

Kreckler. John, F, *From Sydney Cove to Paddington Hill*, The Story of the Victoria Barracks, Sydney 1993.

Larcombe. F, A, *The Stabilization of Local Govt in NSW. 1858–1906*, Sydney 1976.

Lycett. J. *Views in Australia and Van Dieman's Land*. London 1824.

Mackay. Hugh, *Generations. Baby boomers, their Parents and their Children*, Sydney 1997.

Maclehose, James, *Picture of Sydney and Stranger's Guide in N.S.W. for 1839*, Sydney 1997.

Mangold. Michael, *Paddington Bazaar*, Sydney, 1993.

Marriot. Edward, West, *Memoirs of Obed West*, Bowral 1984?.

Marriot. Edward, West, *Thomas West of Barcom Glen*, Bowral 1982.

McCalman. Janet, *Struggletown*, Melbourne, 1985.

McQueen. Humphrey, *A New Britannia*, Melbourne 1970.

Miller. Glen, *Backtrack, -Australia's Twentieth Century*, Sydney, 1999.

Milliss. Roger, *Waterloo Creek*, Melbourne 1992.

Mourot. Suzanne, *This was Sydney. A Pictorial Record from 1788 to the Present Time*. Sydney 1969.

Mundey. Jack, *Green Bans and Beyond,* Sydney 1981.

Nesta-Griffiths. G, *Point Piper Past and Present*, Sydney 1970.

New South Wales Education Department, *Sydney and the Bush*, Sydney, 1980.

Niall. Brenda & John Thompson- *The Oxford Book of Australian Letters*. OUP, 1998.